best sports stories 1971

best sports stories

1971 edition

**A PANORAMA OF THE 1970 SPORTS WORLD
INCLUDING THE 1970 CHAMPIONS OF ALL SPORTS
WITH THE YEAR'S TOP PHOTOGRAPHS**

Edited by Irving T. Marsh and Edward Ehre

E. P. DUTTON & CO., INC. | NEW YORK | 1971

To
Asa S. Bushnell,
Commissioner Emeritus of the Eastern
College Athletic Conference, whose love
of sport is exceeded only by his love of
sportsmanship

Contents

Illustrations

Preface

For the 27th time since the dim, dark days of 1945, your editors are sitting down to the typewriter (they use alternate keys) to inscribe a Preface to *Best Sports Stories.*

But even after 27 years there are a couple of "firsts" in this Preface—first-time winners in two of the three classifications for which the awards of $250 each are presented. The "maidens"—to use a popular phrase known best among the horsey set—are Art Spander of the *San Francisco Chronicle* and Bill Bousfield, a Canadian sportsman who does a little free-lance writing and whose most signal success in this field has come through his winning story in *Outdoor Life.*

But we hasten to interpolate that even though there are "maidens" in two of the divisions, there is a real old-timer, if you can call a man in his late thirties "an old-timer," in the third classification. That would be Bob Lipsyte, the talented sports columnist of *The New York Times,* who this year has chalked up his fifth victory, of which the last two have come in a row.

Since all veteran newspapermen will tell you that the toughest and most important part of newspaper work is writing against a deadline, we have, old-fashionedly, clung to the belief that reportage is the No. 1 prize and have so listed it in all these volumes. But that is manifestly unfair to feature and magazine men, who work equally hard and under just as much pressure to produce their brain children.

So if we mention Art Spander first it's because we are traditionalists and nothing more. Spander won the Best News-Coverage award on the U.S. Golf Open, a story of which one of the judges, Red Smith, said most people would have envied the writer.

Lipsyte's prize-winning effort was a column on Jack Dempsey on the occasion of the great fighter's birthday. Of his previous four victories, three were won in News-Features and one in News-Coverage, and all five have been boxing stories.

Bousfield, who won the Magazine-Story award with his piece on the housebreaking bear, is not exactly a professional writer but the first man to appear in *Best Sports Stories* with a hunting piece. George W. Heinhold was not exactly a professional, either. But his story was later reprinted in *Reader's Digest*. That was back in 1945 and even then the writer was decrying "the national decline of our wildlife, our habit of making sewers out of our waters and our disregard for conservation of woodlands."

It is also worthy of note that the competitions in all three classes were extremely close and none of the winners appeared on all three ballots of our judges. And 22 different pieces of the 50 in the book were deemed worthy of special mention by the judges—the Messrs. John Chamberlain, John Hutchens and Red Smith.

Before we get down to the box score of the judging, it should be mentioned that, as in all previous years, the stories went to the judges "blind"—that is, they were identified merely by a word or two, called in newspaperese a "slug." And so to the box score and the judges' comments:

News-Coverage Stories	Chamber-lain	Hutchens	Smith	*Total Points
Open [Art Spander's *They Were Singing "God Save the Queen"*]	—	3	3	6
Star [Joe Gergen's *Jim Hickman: Authentic American Hero*]	—	2	2	4
Fifth Series [Joseph Durso's *The Orioles Begin Another Dynasty*]	3	—	—	3
Ali [Bill Lee's *Those Three Terrible Left Hooks*]	2	1	—	3
Super [Glenn Dickey's *Super Chiefs Shock Super Bowl*]	1	—	—	1
Third Series [Phil Jackman's *The Brooks Robinson Story*]	—	—	1	1
News-Feature Stories				
Dempsey [Robert Lipsyte's *Dempsey in the Window*]	—	2	2	4
Fats [Stan Hochman's *Florida Fats*]	—	3	—	3
Harlem [Dave Klein's *Harlem Playground*]	—	—	3	3
Laver [Phil Elderkin's *"I Win with My Overall Game"*]	3	—	—	3
Marshall [Jay Searcy's *The Black-Draped Campus*]	2	—	—	2
Pancho [Gene Roswell's *Oh, Pancho*]	1	—	—	1
Baseball [Ray Fitzgerald's *A Solid Vote for Baseball*]	—	1	—	1
Hot Dog [Wells Twombly's *The Hero Sandwich of Sports*]	—	—	1	1
Magazine Stories				
Bear [Bill Bousfield's *The Housebreaker*]	—	2	2	4
Kapp [Al Stump's *Joe Kapp: Football's Fury*]	—	3	—	3

Draft [Roy McHugh's *The Making of the No. 1 Draft Choice*]	—	—	3	3
Jacksonville [Paul Hemphill's *How Jacksonville Earned Its Credit Card*]	3	—	—	3
Indy [Joe Scalzo's *Hell Week at Indy*]	2	—	—	2
Wills [Bill Libby's *Maurice Morning Wills at Twilight*]	1	—	—	1
Columbus [Bob Greene's *Who's on First? Who Cares?*]	—	1	—	1
Bouton [Roger Kahn's *The Life and Hard Times of Jim Bouton*]	—	—	1	1

---

* Based on 3 points for a first-place vote, 2 for a second, 1 for a third.

The judges commented as follows:

JOHN CHAMBERLAIN
News-Coverage Stories

1. Fifth Series [*The Orioles Begin Another Dynasty* by Joseph Durso]
2. Ali [*Those Three Terrible Left Hooks* by Bill Lee]
3. Super [*Super Chiefs Shock Super Bowl* by Glenn Dickey]

1. I like most of the World Series coverage for the year. The writers had comething to exploit: Brooks Robinson. I'm picking *Fifth Series* for No. 1 position because it combined the dramatic story of a single game with a lot of pertinent information about the Orioles over the years. The blend is unobtrusive, the writing firm and good.

2. *Ali* is my choice for No. 2. An honest story of a fight that was something less than magnificent.

3. *Super* for No. 3. "When you can't run and you can't pass, what does that leave you?" It leaves you with a frustrated Joe Kapp, and a superior story about a better team than the Vikings.

News-Feature Stories

1. Laver ["*I Win with My Overall Game*" by Phil Elderkin]
2. Marshall [*The Black-Draped Campus* by Jay Searcy]
3. Pancho [*Oh, Pancho* by Gene Roswell]

1. A feature, to me, should be something to challenge comparison with a magazine piece. Some of this year's crop don't quite measure up. The *Laver*, which I pick for No. 1, is a good portrait of a genius (at tennis) who, out of his own choice, avoids P.R. ostentation. With a longer view of Laver's career, this would have made a first-

rate magazine story. As it is, it's the most skillfully presented feature.

2. *Marshall,* an affecting story of a campus in a state of shock over the loss of its football team in an air accident, conveys a terrible sense of grief without spilling over into melodramatic fakery. A difficult choice for No. 2, for I liked—

3. *Pancho* almost as much as I liked *Laver.* Maybe I'm partial to stories of age outwitting youth, but this story of a middle-aged marvel seems particularly good. Incidentally, if expanded, it would have made an excellent magazine article.

Magazine Stories

1. Jacksonville [*How Jacksonville Earned Its Credit Card* by Paul Hemphill]
2. Indy [*Hell Week at Indy* by Joe Scalzo]
3. Wills [*Maurice Morning Wills at Twilight* by Bill Libby]

There isn't a single second-rate entry for the magazine category, and I hate to exalt any of them over the rest. But the rules of a contest insist on winners. Recognizing that profiles, or close-ups, or whatever you want to call character pieces, are easier to focus than stories of situations or institutions, let's put aside such excellent biographies as *Hogan* and *Kapp* and let's nominate for—

1. *Jacksonville,* the story of a Cinderella basketball team built out of some flavorsomely individual players and a remarkable coach.

2. I liked *Indy* for No. 2. It's a great handling of complex material that was completely new to me.

3. For No. 3 let's go to the biographical interview piece about Maury Wills. The kids would call this "relevant." But the relevance doesn't come from any fashionable exploitation of race; it simply comes from honest probing of a reticent man's feelings.

John Hutchens
News-Coverage Stories

1. Open [*They Were Singing "God Save the Queen"* by Art Spander]
2. Star [*Jim Hickman: Authentic American Hero* by Joe Gergen]
3. Ali [*Those Three Terrible Left Hooks* by Bill Lee]

1. I like this account of Tony Jacklin's triumph for its unforced humor and lively style, along with all the detail so adroitly worked into it.

2. Even for some of the more ardent baseball fanatics the mid-summer All-Star Game is a quickly forgotten episode of no great significance, unless they have bet a bob or two on it or a star is injured. It is to be seen and heard on TV, but not to be hashed over in print like a game having some bearing on a pennant race. So this chronicle of the 1970 interleague caper in Cincinnati gives them a chance to see just how entertaining such a game can be made for the reader by a craftsman who looks at it with good humor as well as authority.

3. A vivid, genuinely absorbing chronicle of a fight that surprised the experts and, for a few moments at least, threatened to provide one of the major sports upsets of our time. I thought it was a fine example of a story in which good reporting is coupled with sound critical analysis.

News-Feature Stories

1. Fats [*Florida Fats* by Stan Hochman]
2. Dempsey [*Dempsey in the Window* by Robert Lipsyte]
3. Baseball [*A Solid Vote for Baseball* by Ray Fitzgerald]

1. A piece both sprightly and informative about an athlete who doesn't fit the standard notion of what an athlete should appear to be—lean, earnest, etc. But Fat Bob Murphy gets there just the same, and perhaps that's why we nonathletes have to enjoy reading about him. There may still be hope for all of us.

2. I cherish this little snapshot of the Old Champ for its warmth and for the skill and economy with which the writer tells so much about why Jack Dempsey is a national institution.

3. This one looks as if its author had dashed it off in a spell of Hot Stove League reminiscence, and perhaps he did. In any case, it's an artful, evocative, even poetic job, the more impressive as coming from one of the baseball writing fraternity, by popular tradition a blasé crew.

Magazine Stories

1. Kapp [*Joe Kapp: Football's Fury* by Al Stump]
2. Bear [*The Housebreaker* by Bill Bousfield]
3. Columbus [*Who's on First? Who Cares?* by Bob Greene]

1. A fine profile, with much of its quarterback-hero's unbelievable, slaphappy toughness. I'll never watch Joe Kapp play again without thinking of a dozen things in this story, including the Kapp growl as he lines his team up against the enemy.

2. An offbeat sports story, perhaps not really a sports story at all, strictly speaking, but a memorable tale of wilderness adventure that leaves the reader with admiration for a brave black bear and his compassionate pursuers.

3. The aforenoted old baseball fanatics will shed a tear as they read this melancholy obituary of baseball in a once renowned Triple-A city. It seemed to me that the author caught perfectly the pathos of the vanishing minor leagues, with all that this implies about the quality of baseball today in the upper regions.

RED SMITH
News-Coverage Stories

1. Open [*They Were Singing "God Save the Queen"* by Art Spander]

2. Star [*Jim Hickman: Authentic American Hero* by Joe Gergen]

3. Third Series [*The Brooks Robinson Story* by Phil Jackman]

1. I'll bet that every subscriber who read *Open* last June envied the writer, thinking, "What fun he has! Imagine watching and writing about something that gives you so much fun, and getting paid for it!" Not a single reader would know what sweat and tears it took to tell the news, capture the spirit of the occasion, and make deadline with such cheerful enthusiasm.

2. *Star* strains just a trifle to be cute, but does a fine all-around job of reporting on an eventful evening.

3. *Third Series.* This wouldn't be legal without a piece about Brooks Robinson.

News-Feature Stories

1. Harlem [*Harlem Playground* by Dave Klein]

2. Dempsey [*Dempsey in the Window* by Robert Lipsyte]

3. Hot Dog [*The Hero Sandwich of Sports* by Wells Twombly]

1. *Harlem.* This one really has it—the mood, the feeling, the facts. There are some fine pieces in this category, but if this isn't a unanimous choice I'll be disappointed.

2. One of those fine pieces, *Dempsey* catches the special flavor of

the subject. If *Harlem* hadn't grabbed me the way it did, I'd make this No. 1.

3. *Hot Dog.* Imagine doing that much good research and that much excellent writing on a wiener!

Magazine Stories

1. Draft [*The Making of the No. 1 Draft Choice* by Roy McHugh]
2. Bear [*The Housebreaker* by Bill Bousfield]
3. Bouton [*The Life and Hard Times of Jim Bouton* by Roger Kahn]

1. As it was last year, this is the most difficult group to judge. I think I could choose any piece in the category as the winner, and find reasons to justify the selection. *Draft* gets my vote because it is a beautiful job of detailed research and reporting, written with fine restraint.

2. *Bear* is just a hell of a good adventure story with built-in excitement.

3. If Jim Bouton had won the attention as a pitcher that he gained as an author, he would have crowded Christy Mathewson out of the Hall of Fame. Of all the words written about his book, those in *Bouton* are the best.

You would have to stand on your head to see as good a picture as the prize-winning action photo *Expos' Last Stand* by Jerry Rife of *The San Diego Evening Tribune.* This is definitely one of the strangest shots ever captured by an alert photographer in the 27 years of this series.

The winning of the feature photo, by Paul Connell of the *Boston Globe,* is imaginative and heartwarming. This marks his third victory and his second feature prize; he also won in this category in 1968. We think you will agree that his photo is warm.

So, ladies and gentlemen, here for your pleasure and edification is *Best Sports Stories 1971.*

Have fun.

IRVING T. MARSH
EDWARD EHRE

The Prize-Winning Stories

Best News-Coverage Story

THEY WERE SINGING "GOD SAVE THE QUEEN"

By Art Spander

From the San Francisco Chronicle

Copyright, ©, 1970, Chronicle Publishing Co.

Sing a chorus of "God Save the Queen" and raise a glass of Watney's Red Barrel. Fortress America has fallen to the British.

Anthony Jacklin, Scunthorpe, England, O.B.E., and magnificent striker of a golf ball, yesterday won the 70th U.S. Open with tactics that would have pleased Admiral Nelson.

He sailed over the wavelike fairways of Hazeltine National Golf Club with his fourth consecutive subpar round, a two-under 70, to shoot a total of 281, seven under, and finish an incredible seven strokes in front of second-place Dave Hill.

Seven strokes. This was a black day for the Daughters of the American Revolution. The way Jacklin plays the game, you'd think he came from a country where they invented it.

Jacklin became the first Briton in exactly 50 years to win the U.S. Open. But breaking precedent is not unusual with Tony. Last year, he became the first Briton in 18 years to win the British Open.

The final holes of yesterday's round were televised to the United Kingdom live, via satellite. And even though it was approaching midnight in England, you can imagine Jacklin's triumphant walk up the sloping 18th fairway was on more tellys than David Frost. "I'm grateful to be an Englishman," Jacklin said into the microphone.

In a country where success of late has been limited to the Beatles and the miniskirt, you had to believe that millions of others were, too.

Jacklin, 25, has good reason, naturally. In a nation where the economy is seldom more than a chip shot away from disaster, Tony will soon be worth more than the Crown Jewels.

First prize was $30,000 from the total purse of $200,000, but that's only pocket change. He's under the management of Mark Mc-Cormack, a man who has helped build Arnold Palmer and Jack Nicklaus into financial institutions that rival the Bank of England.

Jacklin said his British Open win will, in time, be worth nearly $1 million; the triumph in America certainly will not be worth any less. And all this for a lad from the county of Lincolnshire who 10 years ago worked in the steel mills for $9.50 a week.

Jacklin's seven-stroke margin of victory was the largest in 49 years. He also became only the second golfer in Open history to shoot four rounds under par. Lee Trevino did it in 1968.

And Jacklin is the first to lead all four rounds since Ben Hogan at Oakmont in 1953.

His Lordship began the warm afternoon four strokes ahead of Hill, who after three rounds was the only other player in the field under par. But Dave, whose continual criticism of the Hazeltine course earned him the title Prince of Wails, shot a one-over par 73 for an even-par total of 288.

Bob Lunn of Sacramento, playing in only his second Open, and Bob Charles of New Zealand, who tied the course record with a five-under 67, tied for third with 289's. Ken Still was fifth with 291 and Miller Barber sixth at 292.

Gary, Jack and Arnie? They were up there in the 300's. Maybe they ought to go to Britain and learn the game.

After all, it was in America, Land of the Free and Home of the Three-Putt Green, that Jacklin learned. "If I hadn't come here," said Tony, "I'd never learned to play under pressure. I couldn't have won our Open last year, or your Open this year."

Someone had best see about those immigration laws.

Jacklin won "Our Open," as he so tactfully phrased it, because he understands the game of golf. The American golfers, at least the majority, were beaten before they ever put on their two-tone shoes. They said there was no way anyone could play this golf course; to quote Pogo, "We have met the enemy and they is us."

But Jacklin put on his checkered cashmere sweater and went out and played. And played. He opened with 71 in a wind so strong they were ready to post small-golfer warnings.

All right, he's from England, and Englishmen know how to play in the wind.

Friday, however, there was no wind. And Jacklin shot 70. Saturday, there were rain showers, and Jacklin shot 70. And yesterday, there was sunshine. And Jacklin shot 70, 36–34.

As he so poignantly said, "Golf is a game of compromise. You're going to find conditions and courses you don't like. But you've got to get out there and improvise. That's the way I learned to play."

Jacklin also won because he has the resolve of Winston Churchill. Friday and Saturday, he came out of traps and out of the rough for one-putt pars. "I've known him since he was 14," said British golf writer Ken Bowden, "and he has nerves of steel. He's cocky. He believes in himself. A lot of other guys would have given up."

Like on the ninth hole yesterday. Jacklin had bogeyed seven and eight and had his lead reduced to three strokes over Hill.

He hit a bad drive on nine but came out of the rough with a four-iron to the front edge of the green. The pin was in the back and suddenly Hill was looking very good. But Tony dropped a 25-foot birdie putt.

As he climbed to the 10th tee, he passed gray-haired Phil Strubing, president of the United States Golf Association and panted: "I'll be as old as you when I finish this round."

Jacklin said the birdie on the ninth "was the turning point. It eased the pressure on me considerably. I almost let it get to me when I bogeyed seven and eight. But the putt on nine held me together."

Another birdie on 10 made certain he would never come unglued.

"It was hard not to think about the awards ceremony then, but I had to put a mental block over it and just play one hole at a time."

Jacklin is especially friendly with two American pros, Bert Yancey and Tom Weiskopf, who remind him to think—and to slow down. When Jacklin opened his locker to change his shoes before the round, there was a one-word message from Weiskopf: "Tempo."

"Every time I started to rush," he said, "I thought about the note."

He also thought about the climax. As a good many in the gallery of 22,087 broke through the marshals and surrounded the 18th green, Tony hunched over his ball. Then he holed a 25-foot putt for a birdie, dropped his putter and raised both arms in triumph.

Lord Wellington could not have done it better.

Best News-Feature Story

DEMPSEY IN THE WINDOW

By Robert Lipsyte

From The New York Times

A young Puerto Rican tapped on the restaurant window until Jack Dempsey turned and waved. Then the young man carefully took a cigarette out of his mouth and struck a classic boxing pose.

"Hi, boy," said Dempsey, shaking a big fist, and their eyes met and they both laughed.

Dempsey's partner, Jack Amiel, whispered, "How does that boy know the great Jack Dempsey? That boy can't be 21 years old. He's magic, Dempsey's magic." A crowd gathered at the window, tourists, lunchtime strollers, six student beauticians from a nearby school. The girls tapped until Dempsey, sitting on a red banquette with his back to Broadway, turned and then they sang "Happy Birthday." He blew them a kiss.

"Magic," said Amiel. "A guy once came up to us in the Luxor Baths and offered Jack $5,000 to let him knock him into the pool. Just one punch. He wanted a piece of Jack's reputation."

"When did that happen?" a man at the table asked.

"Last week," said Amiel.

William Harrison Dempsey was 75 years old yesterday. He feels good, he says, which he attributes to clean living, honesty and being nice to people. He smokes big brown cigars, but hides them under the table when youngsters march up and thrust menus under his nose. He does not merely sign his name; he makes a social contact.

"What's your name, boy?"

"Benjamin Druss."

"Better spell that last name, Benjamin." As the boy spells it out, Dempsey writes and writes. When he finishes, he says, "That your grandpa over there, Benjamin?"

"Yes, sir."

"Hi, Grandpa," calls Dempsey, and as Benjamin, who is 10, whispers, "Thank you," and begins to slip away, he grabs one of the boy's hands. "Never leave without a handshake, Benjamin."

Dempsey has been sitting in the corner booth of Jack Dempsey's Restaurant, with his back to Broadway, since 1938. The restaurant is between 49th and 50th Streets, next to the Brill Building and across Broadway from the Rivoli Theatre. It is about the last of the Broadway celebrity restaurants and there are usually old songwriters, old prizefighters, old politicians, in a room that seats nearly 300. Dempsey is usually in his corner at lunchtime and at dinnertime every day.

Tall, gray-haired, bright-eyed, Dempsey enhances a legend that did not truly flower until he retired from active prizefighting in 1927. He was not a popular champion, but he worked very hard at being a popular ex-champion. He was always available to speak, to sign autographs, to raise his hands in mock terror when someone pretended to throw a punch.

Sitting in the window, his back to the passing world, Dempsey seems frozen in time. He leans forward suddenly and asks, "Know who named me the Manassa Mauler? Damon Runyon. He was sports editor of the *Pueblo Chieftain* then and he saw me knock out George Copelin in Cripple Creek."

That was in 1915 and Dempsey was an iron bar of a man slashing through the Western mining towns. Someone reminds him how vicious he was in the ring. He shakes his head. "In the ring it was for money: if you don't take him out, he'll take you. But outside I was always nice to everybody; it costs you nothing."

There is a dignity about Dempsey, old-fashioned and courtly, that makes his reticence to offer opinions seem wise instead of shrewd, his enthusiastic hand-pumping gracious hospitality instead of good business. He accepts few speaking engagements, he says, to avoid making enemies of those he refuses. He realizes, he says, it was a mistake to campaign for Gene Tunney's son in a California Congressional election several years ago. He received criticism "from the other side."

"A champion," he says, turning to wave at the ever-present crowd outside the window, "owes everybody something. He can never pay back for all the help he got, for making him an idol."

A man rushes into the restaurant and leans across the table. "Mr. Dempsey, about 26 years ago my dad was working for you and I was going to quit school and he sent me to talk to you. I got that degree and I'm doing good now."

Dempsey reached out and grasped his hand. "Thank you," he said.

Best Magazine Story

THE HOUSEBREAKER

By Bill Bousfield

From Outdoor Life

Copyright, ©, 1970, Popular Science Publishing Co., Inc.

The afternoon was cold but bright with sunshine when Percy King and I cranked up for the run to McKenzie outpost, some 25 miles up the lake.

It was late November, and winter had already set in with its snows and sub-zero temperatures. Scout Bay, the arm that connects our cove with the main body of Lac Seul, had been frozen over for more than a week. A test hole showed four inches of firm ice there. Scout Bay is sheltered, and we knew that we might encounter vastly different conditions before we reached our destination.

We were expecting a bit of trouble, but not the kind we found.

I'm an outfitter and guide. My wife Judy and I operate Onaway Lodge, a hunting and fishing resort on Lac Seul in northwestern Ontario. The main camp and winter headquarters are seven miles north of Perrault Falls, just off the Red Lake highway.

Percy King, an Ojibwa Indian, is our head guide, my right-hand man, a jack-of-all-trades, and, as you might expect, an accomplished outdoorsman in every respect. Percy should be relating this adventure, for it is his story. But Percy never had a formal education. In this part of Ontario the first public school—or a road to get to it—was not built until shortly before his eldest son was born.

Each year at the lodge, our last guests of the season are moose hunters. In previous years moose were legal game until Christmas. This late season was abused by some hunters, who would spot bulls from small aircraft and then land on a frozen lake nearby and make the kill. To prevent that practice, the last day of the 1969 nonresident season was set for November 15, before the lake ice is thick enough to support the weight of a plane on skis.

The resident season, however, continued until December 15. So after Percy and I had bade our last nonresident guest good-bye, we still had a month to bag our winter meat.

For this type of hunting, from the start of freeze-up in the fall until the season is over, we are well fixed for transportation. Ten years ago I built our first scoot—a waterproof metal cab powered by a 65-horsepower airplane engine—to transport my hunters between the lodge and hunting sites under almost any conditions of ice, snow, slush and open water.

With the scoot we can reach all of our outposts, which at certain times of the season would be inaccessible by any other means except helicopter. The scoot can go from ice to open water and back to ice again, taking both in stride. Its speed ranges from about 30 mph on open water to a supposed 100 mph on glare ice. I've never had the nerve to push the throttle that far.

As we crossed the Bay of Islands, the blanket of snow on the ice began to disappear. This portion of the lake had been open water during the snowstorm and had only begun to freeze up later. The ice was thin. Long cracks began to appear ahead of us and snake toward the distant shoreline. We could feel the ice begin to sag under the weight of the craft and could see the frozen surface belly up ahead.

"Hold on!" I yelled at Percy over the roar of the motor and the clank of frozen slush against the scoot's metal skin. "We'll ride her out on top as long as we can."

I hauled back on the throttle, and the guide wedged himself in for what he knew would be a rough ride. We skimmed past the mouth of Shanty Narrows and hit the big open area of McKenzie Bay. There, the ice was not thick enough to hold us at any speed, and we broke through. We plowed along across the open stretch for about a mile until the ice was thicker and we could come out on top again. When we began to pick up snow cover on thicker ice, I throttled back to a more comfortable cruising speed.

The cabin at McKenzie outpost would be our headquarters for the moose hunt. It was owned by our friend and neighboring outfitter, Harry Yoachum, and sat on a clay bluff overlooking the lake. Along one side of the cabin was stacked an enormous pile of railroad ties, abandoned there years ago by a defunct lumber company. Percy pointed these out.

"Harry," he laughed, "use Ojibwa logic."

"How's that?" I asked.

"When firewood around house give out, Indian finds it easier to move house to new supply one time than to bring wood supply to old location many times."

I barely heard his words, for I had noticed something unusual about the cabin. Then I realized what it was. The door stood wide open. I distinctly recalled having checked the locked door when we had stopped by to pick up an empty gas drum just before freeze-up.

"Harry's got visitors," Percy said.

I cut the motor, and we coasted up to the dock. A black bear suddenly stood framed in the doorway. He was tall at the shoulders and looked to be a big one. I could tell by the guide's face that he was as surprised as I was. Earlier in the year, with the berry crop as short as it had been, we would have expected to find a bear looking for food around this or any other cabin. But now it was almost the dead of winter, and this creature should be tucked away somewhere in his hibernating hole, peacefully resting.

Percy didn't waste any time. While I maneuvered for a landing, he crammed shells into the clip of his semiautomatic .30/06. It was mutually understood that we were on a moose hunt, and neither of us wanted a bear. But a bruin walking around in a foot of snow at this time of year was either crazy or otherwise dangerous.

The bear stepped out of the doorway, stood broadside and studied us long enough for Percy to have put in a killing shot if we had wanted the animal. Then the bear retreated fast around the corner of the shack.

We found the cabin in a shambles. Apparently the bear was both hungry and impatient, for he had not stopped outside to reconnoiter. His tracks came straight up an old logging road, now overgrown to little more than a trail, and into the clearing. He had paused at the garbage pit long enough to dig up a few cans and had cut his foot on a broken bottle. From there he'd padded to the door of the cabin and, with raking blows, had ripped off the sign identifying the camp, plus the padlock and hasp and some pretty solid lumber to which it was attached.

Inside, a box of garbage was scattered from one end of the shack to the other, and utensils and food containers had been raked off the shelves and scattered about. A heavy bench was overturned, and the table was knocked askew. The only edibles left in the cabin were a four-pound can of sugar and another of peanut butter. Both bore teeth marks and were bent out of shape. Apparently we had interrupted the black's plan for lunch.

"Lucky we leave our own grub at Marty's," Percy said.

Marty Talgren is a commercial fisherman who lives alone at Shanty Narrows. In the warm months he operates by boat; occasionally in the winter he snowshoes the eight or 10 miles to Onaway Lodge. During the freeze-up and break-up periods, he is completely marooned.

Prior to freeze-up we had stored our groceries for this hunt at Marty's cabin. Though we had passed close by his place earlier in the afternoon, we were carrying about all the load our scoot would haul.

"Speaking of grub," I said, "do you want to go back to Marty's for it, or shall I?"

Percy grinned.

"You go," he said. "I might have a talk with old bear while you gone. Besides, I got to nail door back together."

I parked the scoot on solid ice beside Marty's dock, and while we were having coffee I told him about the bear.

"Most unusual, most unusual," he said. "Something sure wrong there. Keep your eyes open, and don't let that old black get the drop on you."

Marty declined an invitation to hunt with us, stating that he had not yet fully recovered from his last trip to town.

I got back to McKenzie outpost in late afternoon. Percy had the cabin livable again, wood split and stacked inside, and a fresh pail of hot coffee on the back of the tin cookstove.

We fixed supper and at about 8:30 put out the light for a good night's sleep. We'd be up at daybreak.

Most outposts are infested with deer mice, and McKenzie is no exception. As soon as the lights go out, the mice usually get busy and often make quite a bit of noise for their size. In spite of all the activity, I was dozing off when a different kind of scratching sound came from the front of the cabin.

"You hear that?" I called softly.

"Pretty big mouse," Percy whispered. "I hear snow squeaking under his feet."

In cold weather we usually store our rifles in the scoot. Percy, however, must have had an idea that the bear would be back, for his loaded gun was within arm's length of his bunk.

Bear shooting by flashlight is a sport I would hesitate to recommend to my friends, but we held a whispered conversation and decided we'd better finish off our nocturnal visitor then and there. At that time of year perishable food must be left in the cabin, and we often encase it in our sleeping bags to keep it from freezing after the fire goes out. I could imagine what the bruin would do to our bags to get at the food.

The cabin has two windows, one on each side of the door. They are covered with a semiopaque plastic material that lets in some light, but you can't see much more than a shadow through it. The moon was full, and by sound and shadow we finally located the bear under the window farthest from the lake. He would be behind the door when it was opened.

Percy's rifle is equipped with a peep sight, which would make for tough shooting. But we decided to take the chance.

In my long johns and socked feet, I swung the door back and did some fast sidestepping to give Percy room to shoot. When I got the flashlight beam on the bruin's backside, he was going straight away, but then he wheeled to the right just short of the outhouse. Percy got off two fast shots before the bear disappeared into the woods. One shot grazed a foreleg, and the other went through the outhouse wall.

There wasn't any choice now: we'd have to go bear hunting in the morning.

We started out as soon as we had enough light to see the tracks. Percy followed the sign leading away from the cabin and I took the bear's back trail. An old Indian guide once told me that the best way to find a bear's den is to backtrack the critter. A black doesn't like to walk in snow any farther than it has to and will come from its den straight to where it thinks it can find food. Going home, however, the bear may wander all over the countryside to throw a pursuer off its trail.

After an hour of trailing I became convinced that this black did not have a home. I found several places where he had bedded down in the snow like a moose. The sign also told me that he was desperately hungry, for in his seemingly aimless wanderings through the woods, he had paused to dig up and eat dry grass and even the dead roots from upturned stumps.

The sun was clearing the tops of the tall spruce trees and I had turned back toward the cabin to get some coffee when I heard Percy shoot. I paused in midstride, stepped off the trail and stood for five minutes, looking and listening. I heard no more shots, so I assumed that the guide had caught up with our marauder and finished it off.

What really happened, however, was considerably more dramatic than one simple shot.

The bruin had bedded down less than 500 yards from the cabin, with the obvious intention of again investigating our grub supply at his first opportunity. His tracks seemed to indicate that he was not seriously wounded. He left a few drops of blood here and there, but that could have been from the foot he had cut on a broken bottle while digging in the garbage pit.

He had eased out of his bed ahead of Percy, for the trail was dead fresh. He obviously knew he was being followed, for he had picked his way through the densest spruce and balsam thickets instead of taking the easiest course around. Along much of the route lay two trails; one was made the night before, and it occasionally headed off on a tangent. Percy knew that his best bet was to stick with the fresh tracks, even though they led through dense thickets and blowdowns, which he often had to crawl through.

The guide had wormed his way through a brushy top and pulled himself upright to plow through a heavy thicket when the bear charged with a coughing roar. It had been lying in ambush only a few yards away. Percy had no time to aim. He swung the muzzle of his gun and shot from the hip, with the black barely a rifle length beyond the front sight. The animal came to a sudden halt, shaking its head with a jerky motion, but it did not go down. Percy pressed the trigger of his semiautomatic again but got only a click. Without taking his eye off the bear, he tried to work the action with his hand. But the rifle was hopelessly jammed.

Percy was familiar enough with bears to know he had to stand his ground. Moving slowly, he drew his hunting knife out of its sheath and held it ready, waiting for the black's next move. For several seconds the two stared at one another, only a few feet apart. The black was the first to yield. It turned and ran, and, as Percy related later, "I darn sure back up just about as fast the other way."

Percy's unaimed shot had hit the bear at the bridge of its nose and plowed out through the bottom of the throat. From my experience with blacks, I am convinced of two things. First, if that one shot had not given the bruin such a wallop and done so much damage, he most likely would have continued his attack. Second, if in those tense moments of confrontation Percy had shown any sign of fear, the result could have been disastrous.

Normally the black bear is a rather docile animal that will run from a man. Above all else, it is a big bluffer. Usually when threatened it will turn and flee. There are, however, some notable exceptions.

Percy retreated a short distance before trying to clear the jammed cartridge case from his rifle. While he worked, he kept one eye peeled for the black, should it change its mind and come back looking for him. He couldn't pry the case loose. Finally he cut a stick, smoothed it down to caliber-.30 size, and punched out the empty hull from the front end of the barrel.

"After that," he said, "I was so damn mad with bear that I start to look him up a second time. But then I think, maybe gun jam again and bear won't be so polite second time. Better I go get boss."

I was at the cabin having coffee when Percy came in with his story. He flashed a wide grin as he finished it.

"I been trout guide, deer guide and moose guide," he said. "Now take good look at chicken guide."

Percy downed his coffee, and then we set out. This time we had two guns instead of the one. Percy's legs are so long that even when he's walking slow he's hard to follow. A bull moose on a dead run would have been hard pressed to match his stride along the straight path he had made to the cabin from where he'd fixed his gun.

Again we took the bruin's trail, rifles at ready. Normally I do not hunt with my safety off, but it was off now. The blood trail was heavy, and I knew that the bear couldn't have gone far. We found one blood-soaked bed and then another. We proceeded cautiously, trying not to be taken by surprise. The tracks led into a dense thicket, and Percy stopped several yards behind to cover me while I made a tight circle of the brush clump.

I got less than halfway around the thicket when a roar and a crashing of brush told me that we had found our quarry. I swung aside, trying to get a glimpse for a shot, but the cover was too dense. Percy, 30 feet behind me, was in a position from which he could see the animal lunging at me. He put it down with one shot.

When Percy stood in his tracks and pumped a second bullet into the dead bear, I gave him a questioning look.

"One for bear," he said, "and second to see if damn rifle works."

The first thing I noticed about the animal was its thinness. It was a big boar with long legs and feet like soup plates. I guessed the weight at no more than 200 pounds. In prime condition it would have gone over 450 pounds. Then we discovered the reason for the black's emaciation and strange behavior.

In my country we still have bounty hunting for wolves. Many of the wolves are snared by attaching a loop of cable, similar to that used in the controls of light aircraft, to the center of a drag pole and concealing the set in the runway of a wolf.

This big black bear, probably snuffing along, had blundered into one of those snares. We couldn't tell how far or how long he had dragged the log, but it was far enough for the wire to open a slit about two inches deep and two inches wide, completely around his neck. Possibly he had been tied to the snare pole for several weeks without food, though he must have got some water. I would guess that he had broken the last strands of snare wire only days before we met him.

Without question, the bear had been hungry and had known instinctively that he could not survive in hibernation. So he'd been out in the snow, trying to put on as many pounds as possible before his winter's nap.

The stench from the infected neck wound was horrible, and when I suggested to Percy that we skin out our trophy, he gave me one of those you-go-ahead-buddy-I'll-watch looks. But we planned to go back in the spring and bring out the skull. I was anxious to see how it would stack up against heads in the Boone and Crockett Club's book, *Records of North American Big Game.*

Our moose hunt, incidentally, was a success. Three days later I took a nice bull. Percy took me to the main camp and went back in the scoot with his son to bring out the meat. Both of them scored while they were there. The boy got a cow, and Percy knocked over a good bull, about the size of mine. Both bulls were in the 50-odd-inch class, which rates as a good trophy for the average hunter in our part of Ontario. We had our winter's meat, which was what we had gone after.

The highlight of the hunt, of course, was the bear. I'm sure we did the poor old critter a favor and saved him a lot of suffering, for in his condition he could never have survived the winter.

The World Series

THE BALTIMORE BULLS ATTACK THE REDS
(WORLD SERIES GAME II)

By Phil Pepe

From the New York Daily News

Copyright, ©, 1970, New York Daily News

The hitters hit and the fielders fielded and the runners ran for the Orioles and Reds today. Even the umpires stayed on their feet. The story of today's second game of the World Series is a thesis on the erratic and unpredictable behavior of bulls—the ones that marched out of Cincinnati and Baltimore bullpens.

The Baltimore bulls did what they were supposed to do and the Cincinnati bulls didn't do what they were supposed to do, especially in the fifth inning, when Elrod Hendricks slammed an opposite-field, two-run double to left to climax a five-run rally that sparked the Orioles to a 6–5 victory. For the second straight day, the Reds blew a three-run lead and dropped a one-run decision and it sends them to Baltimore trailing the Series, two games to none.

The Reds are reminded that no team has ever lost the first two games at home and come back to win the World Series. It was a fact they didn't need to know to realize they are in trouble.

It was a day for the hitters and a day in which both managers made use of all that bull. Earl Weaver of the Orioles did everything right and Sparky Anderson did everything wrong.

Weaver had Dick Hall and Marcelino Lopez in his bullpen and he had Brooks Robinson sucking up ground balls at third and that was more than enough to offset the home-run power of Bobby Tolan and Johnny Bench. You know how bulls get when they see red.

Game No. 1 belonged to umpire Ken Burkhart, but today, Sparky Anderson had nobody to blame but himself. He chose to bring in 20-year-old Milt Wilcox. A veteran of 22 major-league innings, he came out of the pen in the fifth, and Wilcox ran right into the middle of a five-run inning that turned the game around for the Birds.

"Brooks Robinson beat us both games," said Anderson. He meant Robby's glove, but it wasn't Brooks who brought in the Cincy bulls, and it wasn't Brooks who shut the Reds off in the last few innings. Dick Hall did that. The 40-year-and-two-week-old herky-jerky reliever came on with the Reds threatening in the seventh. He threw one pitch to bail out of the inning and 11 more to retire the Reds in rapid succession in the eighth and ninth to preserve the victory the Red relievers so generously gave away.

The Reds had piled up their usual three-run lead in the first inning, clubbing Mike Cuellar, Baltimore's 24-game winner, for three hits. After shortstop Mark Belanger booted Pete Rose's shot for an error and Tolan forced Rose at second, Tony Perez laced a single to center. Johnny Bench chased Tolan to third with a long drive to right and Lee May followed with a shot he made sure Brooks Robinson couldn't reach.

It soared on a line into the left-center slot, Tolan and Perez scoring, and when Paul Blair let the ball slip out of his hand while attempting to throw, May went to third. It looked like it would be a big play when Hal McRae dared to bunt in the direction of the O's human vacuum cleaner at third. He tapped it softly enough so that Robby couldn't reach it. Cuellar did, and his hurried, back-handed throw home sailed past catcher Elrod Hendricks. It was scored a single and the Reds had their three and it was up to Jim McGlothlin to hold it.

Three wasn't enough yesterday, and, fearing it might not be today, Tolan led off the third and hit Cuellar's 2–0 pitch into the second level in right for a 4–0 lead. Maybe McGlothlin could hold that. He couldn't.

Boog Powell led off the fourth with a tremendous home run, his second in two days, a shot that soared into the second level over the 404 sign in dead center. It probably traveled close to 475 feet and may have scared the stuffing out of McGlothlin. Meanwhile, the Big Red Machine had chewed up another left-hander, and Brooks Robinson had done his part to keep the Orioles in the game.

When Johnny Bench walked with one out in the third, Weaver called on his first bull, Tom Phoebus. The Reds had won 17 of 19 against left-handers at home, and Cuellar looked like just another left-hander to them. The first hitter for Phoebus was Lee May, who keeps making the same mistake. He keeps hitting the ball past

Brooks Robinson . . . and Brooks Robinson keeps coming up with the ball after it passes him. This time, Brooks turned May's "double" into a double play to bail the Orioles out for probably the 9,475th time in his 14 years.

What it all meant was that Robby's play and Powell's homer put the Orioles within striking distance, only three runs down, batting in the fifth.

The fatal fifth started innocently enough, Belanger popping to short and pinch-hitter Chico Salmon getting one up the middle for a single. Don Buford singled to right and Paul Blair singled to left for 4–2 and the menacing figure of Boog Powell, all 240 pounds of him. Something told Anderson now was the time to move. His move was to bring in Wilcox, the 20-year-old right-hander.

Why not ace bull Wayne Granger or No. 2 bull Clay Carroll? Too early.

Then why not Don Gullett, the lefty fireballer who is only 19, but has more experience than Wilcox?

"If I bring in Gullett," Sparky explained, "I got problems if I have to face Powell in the eighth or ninth. I can't give that boy up that early."

So Sparky wound up with problems in the fifth, when the game was on the line. And that's how Powell hit, on the line, a drive to left that delivered Buford for 4–3. Wilcox got Frank Robinson on a drive to deep right, but Brooks Robinson's grounder found a hole between first and second to tie it.

Now the hitter was Ellie Hendricks, lefty. Still no Gullett. Wilcox pitched and Hendricks became a hero without outside help from an umpire. He slammed Wilcox's 3–2 pitch past Perez at third, just inside the line, for a two-run double, and Weaver still hadn't used his prize bulls.

Moe Drabowsky, of 1966 World Series relief fame, worked the fifth and sixth and part of the seventh. He helped make things interesting and frustrating for the Reds—by serving Johnny Bench's first Series home run in the sixth to cut the lead to 6–5. Then things got squirmy in the seventh.

Ty Cline pinch-hit a single to start, and Angel Bravo pinch-hit a sacrifice bunt to put the tying run on second. When Rose walked, it was time for Weaver to get bullish. He brought in lefty Marcelino Lopez to pitch to Tolan. A master stroke. Tolan popped foul to third.

Weaver stuck a "prime" brand on his left-handed bull and called in Hall to pitch to the dangerous Perez. And Hall, throwing like a 40-year-old daddy pitching to his 12-year-old son, got the dangerous Perez to hit the ball to third base. That's where Brooks Robinson hangs out; forget it, Perez, forget it, Reds.

And that was it, fans. For the final two innings, Dick Hall, Swarthmore graduate, carefully dismantled the Big Red Machine. He had one scare, with two out in the ninth. Jimmy Stewart played the role of a pinch hitter and almost took the part of Babe Ruth. He drove Hall's fast ball on a screaming line to straightaway center and deep. But Blair got back there to pick it off and Baltimore's bulls had prevailed. Olé.

THE BROOKS ROBINSON STORY
(WORLD SERIES GAME III)

By Phil Jackman

From The Baltimore Sun

The Oriole third baseman could have overslept and missed the fourth game of the World Series today and it wouldn't have mattered, the 1970 showdown has already been named the Brooks Robinson Story.

For the third game in a row yesterday, The Man did things with the glove and bat that had 51,773 stadium watchers and a few more than that looking in on the tube gaping in amazement. Even a kid with a Jules Verne imagination couldn't dream up the Series Brooks has already had.

And you get the impression he's beginning to realize it. "It is strange," he said, "having the opportunity to make plays three games in a row like that. Sometimes you go a week without a tough play."

After watching B. Robby bash a two-run double in the first inning to get the Birds started toward a 9–3 victory behind Dave McNally, Cincinnati's Sparky Anderson sighed, "Robinson continues to do it in the field . . . and now he's doing it with his bat."

It wasn't what Sparky said, it was the way he said it. Resignation fairly dripped from his words. "If the Orioles win the Series and he doesn't get the car as the Most Valuable Player, they should have a total investigation."

Brooks had a second double to go with his clutch belt in the first inning, but these hits paled next to the three home runs the O's stroked, including a grand slam by McNally, and his daily test of your credulity afield.

This latest bit of larceny occurred in the sixth inning and involved Johnny Bench, who has to be thinking he's as snake-bit as teammate Lee May about now.

In the first two games, Robinson made masterpieces that not only robbed May of base hits but the Reds of much-needed runs. One was a backhanded stop and blind, over-the-shoulder throw from Section 27, Riverfront Stadium, Cincinnati, the second a diving stop and subsequent double play on a ball that should have been a double.

Cincy was still within hailing distance, trailing 4–1, when Bench bashed a liner into left field . . . wait a minute, Brooks has it with a headlong leap into the dust.

Earlier, Dave Johnson had made a diving grab of a Pete Rose belt the Reds' right fielder figured was good for three bases. "Defensively, they're so fine," Anderson pointed out, "that it doesn't matter where you hit the ball.

"Rose said he would have had a triple up the alley on the ball Johnson caught. Then again, Blair might have cut it off, who knows?"

"It wouldn't have got to the fence," the Orioles' center fielder assured. "Fact, I was thinking single if Davey didn't get to it."

So much for defense, except to say Rex Barney came up with the best line of the day when he was asked if B. Robby was back in the clubhouse following TV interviews: "He's not at his locker yet, but four guys are over there interviewing his glove."

This was an offensive game, from the rockets which kept leaving the premises while the home team was at bat to the fierce liners the Reds kept hitting and the O's kept catching.

Baltimore never trailed, which is an oddity in this Series, but it was never out of danger until McNally became the first pitcher in the history of October to bust a grand slam. It was the 12th Series slam and the first by a guy from Montana.

The other homer strokers for the Birds were Frank Robinson, a mammoth shot fielded by one of Baltimore's finest beyond the hedge in dead center, and Don Buford, who reached the bleachers beyond the 360 sign in right.

Considering that McNally's homer went to left, the Birds got great dispersion on their fifth, sixth and seventh circuit smashes of the test.

While Brooks Robby passes off what happened in last year's Series as "one of those things—a calamity of errors," something he did very early this season suggests otherwise, although he denies it.

Emblazoned across Brooks's suitcase all summer has been the identification strip: "Brooks Robinson, Baltimore Orioles, 1970 World Champions."

"I put that on there in April before our first road trip," the third baseman said. "I don't know why, I just did it."

It being done he no doubt figured he had to make good on the claim after going 1-for-19 against the Mets. "I always wish I had done more against New York," he admits, and now it's Cincinnati paying the price.

SAVED BY LEE MAY'S BAT
(WORLD SERIES GAME IV)

By Allen Lewis

From The Philadelphia Inquirer

The Big Red Machine was ready to be hauled to the scrap heap Wednesday, when massive Lee May recharged the batteries with one swing of his bat and saved the National League champions from the humiliation of a World Series sweep.

May, the least publicized member of the Cincinnati Reds' three-man wrecking crew, slammed a three-run homer in the eighth inning to bring his team from behind to a 6–5 victory over the Baltimore Orioles before 53,007 at Memorial Stadium.

The Orioles, who could do nothing wrong in winning the first three Series games, twice came from behind in this contest and seemed on the verge of their 18th consecutive victory when they entered the eighth inning with a 5–4 lead in this best-of-seven-game fall classic.

Before the inning was over, the Reds had the lead, and relief ace Clay Carroll protected the margin to the finish, precluding the 11th four-game sweep in World Series history.

The Reds thus became only the third team to win the fourth game in a World Series after losing the first three. The 1910 Chicago Cubs won the fourth contest from the Philadelphia Athletics and the 1937 New York Giants won the fourth game from the New York Yankees, each victory coming after three defeats.

In an omen that bodes ill for the Reds, neither the Cubs nor the Giants won the fifth game. What's more, Cincinnati manager Sparky Anderson still has pitching troubles.

The rookie pilot said veteran southpaw Jim Merritt, a 20-game winner with an ailing arm, would be his starter Thursday against Mike Cuellar, the 24-game-winning southpaw who was knocked out of the box in the third inning of the second Series set-to.

The most cheering news for the Reds, who still feel they can win the Series if they take the fifth game and force a return to Cincinnati, is a forecast of rain Thursday and possibly Friday, too.

"I could go for a little rain tomorrow," Anderson admitted. "But I think and hope we can come back and win. I honestly think we can if we take them back to Cincinnati."

For a good while Wednesday, a return to Cincinnati seemed very remote. With classy Baltimore third-baseman Brooks Robinson banging out a home run and three singles in four trips to the plate, the Birds overcame Red leads of 1–0 and 2–1 to move ahead, 5–3, behind the steady pitching of Jim Palmer, the first-game winner.

An inside 3–3 pitch to Tony Perez for Palmer's fourth walk and a line single to the left-field corner by Johnny Bench started the Cincinnati eighth and finished Palmer.

Reliever Eddie Watt came out of the bullpen to pitch to May, who said he had never seen the squatty right-hander before.

"I went back to the dugout to find out what he throws," said May, "and they told me he was a sinker, slider pitcher.

"I was looking for something from the middle of the plate in."

May didn't keep the crowd in suspense. The 6-foot-3, 195-pound slugger, who hit 34 homers in the regular season and one in the National League championship play-offs, swung at Watt's first pitch.

From the crack of the bat, there was no doubt about where it was going.

The ball landed deep in the left-center seats for May's second homer of the Series.

"It was a sinker about waist high," said May, who batted in four of the Reds runs. His infield single in the third gave the Reds a brief 2–1 lead.

"I threw a fast ball that started outside and came back over the middle of the plate," mourned the unhappy Watt.

May's homer was the third of the game. After the Reds scored in the second, Brooks Robinson homered to the left-field seats to tie the game at 1–1.

Then, after the Birds chased starter Gary Nolan with a three-run rally in the third, Pete Rose homered into the Orioles' bullpen in left-center in the fifth to shave Baltimore's lead to 4–3.

Rose, the Reds' captain, figured in two big fielding plays, too. The right fielder threw out Brooks Robinson as he was trying to score in the third inning, and Rose's bad-hop throw past third helped the Birds score their final run in the sixth.

The Reds, who squandered leads of 3–0 and 4–0 in the first two games, scored their second-inning run on a walk to May and a triple to right-center by rookie shortstop Dave Concepcion.

After Brooks tied it, the Reds tallied in the third on a walk to Bobby Tolan, Rose's single to center and May's two-out single, which shortstop Belanger stopped with a dive behind second.

Palmer started the big Baltimore third with a single. Two outs later, Boog Powell walked, Frank Robinson singled to left for a run, and Brooks Robinson singled to center for another, with the runners moving to second and third when Tolan fumbled the hit.

Lefty Don Gullett replaced Nolan and left-handed-hitting Ellie Hendricks grounded a single to right. The first Robinson scored, but the slower Brooks was nailed by Rose's accurate one-hop throw, ending the inning.

Gullett blanked the Birds until the sixth when Brooks Robinson singled and raced for third on a single to right by Hendricks. Rose's throw to third skittered into the Baltimore dugout, allowing Brooks to score and Hendricks to take third.

That's when Carroll came on to stymie the Orioles with his moving fast ball and curve and give May a chance to become the big hero.

There's a theory among baseball men that every winning streak is followed by a losing streak.

"I hope it's true," said Anderson.

"No, I don't agree with that," said Baltimore manager Earl Weaver. "Our longest losing streak this year is three games."

Reminded that this was his first defeat in more than three and one-half weeks, Weaver said, "It's not a good feeling."

THE ORIOLES BEGIN ANOTHER DYNASTY
(WORLD SERIES GAME V)

By Joseph Durso

From The New York Times

One year after their memorable loss to the New York Mets, the Baltimore Orioles batted their way to a 9–3 victory over the Cincinnati Reds today and captured the 67th World Series, four games to one.

Spotting the National League champions three runs in the first inning, they charged back with six of their own inside three innings. And by the time Brooks Robinson threw out the last Cincinnati batter to end the game, they had pounded six pitchers for 15 hits and convincingly won the championship of baseball.

It was an awesome display by a team that was upset by the Mets in five games last October, and every man in the lineup contributed to it. All eight regulars got hits, including home runs by Frank Robinson and Merv Rettenmund, and the only Oriole who did not get a hit was Mike Cuellar, the pitcher.

But Cuellar, a 33-year-old Cuban left-hander, lent a hand with the fanciest pitching of the Series. Troubled by a bad hip and rattled by the three-run burst at the start, he allowed Cincinnati only two singles and a walk over the last eight innings and retired 23 of the final 26 batters.

For the Orioles, who dominated the American League the last two years, the victory marked them as the closest thing to a dynasty in baseball—a sport that has become the graveyard for "dynasties" in recent years.

They have played in three World Series in five years, have taken two of them and have won two of every three games during the last two seasons.

They also have become the richest baseball players around. They earned $15,000 in play-off and World Series money last year and will earn perhaps $18,500 this year.

The Orioles reaped these rewards today after a free-swinging Series in which they made 50 hits and scored 33 runs. They also hit 10 home runs, breaking the record for a five-game Series set by the New York Yankees in 1961, also against Cincinnati.

At the outset this afternoon, the Orioles were confronted by rainy weather and an aroused Cincinnati team that had beaten them yesterday after three straight losses. But neither the rain nor the Redlegs' revival proved enough to thwart both starting pitchers— Cuellar, a 24-game winner, and Jim Merritt, a 20-game winner, went to work on an "if" basis: They would pitch if their physical conditions permitted. Cuellar had been bothered lately by a sore hip and Merritt had been troubled for six weeks by a sore elbow.

Both decided to pitch, however, and both were promptly surrounded by trouble.

In the top of the first, the Reds raked Cuellar with four hits, starting with a looping double to right field by Pete Rose. With two down, John Bench singled to left for one run and Lee May, the hero of yesterday's Cincinnati revival, lined the next pitch off the left-field wall for a double.

That sent Bench to third base and manager Earl Weaver to the mound with memories of Cuellar's rough outing against the Reds last Sunday: They got three runs in the first inning then and knocked him out inside three innings.

Weaver went back to the dugout, Cuellar went back to work, Hal McRae doubled to right-center and once more Cincinnati was off to a flying start. It was the fourth time in five games the Reds had taken an early lead, but they were about to lose this one, too.

In the bottom of the inning, Paul Blair singled to left field, with McRae diving and trapping the ball, and Frank Robinson lifted a 3–2 pitch into the left-field seats near the foul line. It was his second home run of the Series, his sixth in three World Series dating to 1961, and just that fast it was a 3–2 ball game.

But that was only the beginning of Baltimore's comeback. Cuellar settled down and retired 11 Cincinnati batters in a row while the Orioles kept scoring in two-run spurts.

In the second inning, they chased Merritt after a long fly by Brooks Robinson, a walk to Dave Johnson, a single to center by Andy Etchebarren and a fly to right by Cuellar that Rose grabbed on the run. Manager Sparky Anderson immediately called to his bullpen for Wayne Granger, who had made 67 appearances and 35 "saves" this season.

But Mark Belanger, a .218 hitter with only one single in the Series, immediately dragged a single past shortstop and Johnson scored the tying run. Then, when Blair lined a solid single to left, Etchebarren scored ahead of a wide throw home and Baltimore was in front, 4–3.

One inning later, the Orioles went at it again with two more runs and this time they chased Granger. John (Boog) Powell opened with a double to right-center and scored sliding when Rettenmund bounced a single through the middle of the infield. Rettenmund took second on the throw home, took third on Brooks Robinson's spinning grounder to Tommy Helms and scored when Johnson singled through the left side.

Now it was 6–3, Baltimore, and Milt Wilcox was pitching for the Reds, trying to calm the Oriole bats. He did, too, retiring five straight batters. But even when they make out, the Orioles hurt with their bats. The last man Wilcox faced was Frank Robinson, who lined a hard shot off the 20-year-old rookie's right hip, with Tony Perez retrieving the ball and throwing to first for the out.

Then in the fifth, after Wilcox had left for a pinch hitter, it was Tony Cloninger's turn to suffer. The second man he pitched to was Rettenmund, who was brushed back by a high hard one and then popped a home run into the right-field seats.

Before the inning was over, Brooks Robinson singled to center, Johnson doubled past third, and Etchebarren drew an intentional walk. But the Reds bailed out of that mess with the bases loaded and were still trailing, 7–3, with four innings to go.

But Cuellar, backed up by an airtight defense, kept the Reds from any late uprising. After a walk to Angel Bravo in the fifth, Cuellar retired six more batters in a row. One of them, Perez, ripped a line drive toward left field, but Belanger speared it with an acrobatic leap.

Then in the seventh, Helms and Dave Concepcion singled with one down, but Cuellar took Bernie Carbo's bouncer and started a double play by way of second base. And in the ninth, Bench pulled a low liner past third, but Brooks Robinson, who had robbed him twice before in the Series, made a diving backhand catch in the dirt.

The Orioles, meanwhile, were still swinging away as they neared the end of their last working day of the season. In the eighth, they got two more runs off Ray Washburn on a walk plus singles by Blair, Frank Robinson and Johnson.

Then Clay Carroll, the 18th Cincinnati pitcher of the Series, struck out two of the last three batters and the Baltimore bats were finally silent.

For the Orioles, the towering figure throughout was the 33-year-old Brooks Robinson, who guards third base like Horatius at the bridge. He not only made spectacular plays with his glove, but also made nine hits in five games (as did Blair), and they included two home runs and two doubles.

Soon after he threw out Pat Corrales for the final out to the cheers of the crowd of 45,431, he was voted the winner of the *Sport* magazine award—a new car—as the outstanding player in the Series.

So the Orioles, who swept the Los Angeles Dodgers in four games in 1966, became the avenging angels of the American League, which had lost two of the last three World Series and the last eight All-Star Games to the National League.

And *The Baltimore Evening Sun* echoed the prevailing mood around Memorial Stadium tonight: "Bring on the Mets again."

Other Baseball

JIM HICKMAN: AUTHENTIC AMERICAN HERO

By Joe Gergen

From Newsday

Copyright, ©, 1970, Newsday, Inc.

It began with Richard Nixon and ended with Jim Hickman. Imagine. It began with red, white and blue bases and ended in a black and blue collision. Imagine. It began with Morganna Roberts failing for the first time and ended with the American League failing for the eighth consecutive time. No imagination necessary.

The All-Star Game played last night in Cincinnati's Riverfront Stadium, a ball park of tomorrow because it isn't finished today, was an All-Star Game for all seasons. The President of the United States and Cincinnati threw out the first ball and waited 12 innings to see Hickman, another former loser, get a winning hit. Hickman, who still can't win them all, didn't get kissed by Morganna. Instead, he was hugged by Luman Harris. At least he didn't get hurt.

Dennis Menke left the park with a deep red spot on his cheek from a throw and a puffy bruise on his hand from a pitch, and Pete Rose needed an ice pack for his left knee. And they were the winners. Ray Fosse, one of the losers, looked so bad, he was sent to the hospital. And to think they call this an exhibition game. "It was fun," Bud Harrelson of the Mets said. "It was really fun."

The final score of the fun was National League, 5; American League, 4. The ending was the same, only different. The National League almost always wins, but they usually don't have to come from behind. Last night, they had to score three runs in the ninth and one in the 12th. And Rose had to run over Fosse at home plate. "Quite a collision," Gil Hodges, the manager, said. "It took a bull-dog like Pete to score."

The game was strictly no contest for eight innings. Morganna had caused the only excitement until then by climbing out of the stands behind third base in the first inning and being pinched, literally, by a cop. She was dressed like Myra Breckenridge, trying to hide her sex and identity in a loose green top and brown slacks. She didn't fool Fritz Peterson, standing nearby in the American League dugout, the park policeman or anyone else in the stadium. "The cop had a real good hold on her," Peterson said. "When she was being led off, she said something into the dugout. I think it was, 'You can't win them all.' No, I remember now it was, 'Better luck next time.'"

Morganna, her baseball record now 5–1, was booked and released in $50 bail. "The first tape-measure job in Riverfront Stadium," a man commented.

Baseball had been saved from Morganna by an alert cop. But, by the ninth inning, it appeared nothing could save baseball from boredom. The American League had scored four runs without much fuss, the National League had scored one on a double-play grounder, Carl Yastrzemski was already being congratulated for winning the Most Valuable Player award, and the President was three outs from Washington. The American League, imagine, was going to win an All-Star Game.

Then Catfish Hunter of Oakland walked in from the bullpen. The first batter was Dick Dietz of the Giants, who had never swung a bat in an All-Star Game. He hit a very long home run over the center-field fence. "The second tape-measure job in Riverfront Stadium," the man said. Harrelson singled for his second single. One out later, Joe Morgan singled and the pitcher suddenly was Peterson. The batter, Willie McCovey, hit a grounder. "I thought it was a double play," Peterson said. It was a single, an AstroTurf single. The score was 4–3, the next pitcher, Mel Stottlemyre.

Roberto Clemente, who didn't want to come all the way to Cincinnati to play in an exhibition game, hit a long sacrifice fly and the game was tied. American League manager Earl Weaver thought about having a relief pitcher, a Ron Perranoski or a Lindy McDaniel, in that inning. He thought, Who needs them? That's what he said, he thought. "What you're trying to get me to say is that I should take one pitcher off and put another on," he said, "and I'm not going to say that."

The 10th passed quickly, the 11th also, and the 12th was in danger of extinction. Yastrzemski had a soft hit, tying him with Ducky Medwick and Ted Williams for an All-Star record, in the top of the inning and the AL had nothing else. The NL had two quick outs before Rose hit a single off Clyde Wright. Then Billy Grabarkewitz singled and the batter was, of all people, Hickman.

That's the same Hickman of whom Casey Stengel once sang, "You can't improve your average with your bat upon your shoulder, tra-la, tra-la, tra-la." The same Jim Hickman who it was said didn't need a bat to play the game. The same Jim Hickman who didn't get to last night's game until 5:00 P.M., who didn't get onto the field until the last National Leaguer was walking out of the batting cage, who was on two flights with mechanical difficulties on the same day in Chicago. In short, the same Jim Hickman.

Jim Hickman swung, the ball went into center field toward another former Met, Amos Otis, and Rose tore around third. Hickman ran into a bear hug from first-base coach Harris. Fosse, the catcher whom Rose had invited to his house for a bull session the previous night, stood waiting for the throw. He never got to catch it. Rose plowed into and over him, and Fosse rolled over in pain.

"He could have slid around him," Wright charged angrily. Rose, who got a bruised knee for his trouble, thought otherwise. "He was two or three feet up the line and straddling it," Rose said. "I started to slide and realized I couldn't make it to the plate that way. I play to win, so that's the way I had to play tonight. I know Frank Robinson would have done it, and that's the best player in their league.

"Besides," he said, leaning back on the training table, "it was Wright's fault. He threw the pitch to Hickman."

And so, Jim Hickman became an authentic American hero. "The biggest hit of my career," he said. And the American League had lost another one. "I'm 0-and-7 now," said Yastrzemski, looking suspiciously at his MVP trophy.

Morganna was dancing in Newport, Kentucky, when the President finally left for Washington.

A SOLID VOTE FOR BASEBALL

By Ray Fitzgerald

From the Boston Globe

Copyright, ©, 1970, Boston Globe Newspaper Co.

Maybe you think, from what you've read over the winter, that baseball was born in a lawyer's office, grew up in a courtroom and flourishes in a bookmaker's shop.

That's not so. Baseball is more than Bowie Kuhn, Curt Flood, Marvin Miller and Dennis McLain. It's more than franchise shifts and lawsuits.

Baseball is grace and talent under pressure. It's Carl Yastrzemski scooping up a single on the gallop in left field at Fenway and throwing the tying run out at the plate.

It's Frank Howard missing and the crowd going "Oooooh," and Howard three innings later hitting the ball 450 feet.

It's Harmon Killebrew's tape-measure homer into the center-field stands and Rico Petrocelli with his short swing sending the ball 316 feet into the left-field screen.

Baseball is Bert Campaneris stealing third on a pitchout, George Scott turning a line drive into a double play. It's a Frank Robinson triple and Sam McDowell's fast ball.

Baseball is also excitement off the field. It's cops on horseback and crowds milling around the players' entrance.

It's kids leaning on a dugout before a game, yelling "Yaz, gimme a autograph." It's a guy in the bleachers with a beer asking "Why do they leave the bum in?" and a lady in a box seat asking "Why don't they take the bum out?"

Baseball is watching the scoreboard for out-of-town results, and fighting for a ball with five people you've never seen before.

It's leaving your seat in the ninth when your team is five runs behind, but lingering in the runway to watch because somehow you think they'll pull victory out.

For a sports writer, baseball is a bunch of memories, most of which have little to do with runs, hits and errors.

It is 10,000 people at an airport to greet a team, and 1,000 people in a Cleveland Stadium that seats 80,000. It is Russ Gibson being told he is not going to make the club and Mike Derrick being told that he is.

It is Tom Satriano standing in a Washington hotel lobby holding this two-week-old baby, no bigger than a show box, and it's Mrs. Jerry Stephenson in a bikini, stopping traffic at the Ranch House Motel swimming pool in Winter Haven.

Baseball is writing 20 paragraphs in 20 minutes in order to catch a plane to Cleveland, and paying two dollars for one egg, three strips of bacon and some toast in the hotel coffee shop in New York.

The game is a chance to meet nice guys like Brooks Robinson, spoiled kids like Tony Horton and churls like Leo Durocher.

Baseball is contrast. It's Sparky Lyle throwing his glove in a trash barrel after giving up a game-winning grand slam, and it's Sparky Lyle surrounded by reporters after striking out the side with the bases loaded.

There is plenty wrong with baseball. Club owners are autocratic and players are greedy. The season is too long and the hot dogs are terrible.

A critic once characterized baseball as six minutes of action crammed into two and one-half hours.

Okay, I'll buy that. Much of the beauty of the game is in the mind of the beholder. What if the batter walks? Will he steal? Can he squeeze? Is the pitcher tired? Can the man pinch-hit? There is plenty of nonaction.

Nonetheless, you can have your blue lines, red dogs and double dribbles. Tomorrow the best of sports in a sports-crazy country returns to Fenway Park and I'll eat a hot dog if it kills me.

MAURICE MORNING WILLS AT TWILIGHT

By Bill Libby

From West Magazine, Los Angeles Times

Copyright, ©, 1970, William (Bill) Libby

Maurice Morning Wills sat in the dugout at twilight, the twilight of another day in his 20th year in professional baseball, the twilight of his controversial career. He was 18 years old when he went pro. He will be 38 years old the last month of this season. Baseball has filled the greatest part of his life and he has not known much beyond the ball field. "It has been my way of life, which someday soon will be absolutely altered," he sighed. "It is the same for all athletes, but for no one else. A person does not stop being a lawyer or doctor or writer around 40. Perhaps he's just entering the prime of his life at that age. But I'm near the end now, and no one ever will know how hard it is to maintain a level of excellence. I can do it, but it takes extra effort. I get tired. No one will ever know how tired I get sometimes now."

He is 5-foot-10 in height and weighs 165 pounds, which is very small for a ball player, but he remains lean and hard. He is no longer young, which is betrayed by a smear of gray in his closely cropped hair. He had been practicing in the late-afternoon sun and the sweat now streamed down his walnut-colored skin, which seemed drawn taut with fatigue over his delicate features. "I'm not a pitcher who works every fourth or fifth day or a slugger who does a job with one swing of the bat, but a hustler who has to use all of his arms and legs and heart and brain every minute of every game to be better than the next fellow. This takes its toll," he said.

He is a complex person, exceptionally proud and sensitive, intelligent and articulate, though this is not generally known because he is not really well known. He does not give much of himself away to anyone and will talk only to the old, old friend or writer who is an old friend. He arrived at the top late and has lingered longer than anyone ever expected. He left L.A. in controversy and returned in controversy and all the while has slipped through the shadows, saying little about what has gone on inside of him.

If he has a single philosophy that enables him to get by it may be that he will not permit himself to regret anything he ever has done. "I have always thought everything through and acted in a way that I felt justified, so I will always accept the consequences of my behavior," he explains. "I don't feel that I have made mistakes. Things have not always turned out as I would have hoped them to, but I always did what I believed the right thing at the time."

His has been a hard life. He was born and reared in a black ghetto in Washington, D.C., one of 13 children of a Baptist minister who had to work as a machinist at the Navy Yard to make ends meet and a mother who had to work as an elevator operator to ensure their survival. "We had all we needed, but not all we wanted," Maury says. "We are not a close family. I doubt most big families are. It is too complicated. I try to see my brothers and sisters when I am in the East, but there are too many of them for me to keep in touch with them. They all lead ordinary lives. They were all brought into a certain world and were caught up in it. They never found a way of breaking out as I did."

His mother is still living, but his father passed away seven years ago. "He only saw me play once on the sandlots and once in the majors in all of his life," Maury says. "I admired my father because he did his best for us, but we weren't friends who did things together the way some fathers and sons do. I am religious, but in my way, not his way. When I was living home and when I first came to L.A. and lived with a minister and his family on West Adams, I went to services constantly, but I don't get a chance anymore. I believe living right is more important than attending church three times a week."

Small, but swift and talented, Maury, who had to use a paper bag for a glove when he first began to haunt the sandlots, developed into a fine all-around athlete in high school. He received college scholarship offers as a T-formation quarterback. However, he married Gertrude Elliott and began a family while still in high school, so he felt he had to make some money. Inspired when Jackie Robinson became the first black in big-league baseball in 1947, Maury attended some tryout camps in hopes of being offered a pro contract as a pitcher.

Although he compiled an outstanding record, most teams rejected him because of his size. The Dodgers offered him $500 to sign and he grabbed it. He went to his first spring training camp at Vero Beach in 1951. The Dodgers had all of their minor-league clubs there, too, and there was an abundance of pitchers among the 400 hopefuls on hand. There was a shortage of infielders, so Maury volunteered to try second base. He was assigned to Hornell, New York, in the Pony League as an infielder.

For the next eight years, Wills bounced around the bush leagues in buses, staying in second-rate hotels and eating hamburgers for dinner. He played various positions before he was settled in at shortstop. He fielded well and hit well and led leagues in stolen bases, but he did not get even a one-game trial in the majors all this time. He started out making $135 a month and after many years he was making only $500 a month and his children were doing without and he was having to play winter ball in Mexico, Puerto Rico and Venezuela.

Once he was promoted to Fort Worth. Here, he was the first Negro player. He had trouble finding places to sleep and eat. He lived alone and ate alone. Travel reservations were made in advance for the others, but not for him. He was depressed and his play suffered. He was demoted to Pueblo and considered giving up.

Another time, he was purchased "conditionally" by Detroit. If he made the Tigers, they had to pay $35,000 for him. He had a spectacular spring training period at the end of which they decided he was too small and returned him to the Dodgers, who sent him to Spokane. Again, he considered giving up.

He sits in a fancy restaurant on the Sunset Strip, his hands wrapped around a fancy cup of coffee, and he closes his eyes for a moment and he remembers when he drank coffee in cardboard containers in greasy dives and he says, "I'm not a quitter, but all those years waiting for my chance tore my insides out little by little."

Every year he went to spring training at Vero Beach with the Dodgers and lived with the minor leaguers, four to a room in double-deck bunks, and dreamed of the day he could move into the major-league annex with a private room with a private toilet, but after a while the dream seemed foolish and he began to give up hope.

Finally, in 1959, in the middle of Maury's ninth season in the minors and the Dodgers' second season in L.A., he was called up.

He walked into the dressing room with his gear tied in a cardboard box, and one of the veterans cruelly asked him if he had brought his lunch. He sat down and picked up a newspaper and read how ridiculous it was for the Dodgers to suppose he could help them. For a while, he did not, but in the end he helped them into the World Series.

Late in the season, there was one big series which was to prove ironic. To celebrate a "Pacific Festival," the best player in the three-game set with the Giants was awarded a free trip to Japan for two. Maury had a big series, won the trip, but didn't take it. He never was much of one for going to Japan.

Reporting to Vero Beach the following spring, he was surprised to see he had been assigned to the minor-league barracks. With tears in his eyes, he protested to team officials, but they laughed him off, told him it wasn't important and advised him to forget it.

Early in his second big-league season, Maury started every game, but seldom finished one. Manager Walter Alston had so little faith in him, he pinch-hit for him often, sometimes as early as the third inning. This was in the Coliseum, and departing players had to walk past officials in the club box to get to the dressing room. "If there had been a hole to crawl through, I'd have preferred that. Those were the most depressing moments of my life," Maury recalls.

He always had done whatever he could to improve. Early in his career he fell away, afraid, from inside curve balls, so he had a coach throw him inside curve balls until he overcame his fear. At Spokane, he had Bobby Bragan teach him to switch-hit so he could bat left-handed, too, and be a step closer to first base. Now he had Pete Reiser pitch to him and teach him new techniques with the bat. For weeks they went out early and sweated in the deserted stadium, and Maury recalls Reiser calling him a gutless so-and-so every time he wanted to quit. Soon, Wills could do tricks with the bat and Alston stopped pinch-hitting for him.

In 1961, Wills was assigned to a private room in the major-league annex at Vero, and if Pete Reiser asked him to jump off a tall building, he would. In 1962, Wills hit consistently and stole bases so successfully, Alston put him on his own. There were faster runners, but few smarter ones. Wills began to threaten records held by old-time ball players which experts had insisted were beyond home-run-oriented moderns.

Seldom has such sports excitement been produced. Attendance rose above two million fans as night after night in Dodger Stadium the people chanted, "Go" every time Maury reached base, and he kept going and records kept falling. On the road, enemy fans thrilled to him, too. But rival teams began to wet down and sand the base paths and pitch low.

The pressure increased until he could not sleep nights. His legs began to swell up and discolor with internal bleeding until it hurt him even to think of sliding on them, and he began to dive into bases on his belly.

He has something of the actor about him, a flair for the dramatic. In his autobiography, *It Pays to Steal,* he compared himself to Manolete, the great matador: "Encouraged by the fans, he became more daring," Maury wrote. "He should have quit, but to please the crowd, he kept fighting. The law of averages finally caught up with him. He was killed."

Somehow, Wills survived. In 1962, he surpassed Ty Cobb's ancient record of 96 steals with a new major league record of 104 and was named Most Valuable Player in the league and the outstanding performer in all of baseball. But the team lost its lead to the Giants in the stretch, and the Dodgers were damned by some writers and fans as "quitters" who had "choked in the clutch."

Much of the satisfaction of his individual accomplishment was erased and Wills was hardened by the experience. When the next season the Dodgers bounced back to win the pennant, Wills and his mates celebrated conservatively. Asked why no rejoicing, Maury, sitting quietly in his cubicle, said, "I remember the guys who are patting us on the back now were stabbing us in our backs last year."

A perfectionist, intense and moody, Maury began to worry that his legs were going and visited a hypnotist to have his confidence restored. "There is little to choose between most major leaguers; it's all in the mind," he says.

He came on in 1965 to exceed his record pace until he suffered such severe hemorrhaging in his legs that he settled for 94 steals. That year, he helped his team into another World Series, where he collected 11 hits as the Dodgers defeated Minnesota in seven games. The next year, another World Series, but this time the Dodgers lost four straight to Baltimore.

Wills had become the captain of the Dodgers and an inspirational leader who was not afraid to take teammates to task whom he felt to be giving less than he was. For example, he once had a bitter rhubarb with Tommy Davis. Wes Parker admits, "Wills' intensity sometimes rubs others the wrong way. He is a hard loser who loses his temper and tells off those who contributed to a defeat. But, you come to see that he simply is striving to stimulate everyone to what we all want, leaving the field winners."

Off the field, Wills kept to himself. While the other players moved about, he sat alone in his room, learning to play a banjo until in the flush of his first fame he became a rather accomplished nightclub performer. Suddenly a celebrity, he did not enjoy the spotlight. He suffered being soiled by pointless scandal when his name was linked with a screen star. "When writers I had trusted passed on such grubby gossip, I learned a lesson not to trust people, which I have never forgotten," he now says.

Following the 1966 season, the Dodgers went on a tour of Japan. Maury's legs were aching and he asked to be excused. Refused, he left with the team, but then left the team to return home. Owner Walter O'Malley and other team officials were annoyed, then angered at reports of Wills playing a banjo in a night club. Shortly afterward, he was traded to Pittsburgh for two mediocre players in perhaps the worst trade the Dodgers ever made.

"My legs really were hurting me, and I felt I was entitled to do what I wished in the off-season," Maury explains. "I wrestled with my feelings before leaving. If I made a mistake, I should have been entitled to one. I had never given less than my best to them and often played in pain when needed. I always understood their problems and gave them loyalty and feel they should have given me understanding and loyalty in return."

He shakes his head, still wistful at the wonder of it all. "When I heard I was traded, all feeling drained out of me. I was like a person in shock who cannot face reality for several hours. Finally, it sank in. I had been in the organization 16 years and the Dodgers had become my family. I rationalized that being traded is part of baseball and I resolved to go on and make the best of it. I always knew there was no sentiment in sports, but I would not then and I still will not now dwell on this harsh side of a profession I love."

Maury puffed on a cigarette, still touched by the emotion of those moments. "In a way, it was good for me," he said. "It took me out of a Dodger uniform and put me into the world. Up until then, my world had been narrow. I began to look to see what was beyond baseball. I began to read books and the front pages and editorial pages of newspapers. I began to broaden with new interest in politics and social conditions and the life that is lived beyond baseball fields by people who do not wear Dodger uniforms."

He played well for two seasons in Pittsburgh, but he was 36 by then, and the Pirates, preferring to protect younger players in the expansion draft, let him go to the new Montreal team last season. Maury insists, "I wasn't bitter. I was only grateful that someone still wanted me. I went to Montreal with a good salary and a good feeling that I was needed. I can't explain why everything went wrong." But it did. The field was heavy from spring thaws and rain, it was cold in the tiny, makeshift ball park, the team was terrible, and so was Wills.

"I swear I tried," he sighs. "I took extra practice like a beginner. Balls I'd scoop up in practice went through my legs in games. Balls I hit in practice got past me in games. When I reached base and tried to run, I felt like I was on a treadmill. It was horrible, as though I'd suddenly gotten old or forgotten all I'd learned. Frankly, I enjoy being a star, cheered by the crowds, celebrated in print. I found it a cruel comedown when I began to be booed by the fans, ridiculed by the writers. I can take the bad with the good, but I'm human and I hurt."

Baseball players are notorious needlers. On a bus one day, Mack Jones decided to have some fun by questioning writer Ted Blackman in front of Wills. Blackman said he liked Wills, but not his play. Wills' temper, drawn thin by his troubles, snapped. He ordered Blackman not only to stop talking about him, but to stop writing about him. Blackman refused. Wills slapped him. Others intervened. Blackman publicized the incident and received a raise. Wills received bad publicity.

He announced his retirement. Then he announced his return. Then his trade back to the Dodgers was announced. He walked into the Dodger dressing room where one veteran embraced him and another helped him dress in his old uniform. "You can't believe how happy he was. God, it was all over him," Wes Parker recalls.

Wills immediately began to play like the old Wills, and by season's end he had sparked the team to a surprisingly high finish. In a way, it made him look bad, as though he had been playing poorly and threatening retirement to force a return to L.A. He admits it looks this way, but denies it was.

"I'm not that smart and I have no power to arrange trades," he says. "I don't know why I did so poorly in Montreal, but I tried everything and just couldn't get going. I don't want to linger past my ability to produce, I don't want to ruin my reputation and I don't want to subject myself to abuse. Impulsively, I quit. And I meant it. But as soon as it was done, I regretted it. I felt I owed it to myself and my team to give it a longer try, so I returned.

"The trade gave me a fresh start. I don't know why I suddenly began to do better, except that I'd be lying if I said I didn't like L.A. more than Montreal and wasn't stimulated by being on a contender. I felt as though I had come home where I was appreciated. I played to a point of exhaustion, but I felt enormously satisfied, almost reborn, by the time the season ended."

By that time, he was thin and drawn and so weary after games he could hardly make it to the showers. "It's always that way with me," he says. "After the World Series in 1965, I cracked up. Flying home, I broke out in a cold sweat and my head and stomach began to ache horribly. I was sick all day. But there was nothing wrong with me.

"All season, I'm wound up tight, not letting myself think about the tough doubleheader ahead on Sunday or the rough airplane flight and long road trip which begins the next day. I just press on, like a man in a dark tunnel, waiting to find daylight ahead. When the season finally ends and I walk out into the sunshine, there is such enormous relief, I come apart for a while."

He is 38 years old and well into the long, dark tunnel of another season. He lives in Los Angeles, while his wife and six children reside in Spokane.

His oldest son, Barry, 19, is at the University of Idaho. He had baseball ability, but gave up the game to point for a business career. "Because he's my son, the coaches wouldn't permit him to make mistakes, and he felt he didn't want to endure that sort of pressure," Maury says sadly. However, Elliott, 17, writes his father letters that he will succeed him as Dodger shortstop and surpass his stolen-base records. "He has enough talent and determination, though I've warned him it won't be easy," Maury smiles.

His other children are girls, Mikki, 18; Anita, 14; Susan, 11; and Wendi, 3. The eldest is in junior college, while the others probably will follow. "I make a lot of money, but I have to keep on doing so to give my kids the college educations I want for them," he smiles. He says he lives apart from his family because long ago he and his wife decided a family needed the firm foundation of a permanent home. "I have them with me sometimes during the season. I go to be with them sometimes during the off-season. It is our way of life." Wills shrugs.

His apartment in the Baldwin Hills area is a nice one. He drives a fancy car and wears quality clothes. He is good for around $100,000 a year and can afford the good life. However, he pursues it in private. He sleeps until noon and seldom answers his phone. Once he takes off, even his business associates have trouble locating him. But he keeps a close check on his interests, mainly his Maury Wills Stolen Base Cleaners which are being franchised nationally and are a success.

An exceedingly neat person, he seems unspoiled by success. There is one place outside Dodger Stadium where the kids line up for autographs, and he is proud that there is no pushing and yelling because they know he will take care of all of them before he leaves. He drinks a little and smokes a little, but he'll conceal this when youngsters come around because he does not want to encourage it in others.

Wes Parker describes him as an exceedingly complex and sensitive person, who needs to feel needed and is generous in helping others, but stingy with his inner self and easily hurt. "He will not let me get too close to him, but he must know I love him," Wes sighs. Told this, Maury made a face as though laughing at himself and admitted, "I really respect Wes, too, but I simply have no close friends. The closest is my business manager, Art Nadler. Yet I consider the Dodgers as much my family as the one in Spokane."

His small, strong hands fussed with the crease in his tidy trousers. He once said, "Someone once told me to act humble and you can get anything you want from people. I've never forgotten this. I'm always the small, humble guy, while the other fellow is always the big man." Now he said, "I may have put on masks and posed at one time in my life, but now I believe in being myself. I try not to take myself too seriously and I do not make judgments of right and wrong on what others do. I wish everyone was this way.

"I may be a little afraid of people. I find the closer they get to me, the more demands they make on my time and the greater the chance they will hurt me in some way. I like to help people. Friends say I'm a soft touch. I feel for people. But I can't bring myself to open up to them. Lots of people really seem to care for me, but I just can't bring myself to let go of what's inside of me."

Asked to whom he might turn if deeply troubled about something, Maury thought a long time and then shook his head and said, "No one." His wife? "No," Maury said. "No one. I would not want to lean on her or anyone else. I'd just have to see myself through whatever it was."

Asked what the great moments of joy in his life had been, Maury also thought for a while before admitting he could not think of any.

The birth of his children? "No," he said. "I'm proud of my family, but I was brought up in a big family and the birth of babies seems like the most natural event in life to me."

Setting the stolen-base record? "No, I never allow myself to get too high in success for fear failure will drive me too low. I was proud of it, but I take such things in stride and let others do the whooping and hollering."

What, then, had been the moments when he had been hurt the most?

"The one I remember most vividly came when a friend invited me to the Turf Club at Santa Anita. I'd never been to the horse races and agreed to go. I was turned away because I was black. This was several years ago and conditions may have changed. But I considered California my home and I felt I had given much to the people of this area. They paid to see me play and cheered me as a hero, but did not consider me good enough to rub elbows with them at such a place.

"I did go to Resurrection City to participate in the musical program, but I've done no marching, no walk-ins, no sit-ins and will not support violence. I believe strongly about civil rights, but believe the best way to bring about change is to set an example by treating everyone equal, regardless of color, and to promote my laundry business franchises, which, while open to all, are set up to encourage the participation of blacks and so the elevation of blacks economically."

Is he happy? Like so many others, he seems startled by the simple question, and laughed wistfully. He was thoughtful for a moment, then said, "A few years ago I might have said I was not. Now I'd have to say I am, though I must admit I don't know what happiness is."

He would like to manage. "Yes," he said, "but I prefer not to talk about it much now because I have talked about it a lot in the past without getting it.

"Frankly, although we've not yet had a black big-league manager,

I think the time has come when we will soon and he will have no problems any other manager would not have. I think I have been denied more because I have been a fighter who was involved in some publicized incidents I wish were forgotten and I've talked about now only because I want to be honest. Although fighters long have been found to make strong managers and there still are some, I think the trend has turned against them, such as Billy Martin and Eddie Stanky. I do feel I've learned the game the hard way, know how to win, and could manage and teach men how."

He will debut as a manager this winter when he manages Hermosillo of the Mexican League. "It is a long way from the majors, but I'm accepting so no one can say I have not had any experience as a manager," Maury comments.

He is more than just another fighter. He has a unique grasp of his game, sharp, swift wits and the sort of personality that inspires respect. He is considered the logical successor to Walter Alston if Alston should retire, but might get another opportunity before that. Alston says, "It is impossible to predict who will prove to be an outstanding manager, but Maury certainly has the qualities that make him an outstanding prospect. Few players, few people in any profession, are geared to give everything they have all of the time, but Maury is one. I'd like him to keep playing awhile because we need him. At his age, he is remarkable. He has lost a little speed, but I honestly believe he is playing the best shortstop of his career."

Wills, who was playing extremely well, was sidelined for a while after he injured his leg on June 21. "You don't bounce back as fast when you're older," he sighed.

It was time for Wills to put on his familiar blue and white flannels and run out on the field. He said, "I want to keep playing for a while because the Dodgers gave up young players to get me back and I want to make their investment in me worthwhile. I can't imagine a time when I couldn't force myself to be outstanding, but I can imagine a time when I will run out of desire to push myself so hard. I need days off now, but I hate to take them. I am terribly, awfully tired sometimes now.

"I don't want to miss the game when I go," he said. "The other night, five minutes before a game, I got a call in the dugout that an ex-player wanted two tickets. At that time, I wouldn't have gotten tickets for my family. But I hustled him up a pair. This fellow had been a star in this town only a couple of seasons back and I want always to be warm and cordial to former players when they return. I see them visiting the clubhouse, standing around ignored, awfully hurt. When my time comes, I want to be able to go without feeling the need to return on visits where I might be hurt. I want to make my own way, not needing anyone or anything."

BLIND SPOT TO THE RIGHT

By Hal Bodley

From the Wilmington Evening Journal

Copyright, © 1970, The News-Journal Company

Bill Schlesinger smiled, but you could tell he was forcing it. Some people can't act.

"I'm scared," he said and there was no forcing that. When you look Bill Schlesinger straight in the eyes, the eyes that are keeping him from making a run at the Phillies' right-field spot, you know he is scared.

Schlesinger is one of two players in the Phillies' spring training camp who were seriously beaned last summer. The other is big first baseman Greg Luzinski who was hit last August while playing for the Phils' Raleigh-Durham team by a pitcher "whose name I didn't even know."

Luzinski insists that except for an occasional "ringing in my ear it doesn't bother me at all. I had some bleeding in the ear and missed a week, but I'm okay now. No problems and I hang in there just as I always did."

Schlesinger, however, is a different story.

Last August 20, just when the future looked bright for him, when he was playing for Frank Lucchesi's Eugene team in the Pacific Coast League, he was hit above the left cheek by a ball thrown by Larry Sherry of Tucson.

At first, nothing seemed wrong. But the next day Schlesinger became very ill in his hotel room and 30 hours after the accident was taken to a hospital.

"It was three o'clock in the morning and they gave me a shot so I'd go to sleep," said the lanky Schlesinger. "The next morning, a Friday, when I woke up, I was blind. I couldn't see a thing. I guess I panicked. I pressed the button for the nurse and when she came into the room, I shouted I was blind."

The blindness was temporary. But now Schlesinger has what they call lack of peripheral vision, and the other day a doctor in St. Petersburg told him it might be like it is the rest of his life. If that is true, Bill Schlesinger will never play major-league baseball.

Schlesinger, whom the Phils obtained in a trade with Boston last spring, says he is not sensitive about his problem. He even goes to lengths to describe the deficiency.

"It's to the right," he said as we talked in a quiet corner of the Phillies' Jack Russell Stadium clubhouse.

He held his hand level with his eyes, to the right, about a foot away. "I can't see my hand at all. But as I raise it, I can see it. Or, as I lower it, I can see it. To my right, there is a blind spot, oh, maybe six inches where I cannot see a thing. It used to be larger, but gradually is getting smaller.

"When I'm batting, I see the ball, lose it, then see it again. I've changed my stance some, but it's not natural."

Bill Schlesinger, a 27-year-old bachelor who will be married later this year, is not bitter.

"There were just 10 days to go in the season when it happened," he said. "I had hit 18 homers and had a chance to win that title. It was the fourth inning and Larry Bowa was on second base. I always crowd the plate and ask for it, but Sherry had been coming close all year.

"It was a fast ball and tailed in. I tried to get out of the way, but couldn't. I didn't freeze."

Schlesinger rubbed a hand over his chin and said, very sincerely, "I just hope it was not intentional. I'll always wonder about that, but will never say anything to Sherry when I see him."

After it happened, doctors were fairly certain the injury could become serious, but they didn't tell him. He was never unconscious, but "after five minutes on the ground, they carried me off the field on a stretcher. I took a shower and went to a Tucson hospital for X rays. They were negative. Then, Gary Wagner and I went out for dinner and I was having a little ringing in my ear. I saw Lucchesi at the restaurant and told him I could play tomorrow night. He said I better take the night off. The next day, I woke up sick to my stomach and was that way all day until they took me to the hospital."

It has all been like a bad dream for the Cincinnati native and resident.

In 1965, his second season in pro ball, the Red Sox invited him to train with the big team and he opened the season with them, but played in just one game. His roommate for that spell was Tony Conigliaro.

"Tony and I became good friends," said Schlesinger. "My accident was so similar to his, it was uncanny. He was hit on August 18, 1967, by Jack Hamilton. Hamilton pitches a lot like Sherry."

Conigliaro had serious vision problems and missed the entire 1968 season. Doctors said he'd never play again, but he came back and was in 141 games with them last summer, hitting .255.

When the Phils played the Red Sox here the other day, Conigliaro and Schlesinger got together.

"I was depressed and told him so," said Bill. "Tony really cheered me up. He told me to have faith, that my vision would improve.

"Knowing that Tony came back, keeps me encouraged. I can't play right field now because I can't see to my right. Center field is okay and left field the best."

Schlesinger is realistic. Today or tomorrow he will leave the major-league camp and begin training with the Phillies' minor leaguers.

"I know I can't help them here," he said, "but I'd like to stick around this summer. I'm hoping I'll remain on the Eugene roster.

"Having been told this may never clear up, I've been giving some serious thought to the future," added Schlesinger, a business administration major at the University of Cincinnati, from where he was graduated in 1964. "I'm hoping I can still make the big leagues. If I can't, I'd like to get some position and stay in baseball."

WHO'S ON FIRST? WHO CARES?

By Bob Greene

From Midwest Magazine, Chicago Sun-Times

At 6:15 P.M., an hour and a half before game time, the only thing moving at Jet Stadium was the creaky revolving metal sign on Mound Street, in front of the ball park. "NEXT GAME TONIGHT, JETS VS. TIDEWATER, ALL KIDS NITE," the sign said. And then, on a small piece of wood underneath the metal sign, "THIS DISPLAY DONATED BY BIG BEAR SUPER MARKETS."

The playing field itself and the stands were empty. The Columbus Jets and the Tidewater Tides were still in their locker rooms, getting taped and putting on their uniforms. The dugouts were deserted. Only a few small boys, blue baseball caps with a big white "C" on the front falling over their ears, leaned over the railing in front of the box seats, waiting for the players and the autographs.

This was minor league baseball, Triple-A, to be exact, the highest form of minor-league baseball, the International League, one step away from the majors. But that step is the biggest one there is in a world where grown-up men prance around in pursuit of a ball, call themselves Jets and Tides and Redlegs and Cardinals and the like, and get paid for it.

These are the 19- and 20- and 21-year-old kids who can close their eyes and see themselves in the uniform of the Pittsburgh Pirates, the club that owns the Jets. These are the 27-year-olds who have had their two and a half seasons in the majors, and now are down in Triple-A again, hoping they can put enough hits together to be sent back up. These are the 31-year-old outfielders who are done, and they know it, but they still spend their summers playing baseball because they can get a little money out of it, and it is the one thing they have ever been able to do well.

The Tides, the visiting team from Virginia and the farm club of the New York Mets, came out of their dugout first. They stood around the batting cage, kidding each other and laughing, tossing balls back and forth, lazily warming up in front of the still-barren grandstand. Their gray road uniforms were almost clean and almost pressed.

They finished up, and then it was time for the home team. The Columbus Jets, looking good in their white uniforms, ran onto the field, but not too fast. The Jets had been up at 6 A.M., riding a bus from New York, where they had played the night before. All day long they rode and they were back in uniform again, on a baseball field again, as they are every night from May to September.

On the public-address system, country music was twanging out. Columbus does not happen to be a country town; it is better than half a million now, and the radio stations play the Stones and The Who and the same groups stations play everywhere. A young guy named Kenny Stone has an all-night progressive rock show on a local radio station. You have to look hard to find country music. But the Jets have a country album, so they put it on the PA system before every game. No one really listens anyway.

Joe Morgan stepped up to the top of the dugout and rested a hand on his knee. He looked out toward center field, focusing his eyes at some point on the Swan Cleaners scoreboard, chewing on a frazzled toothpick. Joe Morgan, who played professional baseball for 12 seasons—but never for a full season in the majors—is the manager of the Columbus Jets.

"Don't ask me about it," Joe Morgan said. "You don't have to. I don't have to tell you what it's like down here. Ask the players, though. Ask any of them. This ain't the majors, boy, you can be sure of that.

"Look at these guys," he said. "Even the good ones, the real good ones, working for maybe $1,000 a month, and that's just for the five months we play. And $7.50 a day for meals, for an athlete. Think about that. This ain't the National League, that's one thing for sure."

About halfway up in the box seats, a balding man in a gray suit was sitting alone. The man's name was Joe Hill. He has been broadcasting baseball games since 1938, and to the people in Central Ohio he is the voice of the Columbus Jets. When the Jets were a new, hot thing in Columbus, Hill's voice went out over WTVN, a high-powered AM station, and everyone knew him and listened to

him. He was quite large in Columbus. Now the Jets draw 700 fans
to a game, and other fans stay home and watch the big-league teams
on television. The Mound Street neighborhood where the Jets play
is not quite as nice as it used to be, and Joe Hill's voice, giving the
play-by-play of every Jets game, can only be heard on an FM station
located just outside of the Columbus city limits, that doesn't send
out all that strong a signal.

Chuck Goggin waits for the game to start, too. Goggin is a 26-year-
old utility infielder, who was a marine in Vietnam. Purple Heart.
Vietnamese Cross of Gallantry. Bronze Star. Bats left, throws right.
Waiting with his arms crossed for something to happen.

A kid in a sleeveless green T-shirt leaned over the railing and
yelled, "Hey, Chuck, hey, Chuck, let me have your autograph. Will
you give me your autograph?" Goggin walked over, not really looking at the kid. He grabbed a program—a red, white and blue
cardboard affair crammed with advertisements—and quickly signed
his name.

"God, that's amazing," said Chuck Goggin. "Simply amazing.
These kids look at us and think it's so great to be a baseball player,
it's so great to get paid for doing it."

It was getting to be time for the game to start, and the Jets were
running in and out of the dugout. In their uniforms they could
have been high-school kids, and the easy talk was out of a high-
school locker room. Ron Campbell, an infielder, yelled, "Hey,
Dougle, where's that first sacker's glove," and the answer came back,
"In the locker, where I told you."

Joe Morgan, the manager, was making some notes on a scrap of
paper. "Naw, it's not like it used to be," he said. "Major-league
expansion is responsible, television is responsible. Now you have 19-
year-old guys who start out in Triple-A. Twenty-five years ago, they
wouldn't have been here."

That is the story. The trouble starts from the bottom and works
up. The lower minor leagues, which used to provide good baseball
for little towns around the nation, are drying up fast. The higher
minors, which used to be a place for young ball players to work up
to and play in just before they hit big time, are feeling it, too.
Crowds are down. Pay is bad. Morale is low.

On the wooden bench, deep in the cool, dark dugout, they were
talking about it. Dick Colpaert, a pitcher, flipped his glove into the
air, caught it, flipped it again.

"It's been nine years for me," he said. "Nine years. I don't know, you just have to figure that some make it quick, some have to wait. But it's always there, in everyone's mind. The majors. That's what everyone is here for. The majors."

Colpaert, a pudgy man with short red hair, said that it was not easy. At the age of 26, Columbus is the highest level he has reached in baseball."What can you do?" he said. "No one makes money . . . with that expense allowance they give us, we lose money, just living. But you just keep hoping, that's all you can do."

A few feet down the bench, Dave Arrington looked at his left hand. Arrington, a young-looking outfielder, had broken a bone in his hand. It had been a month since he had played baseball.

"I can't afford it," he said. "No one can. I'm 22 years old. I think the Pirates like me; okay, I'm in Triple-A, so I'm supposed to be doing all right. But believe me, it's just not worth it unless you're in the majors. I have to make it now. I'll play sick, I want to play when I'm sick, but they won't let you. It kills me.

"Do you have any idea what it's like?" he said. "We get out of spring training, the season starts three days later, and we have to find a place to live. A place to live for five months. Did you ever hear of a five-month lease?

"So we hustle up to Columbus and start looking. Naturally, a lot of the guys can't find a place right away. So they have to get a hotel room, and that costs them so damn much, and then the season starts and they've got to come up with a place.

"And you know something else? We even have to pay our own way to the ball park at night. There's no team bus or anything. So we get our $7.50 a day for food, and then out of that we have to pull cab fare. You end up with five guys meeting together somewhere and squeezing in the same cab, and saying 'Take us to the ball park.' You just have to get to the majors, that's all there is to it."

The stands were getting noisy. There were little kids swarming all over, trying to get on the field for an autograph, yelling, running through the aisles.

"Don't let this fool you," said Frank Brosseau, a pitcher who once appeared in two games for the Pirates. "This looks like a lot of people. They may have a couple of thousand. But that's because it's free night. They let the kids in free, just to have some bodies in the place. Come out there on a regular night. We get 500, 600, 700. It's depressing. Everybody goes out and watches their brother play softball at the playground instead."

A writer for a Virginia newspaper came into the dugout, his notebook out. He asked Joe Morgan a few questions, and Morgan looked straight back at him and returned serious answers about the batting order and lineup changes. It was like a parody of one of those dugout shows before the Saturday Game of the Week. Then the Tidewater writer sat on the bench for a moment.

"You have to understand," the writer said, "covering a minor-league team isn't like covering the majors. Hell, in New York and Chicago and L.A., the writers have a field day cutting up the teams. They can ruin a guy.

"Not us, though," he said. "We help our boys; we don't cut 'em down. We want what they want. We want to give 'em a shot at the majors. I'm one of the few minor-league writers who gets to travel with a team. I'm happy about that. I see some things on the road, but I don't write about that kind of thing. I want our boys to make it big."

Then the batting cage was rolled away and the umpires came out. A game of baseball, the 64th game the Columbus Jets would play in 1970, was about to begin.

The Tides didn't do much in the first inning, but then the Jets came to bat, and the kids in the stands loved that. "We want a hit, we want a hit, we want a hit." Some of the Jets on the bench had their eyes closed.

Gary Kolb was at bat. Kolb is the star of the Jets team. He can play any position. He has the dark, handsome looks of baseball-card athletes. He does not smile much. Thirty years old, he has been in the major leagues on eight different occasions. Now, back in the minors, back in Columbus, he may be working on his last chance.

Kolb stood at the plate, the lights flashing off his blue batting helmet. Then Bill Denehy, the Tides' pitcher, came in close with a fast ball and Kolb went down into the dirt. In a second he was up, charging at the pitcher, grasping the bat. The kids were in ecstasy. It stopped there, though. He walked back to the plate, waited out a pitch, and then cracked a single into shallow left field.

These guys looked good. They all seemed like the all-around high-school athletes, the kids who could do anything with a baseball or football or basketball, now grown up. They moved easily, making difficult plays, all very routinely.

Before the game, in the dugout, there had been tension. But now all the talk about how bad it is was gone, all the talk about the minors and the majors and the meal allowances and the taxis. Now these men were playing baseball. And they seem glad to be out there.

Dennis Ribant was propped on the edge of the dugout, half in and half out. The dugout is unmistakably minor league. Chipped cement, dirty floor, cracked benches. The field, though, is brilliantly lit and well cared for and as green as you could want it. In the middle of Columbus' deteriorating west side, it looked great.

Ribant, a pitcher, leaned against the cement, careful to put his blue warm-up jacket behind him to keep his uniform clean. His blond hair was slicked back, and if he wasn't wearing the number 25, he would have looked like he was heading out for a night downtown. Except that this was Columbus.

"Columbus," he said. "Columbus. You know, this isn't too good. I've been in the minors four years, the majors five years. Back and forth, back and forth.

"The good year, though, was '68," Ribant said. "That summer I had two months with the White Sox, four and a half months with the Tigers. That Chicago, that's a big-league town. There's a place for a baseball player.

"You ever go down to Rush Street?" he asked. "You ever go down to Butch's? That's good. Girls, all you want. That's big league. Money to eat with, first-class hotels, real baseball. Baseball's important there. You feel like somebody there.

"But Pittsburgh likes me; I'll be back," he said. "I know I can do it. I'll be back."   .

Dick Garrett looked bored. He is a photographer for the *Columbus Citizen-Journal*. Before that he was a photographer for the old *Columbus Citizen*. He spends some of his evenings now taking pictures of the Columbus Jets. Before the Jets, he took pictures of the old Columbus Red Birds. He has taken thousands of pictures of Columbus baseball players for his newspapers, and he thinks that it will soon be over.

"Oh, Christ, just look at this place," he said. "Sure, the field looks good. But look up there in the stands. The place is falling apart. Have you been up in the press box? You should see the roof up there, it's all peeling tarpaper. They have to block off part of the roof so you don't fall through it on your way to the press box.

"There's no money to build this team up again," Garrett said. "No one comes out to watch them. You just can't support a minor-league team anymore. It's a miracle they're here this year. I'll bet you something for sure. I'll bet you they won't be back next year. This has got to be it for baseball in Columbus. It's dead."

Out on the field they kept going at it. Tidewater was leading, the children in the stands were getting quieter as it got later, and Joe Morgan sat in the manager's place of honor on the end of the bench, and spit.

Bob Adkins, who has been the Jets' stadium announcer forever, boomed his voice throughout the stadium. "Attention, please," he said. "Attention, please. Will the fan with program number C-10708, C-10708, please report to the head usher. You have won the pony."

And between innings the ushers led a pony past the Jets' dugout as the players sat and waited. Joe Morgan turned his back on it.

Gary Kolb walked back onto the field, to his position at third base, and waited for the Tides' batter to swing. He did, and the ball sailed over Kolb's head, on its way out of the park. He just looked straight down at the ground, a frown on his face, and waited for the Tidewater batter to round the bases. The place was deadly silent. No Tidewater fans travel from Virginia.

The dugout was silent, too. The game was almost over. The players had all had their chances to get up to the plate, so when the Pirates' management would look over the averages, they would be impressed and maybe move a few men up to the majors.

It was the last inning, the Jets' last time up. The fans were still there. Rimp Lanier, an outfielder, stepped to the plate. He swung and hit a loop single toward the lights in right field. The ball dropped in and Arrington, the 22-year-old whose only goal in life is to be a major-league baseball player, scrambled down the line from third base and made one more statistic for himself.

Rimp Lanier rounded first, and in this little green part of Columbus' west side, the people in the stands were standing up and screaming at 10 o'clock on a hot night. They stayed on their feet, happy for the chance to cheer out loud for their team, and in the whole scheme of things that must count for something.

Gary Kolb, the former big leaguer with a last shot at getting back, came up again. He swung hard and the ball screamed at the shortstop. But the Tidewater man made the stop and in a matter of seconds the baseball game was over.

Already the PA system was crackling, "Next Columbus Jet game, tomorrow night, 7:45 P.M., when the Jets once again take on the Tides." The Jets were heading toward their locker room.

Down a gray, skinny tunnel they headed. Some kicked at the floor. Bare light bulbs clung to the ceiling. Bat boys hustled by, on their way to get the towels and the soap ready.

The Jets undressed silently and headed for the showers. The long, narrow locker room steamed up. Some of the players gulped at Cokes. Some just sat in front of their lockers and stared at the floor. Some tried to make quiet conversation.

Joe Morgan paced back and forth. He slapped his hand against one of the tall, gray, ugly wooden lockers. "That shouldn't happen," he said. "We shouldn't lose one like that. That game was too easy for us to lose it."

No one answered, or seemed to be listening. Morgan walked over and sat down by Gary Kolb.

There were two pictures tacked onto Kolb's locker. One showed him crossing home plate after a home run as his Columbus Jet teammates greeted him. The other one, this one bigger, was a color picture, printed on cardboard. It was a baseball team publicity shot. It was an old picture taken when Kolb was in the major leagues. It showed him smiling broadly. He was wearing the uniform of the Pittsburgh Pirates.

"Gary, there's no way that pitcher of theirs can get you out," Joe Morgan said. "No way. I can't understand it. You can hit that guy. No way he can pitch to you."

Gary Kolb, baseball player, age 30, looked up in the air. He slammed his cleats against the locker, in Columbus, Ohio, as the picture of himself in a Pittsburgh Pirates uniform smiled back down at him.

"Damn it," he said. "Damn it. I couldn't hit a damned thing tonight."

"OK, then," said Joe Morgan. "You'll get 'em tomorrow. Don't worry. You'll get 'em. Tomorrow."

The Jets will not be back next year. Club president Ralph Anderson announced that the team would be liquidated after this season. The Jets ended their play-offs last week.

Football

SUPER CHIEFS SHOCK SUPER BOWL

By Glenn Dickey

From the San Francisco Chronicle

Copyright, ©, 1970, Chronicle Publishing Co.

Kansas City, the second-best team in the scorned and soon to be defunct AFL, smothered Minnesota, the proud NFL's best, 23–7, yesterday in the Super Bowl before a capacity crowd that did not quite believe what it was seeing.

It could have been worse. The Chiefs, once ahead by 16 in the third quarter, called off the dogs.

There is no polite way to describe what happened to the Vikings. A locker-room expression applies: The Chiefs kicked the —— out of them. You fill in the missing word.

And it begins to appear that Pete Rozelle goofed. He should have put three AFL teams in the NFL, instead of the other way around, to even the competition. This way, it may take years for the NFL to catch up.

The Chiefs established their superiority early, and only once after the first quarter did the Vikings show the muscle that created terror in the NFL in 1969, when they swept to a 12–2 record, capped by wins over Los Angeles and Cleveland in the play-offs.

Trailing by 16 at half time, the Vikings moved 69 yards to score the first time they got the ball in the third quarter, and their fans came to life for the first time. This was the Minnesota team they had watched all year—a determined second-half club with the poise to come from behind.

It was an illusion, if an understandable one. This time, the Vikings were playing a better team. The Chiefs came back to score as Otis Taylor made a great individual effort on a 46-yard pass play. The rest of the way, the Chiefs sat on their lead, content that the Vikings couldn't catch them if the game lasted three hours.

And at home in front of their television sets, the Oakland Raiders cried at what could have been. Every team they lose to in an AFL championship game wins the Super Bowl.

Before the game, the Chiefs had told anyone who would listen they had beaten the best team in football the previous Sunday and this game would be easier. Nurtured on the myth of NFL superiority, few listened.

Pity. The Chiefs weren't kidding.

(The Chiefs finished second to the Raiders in the Western Division and then defeated them in a "special" play-off game for the title.)

Early on, Kansas City, an 11 to 13 point shortender, destroyed the Minnnesota offense that scored more than 50 points against NFL opponents three times this year. First, the Chiefs cut off the run by presenting an impregnable front.

That isn't the whole of it, of course. Occasionally, the Vikings' offensive line would make a dent in the Kansas City front four, but by the time the Viking running backs got there, several minutes later, the hole would be closed forever.

Those running backs are something. TV viewers probably thought they were watching stop-action every time Joe Kapp called a running play.

The backs seemed to be running in mud all day. On sweeps, the Kansas City defense could have taken a nap and still have awakened in time to make the tackle, at the line of scrimmage.

They do run hard, but when it's all in one place . . .

So, the running attack was no challenge, as long as the Chiefs could keep from laughing, anyway. You could see them chuckling when the linemen caught the backs from behind. Is this really the way they do it in the other league? C'mon, you're putting me on.

The Minnesota passing attack, though, was a little tougher to stop. There have been a lot of silly things written about Kapp. People don't like the fact that he sometimes throws off the wrong foot and his passes don't spiral perfectly.

But he doesn't have a strand of spaghetti hanging from his right arm. He can throw the ball long and accurately. One time yesterday, he threw the ball from his own goal line to the Kansas City 25 to Gene Washington, and the ball was right there.

Unfortunately for the Vikings, so were Emmitt Thomas and Johnny Robinson, and they batted the ball away. That was the story of the ball game. The Chiefs were always there, and usually two of them to every one of the Vikings.

Washington caught only one pass all day, that late in the third quarter for nine yards, and that may have been the most significant statistic of the day. All day, Kapp was forced to go to John Henderson, his other wide receiver. Henderson is a nice fellow—calls his mother daily to check on her health, I understand—but he isn't going to beat you.

Often, too, Joe went to his backs. Usually, you try to isolate backs on linebackers, but not these backs. Not these linebackers, either. Bobby Bell could run in a sack and beat Dave Osborn.

When you can't run and you can't pass, what does that leave you? Right. In the fourth quarter, Kapp went out of the game with an injury to his shoulder, but he may also have been yielding to the inevitable. Joe is a fighter, but he learned in Logic 1-A at the University of California to recognize a lost cause.

The Kansas City defense, although not as publicized as Minnesota's, was recognized as a strong factor before the game. What came as a surprise, though, was the way the Chiefs' offensive line handled the Vikings' front four. As a fan's sign proclaimed at game's end, "The Purple Gang is now black and blue."

For a while, I thought Carl Eller wasn't even playing, he was taken out of plays with such frequency.

The Vikings got the first chance to score, but didn't even recognize it.

Anyway, the Chiefs didn't blow it when they got a chance. Right after the Vikings' Bob Lee punted out on the 17, they moved to the Minnesota 41, and Jan Stenerud kicked a 48-yard field goal.

The next time they got the ball, the Chiefs got a little deeper, to the Minnesota 25, and Stenerud kicked a 32-yard field goal.

Two sequences later, they got to the Minnesota 17 and again called on Stenerud, pro football's most dangerous kicker, to get the field goal, this time from the 25.

The pattern of the game seemed to be set: Stenerud would kick about 14 field goals and Kansas City would win, 42–0. But then the Chiefs upset the pattern by scoring a touchdown, just when everybody thought they'd forgotten how.

This came after a fumble by Minnesota's Charlie West on the 19 after the kickoff, the biggest break Kansas City got all day.

The night before the game, Al Davis told Hank Stram, "If Len Dawson doesn't screw it up, there's no way you can lose." Dawson, who completed 12 of 17 during the game, didn't screw it up this time or any other—although he got thrown for an eight-yard loss on the first play. He fooled Minnesota with a draw to Wendell Hayes which gained 13, and then to Taylor for a 10-yard gain to the four.

Garrett lost a yard and Dawson was stopped for no gain after a mix-up in the backfield, but then Garrett went off tackle, behind Moorman's block, and into the end zone for the touchdown that put the Chiefs up, 16–0, at half time.

The die was cast, and only the most stubborn of Minnesota fans refused to believe it. Still, the Vikings did show signs of life in the third quarter. Coming out of the dressing room, coach Bud Grant's footprints showing clearly on the rear of their uniforms, they moved 80 yards in 10 plays—no one play over 15 yards—to score.

Osborn, going the last four yards in five seconds flat, scored and the Vikings were still alive, barely. But not for long.

Starting on their 18, the Chiefs moved to the Minnesota 46, and then Dawson hit Taylor at the 41 on what was intended to be a short gainer. The Vikings misplayed it grievously.

Earsall Macbee grabbed Taylor's arm at the 41, but he shook loose. At the 19, he cut inside, then outside, then broke an arm tackle by Ken Kassulke. After that, he was home free.

So were the Chiefs.

THE BEST VICTORY

By Si Burick

From The Dayton Daily News

Copyright, ©, 1970, The Dayton Daily News

The little man's innards were so filled with sheer ecstasy that he could scarcely restrain himself. Paul Brown, who, at 62, should have been jogging at best, literally sprinted off the bench in leading his pack to the locker room in the cave under Riverfront Stadium.

After privately thanking the Cincinnati Bengals for their 14–10 victory over the Cleveland Browns, Paul opened the door for the men of the media, who were curious about his inner feelings.

Brown had fathered the Browns in Cleveland 24 years ago. He was their creator in 1946, then took them into the National Football League in 1950.

After the 1962 season, the new ownership of the Browns cast him out. Not like a poor orphan, understand. Paul came out of the Cleveland experience with riches, but his pride had been damaged.

Three seasons ago, Brown returned to football after five years on the sidelines, the founding father of the Bengals, an American Football League expansion club.

Now, in the first year of the NFL-AFL merger, Brown had scored his first league victory over the Browns. All of us wondered what it meant to him, but nobody had to ask. P.B. volunteered the information, sensing with the wisdom that comes to a man of his years and experience what we really wanted to know.

"This is my best victory," he said.

"Best in 1970?" a Cleveland man asked.

"No, my BEST VICTORY." And he meant ever.

So this was the ultimate for a man who started his career in 1931, who had known success in every coaching field.

Going into this year, Paul had won 165 times as a pro. He had won 96 times as a high-school mentor; 18 times at Ohio State; 15 times at Great Lakes. And now he was saying this was the greatest, the man who had known a dozen championships.

Later, I asked him what sweet memory this could have replaced in his football affections.

"The greatest before this came in the 1950 championship game in the NFL. That was the year we [the Browns] beat the Los Angeles Rams, 30–28, in the last 28 seconds on Lou Groza's 16-yard field goal," Paul recalled.

"You must remember that there were emotional impulses in that one, too. The Rams used to be Cleveland's team. They gave up on the city. They moved to Los Angeles. The owners predicted Cleveland would never make it as a football town.

"We replaced them in the All-America Conference in 1946. We were the new team in a new league. In 1950, the NFL took us in. That year we won our division. As luck would have it, we were matched for the title with the team that abandoned Cleveland.

"We averaged over 56,000 fans a game. We'd already proved the town belonged. So there was something quite sentimental about that victory over the Rams."

Sunday's success over the present Browns was "more personal." And Brown frankly explained this "personal" sentiment.

"Look, things happen to you in your lifetime that you can't forget. When Art Modell bought the Browns, he said publicly he wanted this team because I was identified with it.

"But the longer we were together, the more he realized it could never be HIS team as long as I was there."

Eventually, they parted company, which is putting it mildly.

"I was gone five years. In returning to football, I had a strong feeling on this subject. Then, in the league reorganization, we [the Bengals] were put in the same division with the Browns. They beat us up there.

"Now we've beaten them. There's so much satisfaction, as you can see, for so many reasons in this victory."

"Would you give one other reason?"

"Well, yes, there's this thing of calling the signals from the sidelines for the quarterback. You know how much heat I got up there over that. I didn't budge then. I wouldn't budge now. This is my way of running a club.

"So look what happened today. They started a rookie, Mike

Phipps, at quarterback for the first time. And who called the signals for Mike?

"They did, my friend. They called every play."

This happy man talked about the game Virgil Carter had turned in at quarterback for the Bengals.

The strategy had been for Carter to roll out of the pocket on his passes, to throw every pass on the run. An emergency addition to the Bengals after Greg Cook's bad arm took him out of action, Carter had used the roll-out to complete 10 out of 17 passes for 123 yards.

More significantly, the Browns' defense never caught up with Carter for a loss, and there were no interceptions. And even more importantly, he had taken off on the run nine times for 110 rushing yards.

"Those runs," said Brown, "were not broken plays. He's a gung-ho kid for trying this; we're gung-ho for letting him."

"The Bengals," Carter had said, "haven't changed any of the basic things they did before. But they've adjusted some to the things I do."

"Yes," Brown agreed. "What we're doing is tailoring our offense a little toward what he does best. He's quite a kid. The key play on our drive [85 yards in eight plays] for the winning touchdown was Virgil's pass to Chip Myers. [The play, fourth in the sequence, gained 27 yards for a first down on the Browns' 11.]

"That pass," Paul said proudly, "wasn't intended for Chip. He wasn't the primary, or the secondary, choice, but the third. The first two receivers were covered. It takes a fine passer to do that."

It was one of many things Paul Brown was proud of on the day of his greatest victory in his 40th year as a coach.

THE LEPRECHAUNS CHANGE COLOR

By Dwain Esper

From the Pasadena Independent Star News

Copyright, ©, 1970, Pasadena Independent Star News

The leprechauns were painted cardinal and gold on a soggy Saturday in the Coliseum.

Much maligned by friend and foe alike, an aroused band of USC football players took out their frustrations on undefeated Notre Dame while a throng of 64,694 and a nationwide television audience looked on in stunned disbelief.

Beaten four times in this most disappointing season of the last decade, the Trojans exploded for three first-quarter touchdowns and stampeded their way to a 38–28 triumph over the Fighting Irish.

"Everything went right for once," said USC All-America defensive end Charlie Weaver.

"It hurt to lose four games," said the controversial quarterback Jimmy Jones. "Everything rode on this one against Notre Dame. We showed the people what we are capable of doing."

Jones authored the three first-quarter drives to touchdowns as the Trojan offense finally came alive.

Then, when the Irish tried to come back, the USC defense—especially end Willie Hall—rode roughshod over Joe Theismann and his Irish mates. The defense contributed two vital third-quarter touchdowns that pretty well settled the issue.

This was a mighty triumph, make no mistake. Notre Dame's ferocious defense had yielded only 59 points in nine previous games. Yet the Trojans ignored the odds in their final effort of the campaign.

Theismann went down swinging, as might be expected from the all-time Notre Dame total offense leader.

He completed 33 of 58 passes for two touchdowns and an astounding 526 yards.

This was a more impressive effort than Wisconsin's Ron Vander-Kelen delivered against USC in the explosive Rose Bowl game of 1963. On that memorable day, VanderKelen connected on 33 passes for 401 yards. But the Trojans won 42–37.

"We make those passers look good, don't we?" jested USC coach John McKay.

In truth Notre Dame had to abandon its game plan when Jones shot the Trojans out of the gate with his masterful first-quarter performance. In that one period he completed seven of seven passes for 143 yards and one touchdown.

"We had to change once we got in a hole," admitted Irish coach Ara Parseghian. "We went to drop back passes more than normal. The rain hurt us because it is hard to play catch-up football when you can't keep your footing.

"I thought Theismann had a remarkable day, particularly considering the circumstances."

As the 12-point favorite, the Irish looked like money in the bank when they claimed the opening kickoff and rolled 80 yards in 12 plays to a touchdown. Theismann completed four passes for 38 of those yards.

He scored the touchdown himself on a brilliant 25-yard scamper through left tackle. Theismann faked a hand-off to fullback John Cieszkowski going up the middle. Then he moved along the line of scrimmage, cut upfield through left tackle. As the Trojan defense came to him, he broke across the grain and sped unmolested to the goal.

"He is really an elusive runner," admired Weaver.

Down 7–0 after just four minutes, the Trojans certainly appeared to be in for a long afternoon.

But Jones, the junior from Harrisburg, Pennsylvania, and his offensive unit were up to the task.

Taking the kickoff, they immediately marched 70 yards in nine plays to the equalizing touchdown. Two Jones passes ate up 38 yards.

But significant gains were produced by tailback Clarence Davis off the left side. He carried five times, four to the left, for a total of 31 yards, including the final burst into the end zone from the three.

"The basic idea of our offense was to move away from their rover back [Eric Patton]," explained Jones. "It gave them an extra man if we went where he was."

By running away from Patton, extra pressure was placed on left tackle Marv Montgomery and tight end Gerry Mullins.

"I'd have to say they did a great job," praised McKay. "But the whole offensive line blocked extremely well."

The next Irish series ended in disaster when the omnipresent Hall, who had eight unassisted tackles during the day, threw Theismann for an eight-yard loss on third down.

Said Hall: "We wanted to keep Theismann from going to the outside. We knew once he gets outside he can be most dangerous."

Tyrone Hudson returned Jim Yoder's punt to the Trojan 49, setting up another scoring foray.

In five plays the Trojans moved 51 yards to the touchdown that put them ahead for keeps. Key gain was a play-action pass from Jones to Davis for 31 yards. Davis scored the touchdown on a five-yard blast over right end.

Trojan fans gasped when Ron Ayala's conversion kick went wide, leaving the score at 13–7.

The Trojan defense once again stymied Theismann, bringing on Yoder for another punt. Hudson brought it back to the Trojan 43.

Although Jones slipped on the turf for a seven-yard loss on the first play, he got 10 back on a strike to Davis. Another completion to Charlie Evans ate up nine yards to the Irish 45.

Here Jones and the fleet Sam Dickerson collaborated on the play of the game—a 45-yard bomb to a touchdown.

"Sam ran a fly pattern," explained Jones. "If Dickerson goes deep, he is our primary receiver. I put the ball up there, and Sam made a great catch."

Super catch, Jones should have said.

Notre Dame's brilliant cornerback Clarence Ellis was with Dickerson all the way. When the ball came down in the end zone, both went for it. Ellis got his arms on the ball, then Dickerson wrestled it away as they fell to the turf.

Said Dickerson: "We were both moving downfield. Then he looked at me for just an instant. When he took his eyes off the ball, I jumped. He jumped after I did. I don't think he ever really had possession."

Said McKay: "Sam's catch was an extremely big lift for us. Ellis was right there with him."

Another big lift was the diving catch by Bob Chandler of a Jones pass for the two-point conversion, wiping out the Ayala miss.

So here were the Trojans, a 45–20 victim of UCLA just last week, on top of Notre Dame 21–7 with almost a minute to go in the first quarter. Already it was the most points given up by the Irish against any opponent in the 1970 season (previous high: 14 by Pittsburgh and Northwestern).

The day was turning damp and gloomy for Notre Dame. As a concession, perhaps, the lights were turned on in the second quarter.

Theismann responded by directing a six-play, 66-yard march to a touchdown. A 28-yard pass to Tom Gatewood and a subsequent Trojan personal foul penalty moved to the USC 23. Another strike to Darryll Dewan gained 14, and Theismann passed to Cieszkowski, who smashed his way into the end zone from the nine.

Cieszkowski, the burly junior fullback, caught six passes during the day, second only to Gatewood's 10. He had caught only one in the previous nine games.

"It wasn't anything new," argued Parseghian. "We've had the play all season. We like to throw to receivers coming out of the backfield."

Nevertheless, it appeared to many that this was a new wrinkle in the Notre Dame attack.

An interception by Bruce Dyer inspired a Trojan drive leading to a field goal. Moving from the Irish 47, Jones opened fire with a 19-yard pass to Bob Chandler. The Trojans got down to the one with fourth down coming up.

After a lengthy conversation with McKay on the sidelines, Jones returned with Ayala, who promptly booted a 19-yard field goal for a 24–14 margin.

"Let's say we were a long yard away from a touchdown," said McKay. "Jimmy himself said it was too far to make it, and we should go for the field goal."

Future arguments were dispelled by subsequent events.

Although Notre Dame got close enough for Scott Smith to try a 49-yard field goal (it was short), the Trojans held their 10-point lead at intermission.

Three big defensive plays by Willie Hall in the opening five minutes of the third quarter probably determined the final outcome.

It was Hall who slammed into Dewan, forcing a fumble recovered by Trojan Kent Carter at the Irish 17. Jones passed to Dickerson to the four. Evans picked up two more.

Mike Berry smashed into the line, lost control of the ball which squirted into the end zone. Offensive tackle Pete Adams recovered for a Trojan touchdown.

Obviously shaken by this turn of events, the Irish lost their poise. Bob Minnix fumbled the kickoff, setting up poor field position on the 18. Theismann fumbled, recovered the loose ball and suffered an 11-yard loss when Hall nailed him at the seven.

Theismann once again faded to pass, but Hall crashed into him in the end zone. John Vella picked up the loose ball for the touchdown and a resounding 38–14 lead.

Said Parseghian, witnessing the most points ever registered against one of his Notre Dame teams: "We gave up two touchdowns by playing greasy football. I had expected the game to be a moderate scoring affair. But our errors gave them two easy scores.

"Those two quick touchdowns prevented us from catching up all the way."

Theismann got one of them back immediately on a five-play, 72-yard march, culminating in a 46-yard bomb to sophomore halfback Larry Parker.

With a minute gone in the fourth period, Theismann ended a 17-play, 69-yard drive with a dive from the one to narrow USC's lead to 10 points once again.

The rest of the game was played in a virtual quagmire with the rain pelting the players as hard as the opposition.

Three times the Trojans rose up to intercept Theismann after he made penetrations across the midfield stripes.

In all, Theismann suffered four interceptions. He also was sacked six times for 60 deficit yards. In addition, Notre Dame lost four fumbles during the dank day.

So the frustrations that had played so much a part of USC's season now belonged to Notre Dame.

And when the gun finally sounded, the remnants of what had been a good-sized crowd cascaded down to the playing field and gathered the Trojans in their hearts once again.

And the painful memories for Notre Dame were rekindled.

It was USC that nipped the Irish, 16–14, in 1931 to end a 26-game Notre Dame undefeated streak.

It was USC that slugged previously undefeated Notre Dame, 13–0, in 1938.

It was USC that rallied from a 17–0 deficit to dent another previously undefeated Irish squad, 20–17, in 1964.

Wet and nasty November 28, 1970, certainly was. But the sun shone on the Trojans on this day. A day they'll cherish for years to come.

JOE KAPP: FOOTBALL'S FURY

By Al Stump

From True Magazine

Copyright, ©, 1970, Fawcett Publications, Inc.

Cesar Chavez has waged war for 15 years now with California's agricultural interests in behalf of the West's most hapless labor force—300,000 Mexican-American crop pickers. And Chavez has been a loser. So many battles have been dropped to the grape, citrus and cotton industry that in 1969, feeling cocky, publicists for the products sloganized Cesar.

"UFWOC you, Chavez!" became their taunt (former crop-hand Chavez calls his group the United Farm Workers Organizing Committee).

Early this year, however, to their shock, the land tycoons got UFWOCed themselves. Suddenly they were blitzed and they still aren't sure what hit them. The attack came from a broken-nosed newcomer with the German name of Kapp, whose address is Bloomington, Minnesota, and who previously was known only for throwing footballs to receivers, not overripe kumquats into official faces.

All at once in the seventies, Chavez' losing *La Causa* (The Cause) begins to look like it could become a winner.

"Where does Kapp get off, butting into this?" asked the industry.

Appearing in Los Angeles last May to address a full-house crowd of protestors, after drawing standing-room audiences wherever he appeared in the state, Joe Kapp replied, "What's my interest? My mother is a Garcia from California who was a crop hand. I'm half Mexican and maybe I owe my people something. I grew up with the poor chicanos and picked the damned grapes and lettuce, myself. . . . I've seen their agony . . . why, shit, Steinbeck didn't describe half the scene."

Thirty-two-year-old Joe Kapp of the Minnesota Vikings is a rare sight in sports, a quarterback who is a practicing cynic and a socially conscious, hard-fisted activist. He doesn't talk fancy; he barks at crowds as if they were in a huddle with him. Kapp never could make the sweet spiels for luxury goods you hear on TV from the Giffords, Rotes and Garagiolas. He comes on mean, loud, menacing. Watching his act in the Los Angeles Sports Arena, close observers saw a 6-foot-3, 218-pounder with black brows and a long scar tracking his jawbone. Once, during a brawl in Canada, one of his own teammates hit Kapp with a bottle and laid open his jaw from ear to ear, good for 108 stitches.

Yet, the "Big Mex" (his pro football nickname) also is beautiful. He often wears Yucatán sandals, flat black gaucho hats, gaudy ponchos hanging to his knees, and more neck chains and buckles than Pancho Villa. On this particular L.A. night he was togged formally, in a black Edwardian suit with crimson shirt ruffles, and he drove up to the arena in the only car he owns, a 1939 black LaSalle, once used in Hollywood gangster films. Curly black hair flowed over his 18-inch neck. Mexican-born actor Anthony Quinn was standing next to Kapp in the wings and said, "Joe's a real animal. You can hear him *hum* inside. He's the way I was when I was young and went around punching guys stiff and taking women all over town. And he's dedicated to *La Causa*."

Leaping onstage, Kapp drew an ovation from 15,000, the largest local turnout of Spanish-speaking people in many years. "Get off your knees, unite!" he told them. Legs spread, fist raised, he was the symbol of machismo, of leadership of the rising brown tide in fields and in urban barrios.

"Above all, have teamwork. Organize your vote and elect your people!"

Since the jaw-slicing accident, Kapp's voice has been a rasp, almost a croak. "Never give up on Chavez and your pride . . . *fight! . . . fight the bastards!*"

Even Quinn, longtime supporter of Mexican emancipation, became nervous at the way the crowd roared and stomped. "Hope they don't tear down the place tonight," he said.

You could feel the building shake before Kapp finished, which is the way it always goes with him and a reason why he's talked about as the "people's replacement" for Governor Ronald Reagan, whose ancestors sure as hell didn't found and "culturize" California.

"I gave 'em my No. 2 speech," Kapp said idly, later. "I only slapped the power structure. When I'm mad, I give my No. 1 talk, called 'Remember the Alamo, the Only Goddamn Thing Mexicans Ever Won in the U.S.A.' "

Conservative editorial writers call Kapp "a race-baiter looking for headlines" and say that as a sociologist he should stick to calling trap plays against the Packers. Still he is a big force in two states, in two fields.

In Minnesota, now, they say that not since Bronko Nagurski have they had such a rugged performer and that the Vikings still would be a last-place team if Joe hadn't rescued them. When he first showed up in 1967, the Vikes were torn by internal trouble and in the basement. Two seasons later Kapp's passing, his clumsy but brutal ability to run the ball and his knack for firing up a squad made them division champions. Last season Minnesota scored 379 points to 133 for opponents, won 12 of 14 games and took the NFL title. In coming from the bottom, the team posted scores unusual in an age of defense: 52–14 over Baltimore, 51–3 over Cleveland, 27–0 over Detroit, 31–0 over Chicago, 52–14 over Pittsburgh, and again over the Browns, 27–7 for the title. Baltimore's pass defense was considered just about the finest until Kapp ripped it for seven touchdown passes, tying the all-time NFL record. Sticking up eight fingers to the anguished Colts, he asked, "Shall we go for the record? Just hang around and keep screwing up like you've been doing."

Number eight eluded him, but it was a year when the verbose ex-asparagus-plucker averaged close to five yards per play running, passed for as many as 449 yards in one afternoon and insulted ball clubs in a way that got him hated.

Insolent throughout, he completed but four passes for only 41 yards gained against Green Bay in November, yet maneuvered enough field position to win on place kicks, 9 to 7. "You cruds," Kapp kept telling the Packers. "You can't even beat me when I've got one arm." He was playing with a fractured left wrist in a cast.

Normally, tough talk across scrimmage lines reflects only humor, temporary anger, or psychological tactics, yet there have been such gutty quarterbacks as Bobby Layne and Norm Van Brocklin who openly challenged tons of beef to come and kill them. With maturity (enough time spent in hospitals) they became civil. With Kapp, although he's a veteran with knees that creak after three operations, the game isn't fun without needles and insults; his linemen, Mick Tingelhoff, Jim Vellone, Ed White and others shudder, as they crouch down, at what they're hearing. "Once," says Vellone, "Kapp was hit by three Colts. They buried him six inches in mud. They saw he was bleeding, and Billy Ray Smith offered him a hand up. Joe knocked Smith's hand away hard enough to break his wrist and yelled, 'Don't ever touch me, you whore! You're also a ———— and a ————.' "

Smith is from Alabama where you don't speak of mamma and sister like that. "He'll never retire happy until he fractures some part of Joe," the Vikings say, wonderment in their voices.

The Los Angeles Rams dislike Kapp for (a) hurdling over them when carrying the ball, a rules violation, and (b) holding them cheaply, despite their 32 wins and three ties in 42 games the past three seasons. "We aim to macerate him," says Deacon Jones, the well-read 270-pound defensive end.

"First time we ever saw him, in '67," says Jones, "Kapp made a speech. He was in his first NFL year, but he leaned over the line and said, 'F—— you, Rams. You're not much. Here I come.' We couldn't believe what we were hearing. Only a crazy cat would talk to us like that."

That night the Rams wrecked Minnesota, 39–3, Kapp having little support in those days. He was flattened 11 times, cleat-stomped and half knocked out. "But he was fighting harder and talking more than ever at the end," adds Jones. "We could see he'd be trouble if his club ever got him some help."

Jones and other Ram chargers theorize that Kapp "likes hurt."

Linemen, leaguewide, agree they've never seen Kapp even flinch and that in him the ultimate masochist has appeared. Ken Kortas, 285-pound Pittsburgh tackle, thinks, "He's got a suicide complex. Or, at least, some weird thing going. He doesn't know anything about fear."

Minnesota's play-the-safe-percentages coach, Bud Grant, met him at the sideline during the championship game with the Browns last January and asked, "Why'd you do that?" Kapp's head wobbled on his neck. He groaned with each step. His eyes were out of focus.

"Didn't I get the damned yards?" returned Kapp.

He had, but in a way that went out of style when the QB became a priceless 75 percent of the offense. In the third period, the Vikings had it won, 24–0. Here was the time to stay on the ground, use up time, play safely for the Super Bowl coming up. With his lumbering washerwoman's gait, Kapp retreated to pass, then suddenly raced to his right, turned upfield and found, confronting him, Jim Houston, 250, toughest of Cleveland's linebackers. Out of bounds was handy to Kapp.

"I never even thought of going out," he said recently. "Jim Houston? Hell, he's one man, not a city. So I popped him one." Only one body got off the ground after the fearsome head-on crash. Houston was carried away, out cold, unable to play anymore.

Thrown six feet into the air, Kapp stayed in the game, completed a 20-yard pass to fullback Bill Brown which set up a Viking field goal, then went to the bench where he was very sick.

In the Super Bowl, later, the Kill Kapp Klub had a field day. He was forced to quit with a sternothoracic shoulder dislocation. The Kansas City Chiefs not only upset the Vikings by 16 points but put Joe out of action for one of only two times in history. Back in 1957 in a California-Michigan State game he suffered two broken ribs and a punctured lung, which sidelined him for a couple of Saturdays. Other than that and the Super Bowl injury, he has never failed to complete anything he started, which covers some 250 high-school, college, United States and Canadian pro games over 17 years. This may be a record for passers.

Those who knew he'd get it someday still celebrate what the Chiefs did to him, but if you ask Jerry Mays, Kansas City's All-Pro end, nothing about Kapp was dimmed. "He's different," admits Mays. "Once I dived for him and his hand hit my helmet when he followed through on the pass. The helmet was cracked open over the earhole. He didn't even feel it. Or at least I don't think he did. On the next play he faked and ran a draw play himself for six yards."

As new leader of what has become the most straight-power-conscious, yard-crunching-out, old-fashioned of teams, Kapp warned his wife long ago that she might see him stoned out of his head about one hour after a game had been lost. She was a Miss California candidate when they met, a slim brunette beauty. The romance began in Joe's postcollege years when he had a job hauling $50,000 at a crack from the South Lake Tahoe, Nevada, crap tables to a bank, revolver on his hip. Marcia was a dancer in club shows.

"I'm a real bad loser," Joe warned. "And I'm also one of the country's greatest tequila drinkers."

"Okay, don't brag," said Marcia. "Do you fight when you're drinking?"

"Profusely," said Joe.

It's too bad, in his opinion, that his wife wasn't around to catch his action one Christmas Eve in New York when, leaving a bar with friends, he hailed a cab. A blizzard was going on, and when a taxi stopped, three men rushed out of the bar and took possession of it. Joe's associates cursed but did nothing.

Kapp made no other objection than to reach in, pull out the transgressors, one by one, and belt them all over the street. "Now proceed on," he told the cabby.

"Never once have I heard the Big Mex blame his blocking for a defeat," points out Carl Eiler, All-Pro Viking end. "And nobody else better do it, either." An example was a 30–27 loss to the Packers in '67, the only time a Kapp-led team has lost to Green Bay. Three years ago he had what opponents called "watch-out blocking" going for him. Guys would miss a block and yell to him, just before Kapp was swarmed under, "Watch out!" Following the Packer loss, a bitter Kapp and his close friend, linebacker Lonnie Warwick, headed for a saloon, where they traded 12 straight shots of tequila.

Remarking that the defeat was his fault, Kapp was contradicted by the huge Warwick. "No, the boys up front let you down," said Warwick.

"Nuts," growled Kapp. "I blew it with that last-minute fumble." Warwick still disagreed.

"Listen, don't argue with me. If I say I lost it, I lost it!" roared Joe. The two became so hot that they invited each other outside.

It was a fight to remember. Warwick at 245, was up and down and suffered a split lip; Joe was up and down and had a closed eye and lacerated nose. When they were exhausted, their clothes wrecked, they returned to the bar for more juice of the century plant.

"Ahhhhh, tequila," Kapp says, with relish. "That's beautiful stuff. Makes you crazier than peyote—which by the way is another Mexican product."

Exuberance of Zorba dimensions, rather than standout skill, explains Joe who is a below-average passer and a plodding runner.

"I win because winning is right on, it's honest. Your blood turns sour and sticky when you lose," he says. Asked what he thought of a recent Roman Gabriel statement about NFL athletes, Kapp croaked, "That's bull." Gabriel of the Rams had claimed, "A pro isn't an animal. They call us that, but we'd rather be known for ourselves—normal persons with good feelings."

Kapp says, "It's an animal game. I'm an animal. Any guy good at it is an animal. Sure, I love my wife and son, but there's another kind of love. Is it normal to wake up in the morning in a sweat because you can't wait to beat another human's guts out?"

When he reached college, Kapp had never met a Communist, didn't know what a Jew was, had no concept of racial problems of United States Orientals or Indians. He did know that Mexicans were looked down upon. He was born in Santa Fe, New Mexico. His mother Florence Garcia (whom he has set up in a business of her own, in San Jose, California) worked as a farm stoop laborer and as a waitress. His father was a traveling salesman. Kapp says, "He was an early-day hippie. We didn't see much of him."

Moving to the San Joaquin Valley of California, the family of six knew hard times. Joe graduated from the broiling crop fields to high-school stardom in three sports, then to California U. and more honors. Kapp signed a $15,000 contract with the Calgary Stampeders in 1959. Bad knees seemed to have finished him in 1961, but he wouldn't accept the medical verdict.

Another setback came one night when Kapp and his Calgary mates were guzzling whiskey and one of them threw a sneak blow at him—with a bottle. "You never saw so much blood," says Vikings' general manager Jim Finks, then running the Calgary team. "Three of us were soaked in it when we got him to a hospital. His lower jaw was split wide open. Another half inch down and he'd have died of a severed jugular vein."

Kapp played two games later—despite his 108 stitches and more bandages on him than a mummy.

"Calgary traded me for a case of jockstraps to the Vancouver Lions and I got going," he smiles. Six years later the Lions had two all-Canada titles, Joe was a hero who'd passed for 137 touchdowns and 22,725 yards, and now NFL owners wanted him, on any terms. Kapp made the terms harsh.

Before he stopped dealing, he'd signed with the Houston Oilers (forcing Vancouver to suspend him), collected Houston earnest money, incited a threatened Canadian-NFL lawsuit, maneuvered the merged NFL-AFL to pay reparations to the CFL for waiving him out of the northland, squeezed another, larger payoff from Minnesota when Houston's claim to him was denied—and stepped into the best opportunity then open in football. Fran Tarkenton, the Viking passer, had feuded with his coach and had been traded to the New York Giants.

"The negotiation was unprecedented, and when I had a poor first year they almost booed me out of the park," rattles off Kapp. "They said my long ball fluttered, that I was bowlegged, a dipsomaniac, a mental case and that I didn't have enough teeth. The fact is, I have all my teeth. As for the rest, who's perfect anyway?"

With many a jest and a lot of first downs made in third-and-eight situations, Kapp soon won over the customers, and now he's one of the best-known sights in Minneapolis and St. Paul—not to mention Acapulco, where he lets himself be strapped into a harness and towed 200 feet in the air under a parachute behind a speedboat.

Early last season he reinjured his knee, which was casted, and for days he drove around Minneapolis one-legged, with the other leg draped over the console. No policeman gave him trouble. No doubt they were thinking of how he turned down the Most Valuable Player award of his club at a banquet, leaving the banquet chairman standing there with the cup in his hands. Joe said, "All the Vikings are most valuable."

Or perhaps they thought back to the day against Detroit when he was knocked cold in the second quarter and then his replacement, Gary Cuozzo, broke his collarbone. Back came Kapp, with no legs under him and unaware of much of what was going on. He finished the game and later, when they asked him about the fourth period, he couldn't remember any of it. In this condition, he unloaded a 51-yard bomb for a touchdown after four times personally running the ball into the center of Detroit's line.

The guess on Joe Kapp's future is that he'll be around longer than most. Quarterbacks past 30 talk yearningly of retirement, but he'll quit when they drag him away. After that he might turn to helping Mexican-Americans improve their lot. "Maybe I'll get some ragged clothes and go back to picking peas with the peons," he speculates. "If you're going to be in a war, you want to be where it's happening."

And what happens if some grower's foreman pushes him around? *Wham! Oooof! Crunch!*

WHO'S GOT A DIME?

By Frank Dolson

From The Philadelphia Inquirer

A coin flip to decide one of the play-off berths in the National Football League's complicated system became a very real possibility Monday night because of Detroit's victory over Los Angeles.

If Detroit, Dallas and the New York Giants all win their final games Sunday, Detroit and Dallas will be tied for the best second-place records in the National Conference at 10–4 and will have to flip a coin to decide a play-off spot.

How about that, sports fans? A 14-game season (not counting exhibitions) may not be enough to determine the eight NFL teams that will qualify for the play-offs—and a shot at the Super Bowl. So the play-off lineup could be decided by a coin flip.

Not an extra game, mind you. A flip of a coin!

Think of it. All those preseason games, 14 regular-season games, God knows how many knee operations, and then the moment of truth: a coin flip.

Under the circumstances it can be assumed that no normal, everyday coin flip will do. After all, a $25,000-a-man championship is at stake. Chances are Pete Rozelle has already sold the television rights to the highest bidder.

We take you now to the National Football League's first annual Super Flip, pitting the Dallas Cowboys against the Detroit Lions, exclusively on NBC:

DAVID BRINKLEY: Good afternoon. I'm your Super Flip anchorman. Frank McGee, Curt Gowdy, Hugh Downs, and I will be with you for the next two hours describing all the action as a representative of the Dallas Cowboys and a representative of the Detroit Lions flip. Now, down to the field to Curt Gowdy . . .

GOWDY: Thank you, David. With me is Commissioner Rozelle, who will personally referee today's contest. Commissioner, our audience is waiting eagerly to learn the identity of the men who will call today's big flip.

ROZELLE: Yes, Curt. As you know, their names have been kept a very closely guarded secret until this moment.

GOWDY: THE ENVELOPE, please, Mr. Commissioner.

(*Drum roll in the background as Rozelle hands the sealed envelope to Gowdy, who rips it open immediately following a one-minute TV time-out.*)

GOWDY (*his voice rising dramatically*): Introducing from the Dallas Cowboys, 6-foot-3, 206 pounds, Don Meredith . . . And from the Detroit Lions, 6-foot-2 and 245 pounds, Alex Karras. Now back to the booth.

BRINKLEY: And so it is time to flip. Will the Dallas Cowboys qualify for a place in the championship play-offs, or will it be the Detroit Lions? Come in, Hugh Downs . . .

DOWNS: With me David, is J. P. Morganbucks, a lifelong employee of the U.S. Treasury Department. Mr. Morganbucks has handled countless coins in his career. Tell me, sir, in your considered opinion, which has the better chance of coming up—heads or tails?

MORGANBUCKS: As you know, Mr. Downs, my department has studied this matter carefully. We have left no margin for error. In our considered opinion, if a silver dollar is used there is a 50–50 chance it will come up heads.

DOWNS: And if a smaller coin is used?

MORGANBUCKS: Also 50–50. It's a toss-up.

DOWNS: Thank you, Mr. Morganbucks. David?

BRINKLEY: The commissioner is now reaching in his pocket for a coin, so back to Curt Gowdy on the field.

GOWDY: There seems to be some delay, David. Uh, Mr. Commissioner, did you want to say something?

ROZELLE: Yes, Curt. Do you have a quarter?

GOWDY: I believe so. Here . . .

BRINKLEY: Ladies and gentlemen, the big moment has arrived. Commissioner Pete Rozelle is holding Curt Gowdy's quarter in his right hand. Don Meredith has been given the privilege of calling the flip. The preliminary signal is that he has called "tails" . . . And now the coin is in the air. We switch you to Frank McGee.

MCGEE: David, our RCA computer indicates the flip's trajectory looks good. And we have a projected winner . . . Heads, David! Our computer projects heads will win.

BRINKLEY: And so, the Detroit Lions have won the first annual Super Flip, as you can all see clearly now on our NBC isolated, stop-action, slow-motion, living-color camera. Before we sign off, do you have any final comment from the field, Curt?

GOWDY: Just one, David. If you see the commissioner, would you ask him to return my quarter?

GREEN AND LEAFY FOOTBALL

By Stan Isaacs

From Look

Copyright, ©, 1970, Stan Isaacs

With six seconds remaining in the first half, and Worcester Tech leading the Coast Guard 13–0, Worcester quarterback Dave Alden came to the sidelines to ask coach Mel Massucco what to do next. "Do what you've been doing," Massucco said. "Take the ball and run with it. Kill these last six seconds."

Alden, a halfback who had been moved over because of an injury to the regular quarterback, took the snap, wheeled and ran toward the sidelines. To avoid running out of bounds before the clock ran out, he then turned and headed back into his own territory. At that point, the Coast Guard cannon boomed out from behind the end zone, signaling the end of the half. The fledgling quarterback, believing play was dead, stopped running, shouted, "Yippee!" and threw the football into the air. An alert Coast Guard lineman gobbled up the loose football and ran it some 30 yards into the end zone for a touchdown.

Somehow, Worcester went on to win one for Massucco anyway, and he recalls that 1967 game, his first win as a coach, as "the only game I saw that started and ended with the national anthem." That bit of patriotism stemmed from the pregame vow of the Coast Guard coach to his players that the game ball, emblematic of victory, would not leave the Coast Guard. This made an impression on the Coast Guard manager. When the game ended, and the captain of Worcester went over to an official to claim the ball, there was opposition. The Coast Guard manager, a plebe who didn't quite grasp the significance of the game ball, was determined to retrieve it. So they both clutched at the ball in the middle of the field. A tug-of-war ensued. Players from both teams joined in a grand free-for-all. "The bandleader started playing the national anthem," Massucco said, "and only then did the guys stop fighting and come to attention." And Worcester got the game ball.

A quarter back who doesn't know when the half ends and a manager who doesn't understand the significance of the game ball are among the giddy aspects of the raging action every Saturday on small-college football gridirons. "It's a challenge," says Wesleyan coach Don Russell. "It's a lot of teaching," says Glenn Drahn of Coe. "It's hard work," says Rocky Carzo of Tufts.

Carzo remembers his first victory vividly. "We were playing Bowdoin. We hadn't won, and we hadn't scored often either, so when we scored first, we had a disorganized discussion on the sideline whether to kick the point or go for a two-point conversion. While we were debating, our kicker, Bob Froehlich, unknowingly rushed into the game and lined up to kick the point. It was only his third attempt of the season. He made it, and we won, 7–6."

If Tufts beat Bowdoin that day, it meant that Bowdoin was not playing Bates. Let that be noted because some keen observers of the sporting scene have the impression that Bowdoin always plays Bates. Comment: "Every time I listen to those Saturday night football scores, they are giving a Bates-Bowdoin score." There also used to be the feeling that "as Maine goes, so goes Colby," but the University of Maine has moved onto a more ambitious level of play, leaving Bates, Bowdoin, and Colby to battle among themselves for the coveted championship of the State of Maine.

If your ear is attuned only to the names of the 118 schools that play big-time football, then it's not unlikely that the small-college football scores will all come out sounding like Bates-Bowdoin. And one man's Bates-Bowdoin is another's Wooster-Muskingum, Luther-Wartburg, Morris Brown–Bethune-Cookman, Pepperdine-Occidental, Upsala-Lycoming, or, lest we forget, Hope vs. Defiance.

College football conjures up movie-like montages of mammoth stadiums, inflated coaching staffs, specialization, keen scouting from luxurious press boxes, tumultuous television coverage, and, of late, the titillation of a visit from that most enthusiastic jock, the President of the United States. But small-college football is a different matter—no TV cameras, no President, smaller squads playing on windswept fields with wooden grandstands, sometimes before nonpaying (and when the going is bad, nonexistent) spectators.

The question, though, is not which is better, which registers higher on the football pleasure meter. It is which is more consistent with the basic aims of an academic institution.

The people who were a part of the cozy Wesleyan-Williams festivities last year—coaches, players, and spectators—will argue, with justice, that nobody came closer to the best of football times than they did that crisp fall afternoon. Wesleyan, founded in 1831, is a privately endowed school of 1,700 students, 285 of them women, in Middletown, Connecticut. It is one of the small New England prestige schools, among the most liberal and innovative of American liberal arts colleges. Its significance athletically is that it is one of the Little Three, along with Amherst and Williams. Its alumni have no trouble looking the alumni of the Big Three (Harvard, Yale, Princeton) straight in the eye.

Wesleyan is usually the weakest of the Little Three. Last year, though, Wesleyan beat Amherst and strung together six victories. It went into the Williams game with a chance at its first undefeated season in more than a decade.

At Wesleyan, the field is laid out for the football season between temporary stands on a greensward smack in the middle of the campus. On a football afternoon, the sense of leisure is typified by a terrace behind the end zone on which nonpaying spectators spread out on blankets to picnic and gossip. Dogs frolic among them, and it's deliciously anticipated that a mongrel will, at any moment, romp onto the field and join the action.

The 1969 Wesleyan-Williams game developed into one of the epics of the 75-year series. Williams took a 14–0 lead, led 14–6 at the half. Wesleyan kept up a fraught-with-frustration chase most of the game, and there was a shamble of intercepted passes, fumbles and nullified touchdowns. One sequence: Williams intercepted a pass; a few plays later, Wesleyan intercepted; and on the very next play, Williams intercepted back. As onetime Stanford coach Jim Lawson says, "You have to get out in the bush leagues to see those what-the-hell triple reverses and lateral forwards."

Wesleyan eventually won, 18–17, scoring a touchdown in the final minutes, and putting a partial block on Williams' would-be game-winning field-goal attempt on the final play of the game. The players paraded coach Don Russell off to the locker room, while the Wesleyan swing band (complete with battered upright piano) played raucously. Students—long-haired and short-haired—ran from the stands and the terrace for squealing embraces. Alumni—Lord & Taylor tweedy—cheered.

At small schools, the players, essentially unrecruited, are very much a part of the student body. On the Wesleyan team, there were extremes of longhairs and crew-cut jocks. In 1968, star end Stu Blackburn led a protest against the war in Vietnam. In the midst of the protest, Blackburn's pal, Steve Pfeiffer, the quarterback, was collecting signatures for a petition urging that those protesters staging a sit-in at the president's office be forcibly removed.

"Despite this, they remained friends and left here as friends," coach Russell said. "I think there is a willingness on all sides here to respect the other fellow's view."

Quarterback Pete Panciera, the boy whose line-drive passes moved Wesleyan to victory, said, "Sometimes it gets me angry that the students here aren't excited about football and that we don't get the write-ups that we would get at a big school. But this is not a rah-rah place. As much as you are wrapped up in football, you realize there are more important things for most people."

Frank Navarro, ex-Williams, current Columbia coach, says, "The difference between a big school and a small school is that you have more time with the players at a small school. You have closer relationships with them. And at a small school, you are more likely to be measured by the impact you have on the life of your students than by your football record."

The best of all sporting fare comes in games where the spectators enjoy a sense of nearness and participation. Never is this more available than on the crisp fall afternoons when the traditional meetings between teams like Denison and Oberlin, Hamline and Macalester and Cornell [of Mount Vernon, Iowa] and Coe take place. Spectators mingle with the players, sometimes right up to game time. Afterward, they walk off arm in arm to social gatherings. At Coe College in Cedar Rapids, where the get-togethers among players, parents and faculty are called "a coffee," coach Glenn Drahn says, "People often come up to me and say, 'I never realized how much fun you could have at one of these games.'"

The fun and games of the Lafayette-Lehigh series often revolve around the fringe activity, lending a quality of lasting insignificance to the games themselves. Until they were banned in Bethlehem, Pennsylvania, home of Lehigh, the students built huge bonfires for the pregame pep rally. This often inspired enemy raiding parties to set off the fire prematurely. One year, Lafayette students gathered outside the enemy campus grounds to shoot flaming arrows into the woodpile.

In 1933, the grand statue of the Marquis de Lafayette, the pride of the campus, was stripped of its sword by a Lehigh raiding party. Ever since, the marquis has been standing there clutching an empty hilt. Events at Lafayette once were spiced with a tug-of-war between the students of both colleges, but this was discontinued when the Lafayette scalawags tied their end to the baseball scoreboard, and the Lehigh stalwarts pulled it loose from its moorings. Lehigh also looks back with some pride to a chemical raid on Lafayette that puzzled the victims until, in succeeding weeks before the game, a great L E H I G H emerged in the grass of the football field.

Alumni gabfests are rich with recollections like the one that Richard Harding Davis scored Lehigh's first touchdown in the first game of the 86-year-old series, and that, in 1918, a Lehigh man named Snooks Dowd ran the wrong way, discovered his error, reversed his field and scored a touchdown in a run that was charted to be 210 yards—later cut down to a mere 160.

The Lafayette-Lehigh series started later than Yale-Harvard, but it is the longest now because the teams played each other more than once a season in the early days. Nor do they budge an inch to the big boys when it comes to legends. There's a fine tall tale that Harvard coach Percy Haughton once evoked the proper mental attitude against the Bulldogs of Yale in 1908 by bringing a live bulldog into the locker room and strangling it to death with his bare hands. In the Lafayette Leopards vs. Lehigh Engineers version, Tom Keady, a strong silent type who coached Lehigh in the World War I era, throttled a leopard and threw the carcass at the feet of his players. He did it, a Lafayette man said, "to appeal to their intelligence."

There is an abundance of good cheer on Philadelphia's Main Line when Swarthmore meets Haverford in what they unabashedly call "The Game." It overcomes many of the frustrations of playing football at Haverford and Swarthmore (though coach Lew Elverson talks about Swarthmore's 17-game winning streak in 1965-66 with great wistfulness). "The night we beat Swarthmore a few years ago," says Haverford hero Don Evans, "the whole cafeteria stood up and applauded."

The most recent "Game" was played on Haverford's Walton Field in the ankle-deep-in-fallen-leaves, russet-and-brown suburban countryside outside Philadelphia. In the late afternoon, the sinking sun's rays filtered through five huge oak trees behind the grand-stand, casting speckled shadows on the darkening football field.

The organized anarchy on the sidelines featured the Haverford musical ensemble, acclaimed by the PA announcer as "The Haver-ford Varsity Marching Society & Auxiliary Fife, Drum and Kazoo Corps, locally famous." Haverford president John Coleman, re-spendent in a black sweater with a large red "H," led impassioned cheers in front of the Haverford stands. The PA man said, "The kazoo band, through an intricate application of geometry, will now undergo a complex maneuver that will describe the Swarthmore social life." The kazooniks arranged themselves into a large square. (In its tribute to writers last year, the Harvard band paid homage to Philip [*Portnoy's Complaint*] Roth by playing "He's Got the Whole World in His Hands.")

Despite the yeoman efforts of Haverford's 5-foot-4, 135-pound tailback, a black freshman named Charlie Cheek, Swarthmore prevailed by dint of grit, pluck and a line that outweighed its opponents 10 pounds per man.

Kalamazoo and Olivet of the Michigan Intercollegiate Athletic Association started their rivalry in 1892, but the most famous game took place in 1958. Olivet went into it with a losing streak of 29. Kalamazoo was winless for the season. A downpour on the day of the game turned the Olivet field into a mud bowl. The teams played into the final minutes, tied 13–13, when Lee Soncrant of Olivet got away on a 66-yard run. League historian Dick Kishpaugh calls it "perhaps the slowest run in MIAA history. He got a step ahead of the nearest defender, and both the runner and his pur-suers plodded through the mud in slow motion. He scored and Olivet won. There's a victory bell in the chapel on the Olivet campus. It was rusty from disuse, but it rang the entire night."

The MIAA football schools also number Alma, Albion, Hope, and Adrian. Hillsdale is a former member of the league, having been suspended in 1960 for violating a group vote against post-season bowl games by participating in something called the Mineral Water Bowl. This kind of conference arrangement among equals gives meaning and direction to a football program, providing the goal of a championship as an incentive for boys to put in the hard work that football piles on top of heavy academic loads.

There are, admittedly, differences among the small schools about what constitutes a sane approach. On the wings of a successful season, a Wesleyan public-relations man says, "We think our football program is appropriate. We don't treat it as a joke the way they do at Swarthmore and Haverford." The PR man at Haverford responds, "Wesleyan is more of a button-down school, with more of a life-and-death approach to the game of football. Here, we have The Hood Trophy; it goes annually to the school that wins more events in the competitions in nine sports between Haverford and Swarthmore."

Swarthmore coach Elverson, a burly, physically impressive man, has the difficult job of handling young men whose commitment to football is marginal. "Sometimes the frustrations send me up the wall. The kids have labs that cut into practice, and on seminar days, you don't see them all. There's tremendous pressure on them because at the same time that they're out on the football field practicing, their pals are in the library studying. And with only 30 or so kids on the squad, you can't knock their brains out in practice." Says Haverford's coach Dana Swan, "Sure we have two-platoon football here. We run our offensive team off the field, run them around the bench, and send them back as the defensive team."

The players on a small-school squad don't have to play football to keep their scholarships, so a coach of a losing team is often faced with a morale problem and dropouts. Swarthmore once reached out to Oberlin, in Ohio, for a home-and-home series because both presidents were anxious to dispel a mutual problem: the prevailing feeling that both were girls' schools. Swarthmore recently had a sophomore who decided in preseason practice to quit football because it was a dehumanizing game. He went through the agony of finishing the season, though, because he felt he had a commitment to his teammates and coach. Haverford lost one of its starting guards when he transferred to Sarah Lawrence, then a girl's school, as part of an exchange program.

Haverford needs to win with more frequency before coach Dana Swan would want his school to be pointed out as any kind of football paragon. Yet he insists that unsubsidized football is the answer to many if not all of the problems facing educators. Swan, a short, mild young man in his late thirties who could be taken for a graduate fellow, has written: "For the player who chooses to participate in an unsubsidized, student-centered program, football can be the key . . . to much broader experiences. For it becomes a tool, not master. Through football, he finds friends, identity and release. . . . If, as he matures, he finds that football no longer meets his needs, he is entirely free to retire from the field without the conse-

quences of having to leave college through loss of financial aid."
One of the Haverford boys, halfback Art Baruffi, says, "In high
school, the football program was run on fear. We needed policemen
to keep us apart after games. Here, Swarthmore is our arch rival,
and we invite each other to parties after the game."

Henry Steele Commager, the historian, once said, "It is as illogi-
cal to expect the young men of Princeton or Notre Dame to provide
[spectators] with sporting entertainment as to expect young ladies
of Vassar . . . to provide them with nightclub entertainment."
Haverford's Swan says, "With the advent of television, football
really went into business—the entertainment business. Beneath all
the flag-waving, breast-beating and educational gobbledygook, the
business ethic has become synonymous with the football ethic for a
significant portion of the football world."

As a business, small-college football is a failure. There's no money
in it. On the other hand, it doesn't cost very much. The whole
football program at Wesleyan costs $25,000, including $5,000 for the
erection and dismantling of temporary stands. Haverford fields a
football team for $11,000. (At Ohio State, the football staff spends
$23,000 every year just on telephone calls.)

The high cost of football has taken its toll of schools that have
attempted to operate ambitious programs. Detroit, Saint Ambrose
and Loras are among those who have fallen by the wayside in recent
years. Manhattan College must settle for club football because,
explains coach Larry Kelly, "We are caught up between our football tradition and the schedules of our [existing] varsity teams.
Our fans and alumni would not tolerate our playing Hobart and
Union." (And what's wrong with Hobart?)

The big-time mentality afflicts many athletic people who are
small time not because of intent but because of an inability to cut
it on the big-time scene. They wistfully ape the big guys. A few
years ago, Rensselaer Polytechnic was working on the longest losing
streak in the country. Its dogged pursuit of victory had earned the
attention of people beyond the Troy, New York, campus, inspiring
the ditty:

> You can rail at Yale,
> And pooh-pooh Purdue,
> But do not sneer
> At Rensselaer.

When RPI finally won, there was much rejoicing. The New York
Football Writers Association invited the RPI coach to speak before

one of its weekly gabfests. He proceeded to deliver a keen depth-chart analysis of his squad, as if he were a Rose Bowl coach providing deathless information for the big game. He seemed unable to grasp the merriment of the turnabout.

When a school is bogged down in defeat, there are inevitably questions about dropping the sport. Columbia, which has had a long losing tradition, began to hear this kind of opposition last year in a student editorial. The editors presented a low-key argument that the university begin "setting its priorities and decide what it can and cannot afford." It pointed to football as an expensive activity "which does not serve any essential purpose of the university."

The experience of the University of Chicago may serve as the example for many schools staggering under the load of big-time football. Chicago once was a proud member of the Big Ten, but dropped football in 1939.

Last year, following a 30-year absence, football returned on a modest scale to Chicago. One of the star substitutes was Mitchell Kahn, also the football correspondent for the *Maroon,* the undergraduate newspaper. Anticipating Chicago's return to the game, Kahn wrote: "The Monsters of the Midway take on a Baptist bastion at Wheaton College [Illinois] in a vigorous attempt to regain the football stature which at times past have made them the most feared team in the sport. . . . Lusting after victory as only a U. of Chicago team can, the varsity-grid jocks seek to snap a losing streak which began Nov. 26, 1939, with a 46–0 obliteration at the hands of the Illini." His postgame newspaper story began: "The Monsters of the Midway turned out to be nothing more than paper dragons, slain by those knights in shining armor who call themselves the Wheaton Crusaders by the scandalous score of 6–0 . . ."

Laughing, Kahn said, "When I met the guys in the locker room after the paper came out, I thought I was going to get killed. If they had shown half as much fight against the other team on the field as against me in the locker room, we would have won the game."

Kahn is a 19-year-old junior, a pianist and trombonist. He was unimpressed with the mystique of college football although enthusiastic about his newfound challenge. He said, "I was too small in high school to go out for football, and I was sort of introverted. But I'm settled down now. I'm not worried about my ability to get into graduate school, so I can play football. And where else in the country could someone like me come out and play college football?"

In Chicago's last season before it gave up football, it was humili-ated in games against the big boys, losing to Illinois, 46–0; Virginia, 47–0; Harvard, 61–0; Ohio State, 61–0; and Michigan, 85–0.

In resuming football 30 years later on a scale accommodating ordinary students, Chicago played Valparaiso, Wheaton, North Park, and Marquette's club team, actually beating Marquette, 14–0. College is for learning, and it took the University of Chicago only 30 years to understand that there is green, leafy, fall-afternoon foot-ball fun available—if you don't mind being one of the hundreds of little schools that come up on the Saturday night football newscasts sounding like Bates vs. Bowdoin.

AS THE COACH LAY DYING

By Bob Addie

From The Washington Post

Copyright, ©, 1970, The Washington Post

Monday, August 31, was the 30th anniversary of the marriage of the former Marie Planitz and Vincent Lombardi. The marriage took place on Saturday afternoon, August 31, 1940, in Englewood, New Jersey, where Lombardi was busy teaching chemistry, Latin and physics at St. Cecilia's High School as well as coaching the football, baseball and basketball teams (all won state championships). In addition, Lombardi was attending Fordham Law School.

Mrs. Lombardi permitted herself a few reflections the other evening at Georgetown Hospital where she has taken a room across the hall from the seriously ill coach and general manager of the Redskins.

It was dusk at the hospital and people were busy visiting patients. But none found his way to the coach's room. These days, Lombardi sees few people outside his wife.

"People have been wonderful," Mrs. Lombardi said. "At one time Vin was getting over 500 letters a day, Mass cards, and all kinds of suggestions from healers as well as encouragement from rabbis, priests and ministers.

"Some well-meaning people sometimes cause problems. Two girls came by one day and wanted to pray in his room. I told them the prayers were just as effective if said in the hall. I finally convinced them."

Mrs. Lombardi picked up a "flower lamp" which had come from Ethel Kennedy. The floral arrangement resembles a floor-to-ceiling lamp with various objects attached such as candy, a miniature brandy bottle and other trinkets. "What's this I've been hearing about you running to daylight with the nurses," read the card. "Love and kisses from Ethel."

Mrs. Lombardi is a chain smoker and her vigil has not diminished her habit. "We had a coaxial cable which brought the first three Redskin games to Vin," she said, lighting one cigarette from another. "Those people from CBS who put in the cable couldn't have been sweeter. The Washington press has been wonderful, too. Vin watched about one half of each game. When some of the players didn't do things right, his language really blistered the ears of those nurses. I remember he looked asleep watching one play and I said something about Charley Taylor dropping a touchdown pass. 'I can see,' he growled."

Mrs. Lombardi revealed that the coach's hair has grown long in the last few weeks. "Vin a longhair, that's beautiful," she said. "Vin always has his hair cut every week. He has the type of hair hard to cut. His father, who is 81, has a beautiful head of hair."

Marie Lombardi has been more than a football coach's wife. She has been his permanent assistant, his critic, his haven, his partner, his constant companion.

"I miss the travel—the buses, the planes," she said. "I went everywhere with the Packers. I was the only woman on the trips. But, you know, Vin likes women around. That famous five o'clock happy hour of his always included women. He always believed that women take a lot of abuse from their men during the season and it's only right that they share some of the fun and the glory.

"I shared the championship souvenirs. I'll tell you a funny thing. Young Vincent, my son, was given two rings and a watch as souvenirs of the Packers' championships. He refused to wear them. He told his father: 'I didn't earn them.'

" 'I wore a ring of my father's for years,' Dad told young Vincent, 'and I didn't earn it either. All right, I'll give the stuff to my grandchildren.' "

Mrs. Lombardi wears a charm bracelet made entirely of miniature, gold footballs. "There's a story in these," she explained, "and maybe it tells something about Vin Lombardi, the man.

"He's different from most coaches because he believes that a football team is a family. He is the head of the family and he shares the players' problems and joys as if they are his own children. They often say Vin is like the commander of a Roman legion, but if he is, he commands a legion of love.

"Anyway, one of my delightful duties every year at Green Bay used to be hosting a luncheon for the wives of the players. One time I was ill and got to the luncheon a little late. There were 40 women there and crazy Max McGee, the end, who is a bachelor. I love that man. It turned out to be a surprise party for me. The girls gave me this charm bracelet and I was so touched I nearly cried—and I hate to cry in public.

"They're all gold footballs and each means something. Two are Army-Navy footballs. That's when Vin was an assistant to Red Blaik at Army. During that time we beat Navy two out of five—not much but we got two. Two are Fordham footballs when Vin was one of the Blocks." (The famed Fordham line with which Lombardi played was known as the Seven Blocks of Granite.)

"Six of the footballs," added Mrs. Lombardi, "represent Green Bay titles. It was a sweet gesture."

Mrs. Lombardi has been something of a "den mother" to the Packers and Redskins. "I always was a friendly soul," she confessed. "Sometimes, I'd see a boy who looked down. You know, they're big strong boys but they are, after all, only boys. So I'd cheer up the poor boy. Most times it turned out Vin had chewed him out so the boy felt better after we talked. Vin never put me up to it."

There was the time, she says, that Dan Currie, the big Packer linebacker, asked permission to take two of his four children on the Green Bay charter.

"We were going out to play Los Angeles in 1964," Mrs. Lombardi recalled, "and one of the Currie children was a baby. Our team doctor discovered the baby had measles. The information got all over the plane. I picked the baby up and put him in Vin's lap. Both screamed. Fortunately, nothing came from that, although the Rams did hold us to a 24–24 tie."

Mrs. Lombardi reveals that when the coach went to New York during the recent player rebellion, he overtaxed himself. "Coming back on the plane from New York was a nightmare," she says. "I pleaded with the clerk at LaGuardia in New York to put Vin aboard ahead of the crowd so he could relax. It was a long time before he got on that plane, and when he did, the stewardesses ignored him. I know this is an isolated example because we always received wonderful treatment—but of all times to be ignored.

"I had two big bags and I was struggling when we got back to Washington. A nice young man passed by and asked Vin if he could help. You know Vin. He never needed help. But he turned to this young man and said: 'Help me.' I almost cried right there.

"I never met a football player I didn't like," she continued, "although I must admit that at times I've come close. One boy I loved was Donny Anderson, but I didn't think he was much of a halfback and I told Vin so when we got Donny at Green Bay.

" 'You're wrong, you're wrong,' Vin said. 'This boy is going to be great.' A week or so ago I was giving Vin a rundown on the scores and he was obviously pleased when Donny scored three times in the exhibition game against Dallas. 'How about that lousy halfback, Donny Anderson?' he said."

Mrs. Lombardi says the coach has been buoyed by the visits of his former players including Bob Skoronski, Forrest Gregg, Paul Hornung, Jim Taylor, Tommy Brown, Bart Starr, Bob Long and Jerry Kramer.

"I think Bill Austin will do a great job with the Redskins if they leave him alone," Mrs. Lombardi reflected after a pause. "I like the Redskins. I think they can win the title."

It was dark now and the hospital sounds had stilled. There was only the oppressive silence of the hot summer evening and the sounds of cars leaving the hospital. The door across the hall, 6100, had remained undisturbed.

"I keep thinking," the coach's wife mused, "about Vin staying in football as a coach and general manager. In the end, I think football will break his heart, because he'll have to fight the owners for being too permissive to the players. He would lose his fight to prevent the players from dictating terms.

"But I mustn't think. Vin always tells me: 'Don't think, Marie.' Right now, I don't think."

She put her head down, but even then she didn't cry in public.

THE MAKING OF THE NO. 1 DRAFT CHOICE

By Roy McHugh

From Sport

Copyright, ©, 1970, MacFadden-Bartell Corp.

On this last Tuesday morning of January, in a small room illumi-
nated by harsh winter sunlight, Art Rooney, Jr., sat at the foot of a
T-shaped walnut table and waited for a telephone to ring. Neat
lists of football players' names were chalked on blackboards hanging from the walls. A football player when he attended St. Vincent
College, bushy-haired at 34 and wearing oversized black-rimmed
glasses, Art Rooney, Jr., is personnel director of the Pittsburgh
Steelers, the professional team owned by his father, and in bulk he
compared with the coaches in the room. As 10 o'clock approached,
the room was silent. Exactly at 10, the phone rang. Art Rooney, Jr.,
the receiver cupped to his ear, listened for a moment and said,
"Bradshaw."

The Pittsburgh Steelers, first team to choose in the 1970 pro
football draft, had announced their selection. At a desk in a ball-
room of the Belmont Plaza Hotel in New York, facing television
lights and platoons of reporters, a Steeler representative sped the
word to commissioner Pete Rozelle, who stood by. And soon, with
dramatic pauses, Rozelle was talking into a microphone, saying:

"Pittsburgh . . .

"First choice in the first round . . .

"Terry Bradshaw, quarterback from Louisiana Tech . . ."

When the news reached the offices of the Philadelphia Eagles,
draft headquarters for BLESTO-V, a talent scouting service available to the Chicago, Detroit, Philadelphia, Pittsburgh and Minnesota teams, 11 men jumped to their feet and cheered. BLESTO-V is
a name that resulted from compressing the initials of something
once called the Bears-Lions-Eagles-Steelers Talent Organization, the

V at the end standing for Vikings, who joined the group tardily. At a meeting in Pittsburgh six weeks before the draft, having assessed and minutely graded a thousand college football players, the BLESTO-V scouts, gathered now in Philadelphia, had pronounced Terry Bradshaw the best of them all.

BLESTO-V's appraisal of Bradshaw was a trade secret. In those considerable areas of the nation where Louisiana Tech is not a household name, it would have dumbfounded the average football fan. Louisiana Tech—officially, Louisiana Polytechnic Institute—is in Ruston, Louisiana. Its games with Northeast Louisiana and Southeast Louisiana, Northwest Louisiana and Southwest Louisiana, McNeese State and East Carolina merit one line of type in the Sunday morning editions of big-city newspapers. Accordingly, the world for the most part was unaware of Terry Bradshaw until *The New York Times,* early last November, identified him as news fit to print. A feature story on Bradshaw appeared in *The Times,* but the BLESTO-V scouts and their professional rivals had no need to read it for educational purposes. "Lord God," said Jess Thompson, the BLESTO scout who covers Louisiana, Texas, Mississippi and Arkansas, *"all* of us knew about him."

Scouts are reverent, brave and possibly also trustworthy when they describe Terry Bradshaw. He reminds them, simultaneously, of Joe Namath, of Roman Gabriel, of Sonny Jurgensen, even of Li'l Abner. Will Walls, a BLESTO scout who caught Sammy Baugh's passes at Texas Christian University, says that Bradshaw has a "better arm" than Baugh did. Scouts use such adjectives as "better" and "best," "strongest" and "quickest" glibly in discussing Bradshaw. The very sight of him spurs them to hyperbole. It was Jess Thompson, at his first glimpse of Bradshaw in the flesh, who saw him as Li'l Abner come to life. Bradshaw has extravagantly blond hair, resembling, in that respect, Daisy May rather than Li'l Abner, but a square-jawed, snub-nosed, ingenuous face with deep-set blue eyes. He is big and rawboned. His mere dimensions, however—6-foot-2½ and 215 pounds—do not convey an adequate idea of his appearance, for the massive upper arms, developed by weight lifting and summertime ditch digging, contribute indeed to an impressive top-heavy look suggestive of Li'l Abner. His actions, in the heat of a football game, are brisk and decisive. Even when he is scrambling or improvising, he always seems sure of his next move. And he throws with a snapping overhand delivery, cutting the ball through the air at high speed for great distances.

Y. A. Tittle, no scout but an authority on quarterbacks, having been one, has seen Bradshaw play, and he says the Steelers should charge admission to watch him warm up.

In Art Rooney, Jr.'s, office, there's a gray metal filing cabinet. It contained, in the fall of 1966, on a small sheet of paper called an underclassman form, two expository sentences about Terry Bradshaw: "Best arm on freshman quarterback I've ever seen" and "World's high-school javelin champion." (The latter may have taken in a little too much territory: Bradshaw merely held the United States high-school javelin record—244 feet, 11 inches.) The author of that report was a BLESTO-V scout named Jim Palmer, Jess Thompson's predecessor in the Louisiana-Texas-Mississippi-Arkansas area. No one had read it except the filing clerk, a gray-haired, middle-aged woman. Terry Bradshaw was a freshman in 1966, and for a scout to report on a freshman is almost unimaginable. Art Rooney, Jr., never looks at underclassman forms. "We have a thousand seniors to think about," the personnel director explains.

If Louisiana Tech was an unlikely place for Jim Palmer to discover the best arm he had ever seen attached to a freshman, the reason Bradshaw was there had nothing to do with anyone's lack of perception. During Bradshaw's last year at Woodlawn High School in Shreveport, Louisiana, he attracted the favorable attention of Baylor University's head coach, Johnny Bridgers, later to become the backfield coach of the Steelers. Bridgers inspected films of Bradshaw, and, certain that he could play in the Southwest Conference, made phone calls and visits to Shreveport and invited him to the Baylor campus.

Baylor is rigidly Baptist and so was Terry Bradshaw's upbringing, with its curfews and rules about Sunday school attendance, its prohibitions against smoking and drinking. Terry's father, Bill Bradshaw, was a self-made man who had been on his own since the age of 13, after running away from his home in the Tennessee hills when his parents split up. Construction worker, bus driver, short-order cook, he had staked himself to a patchwork education of numerous correspondence courses and 57 credit hours in "colleges all over Louisiana," his path leading eventually to a plant manager's job with the American Machine and Foundry Co. But Baylor was not for Bill Bradshaw's son. On a trip through the dormitories, Bill Bradshaw said later, Terry had noticed whiskey bottles. Another story, never formally authenticated, was that Baylor had lost interest in Terry because of his score on the college boards test. In New Orleans it has been printed that Terry had failed the test for admission to Louisiana State, which was also recruiting him, but turned down a chance to take it again, having decided on Tech.

With the slightly strained patience of one who is forced to repeat the same explanation over and over, Terry spells out the advantages of Louisiana Tech—its location, "70 miles from Shreveport," the "real good brand of football," the pro-style offense favored by the coaching staff, the new stadium, "seating 25,000." The lack of publicity never bothered Terry. "I figured if I was good enough to play pro ball, I'd get my chance," he says. "The scouts come around to the small colleges, too."

He was still just a freshman, trying to make the varsity team in spring practice, when Jim Palmer went back for another look. Projecting six months into the future, Palmer wrote: "Has quickest delivery and strongest arm I've ever seen on a sophomore." Filing clerks in the various offices of BLESTO-V clients may have discerned a faintly monotonous quality in Palmer's literary style, but there were also these negative notations: "doesn't scramble well" and "needs game experience."

The game experience came the following season, when Bradshaw divided the quarterback job with a senior the scouts referred to simply as "Robinson." Jess Thompson, replacing Jim Palmer, carefully recorded Bradshaw's passing statistics and labeled him "a fine future prospect." The passing statistics were nothing remarkable, but Thompson, looking back on it, drawls, "Ah don't know, you kind of feel 'em or smell 'em. He was a pro all the way."

In the spring of 1968—Bradshaw would be a junior that fall—the sniffing of the scouts became audible to him. He observed them at practice—big, quiet men with the screaming unobtrusiveness of hotel detectives. The head coach, Maxie Lambright, would say to him, "So-and-so's here for a look at you. Don't worry about it; just get out there and throw the ball like you can." Bradshaw understood that Maxie Lambright was scrutinizing his poise.

"He's a very humble young man," Maxie Lambright once said of Bradshaw. "If he's got any bad habits, I don't know about 'em. He doesn't smoke or drink, but even if he did I think he'd play for us." Enthusiastically, Bradshaw had joined the Fellowship of Christian Athletes. Youth director of the Baptist church in Ruston, he enjoyed giving inspirational talks to audiences of children, telling them that by hard work they could achieve their goals but to bear in mind that the glory belonged to God. Early in life he had thought of the ministry, but decided that "God would rather have me play football," God's eye for a quick delivery and a strong arm being equal, apparently, to Jim Palmer's.

For the preservation of that arm, Bradshaw had given up the javelin. As a junior, he passed for 22 touchdowns and almost 3,000 yards, Louisiana Tech winning eight of ten games. Before that season was well along, Jess Thompson had sent a message to Will Walls, a BLESTO-V superscout whose job is to check on the area scouts. "We've got a dinger over here," Jess Thompson said, "I think I've seen the best arm I ever saw."

Will Walls was the first scout to say positively that Bradshaw would be a first-round draft choice. There was a striking repetitiousness in the observations the scouts collected from college coaches who had seen Bradshaw play. They were all of the same opinion: that Bradshaw's arm was extraordinary, that his vision was keen, his wrists flexible, his ability to "set up" unexcelled. Art Rooney, Jr., began to read the reports when the 1969 draft was out of the way and Bradshaw's underclassman forms went into the thick, loose-leaf, black-covered notebook in which Rooney keeps track of seniors. And Chuck Noll, the new head coach of the Steelers, requested films from Louisiana Tech. His verdict on Bradshaw was: "Boy, he has a real rifle arm!"

Jess Thompson noted that Bradshaw was getting "actual pro-type instruction" from Maxie Lambright, who had been a quarterback at Mississippi Southern when Thompson was line coach there, and from backfield coach Mickey Slaughter, who had played the position at Louisiana Tech and with the Denver Broncos. Last fall Thompson sat in the stands on the Saturday afternoon that Louisiana Tech lost to his and Lambright's old school, now the University of Southern Mississippi; it was Tech's only defeat until the postseason Grantland Rice Bowl. Then and there, Thompson said, he realized Terry Bradshaw was "the No. 1 boy in the country. Southern Mississippi," he remembers, wincing, "just physically whipped Louisiana Tech's line and Terry got racked something awful. But he just never quit, he never slowed down, he stood in there throwing the ball like he owned the park, throwing on target all the time, and he passed for 248 yards." Bradshaw, Thompson put down on paper, "could be a superstar."

Art Rooney, Jr., willing to believe, headed for Ruston. He stopped first at Grambling College, three miles outside of Ruston, which in recent years has been an assembly line for draft choices. Eddie Robinson, the black head coach there, said, "Oh, you've got to see this guy Bradshaw, he's the greatest thing going." Rooney drove into Ruston with pleasant expectations.

Ruston is a placid college town, undefiled by the smokestacks of industry. Up North, the weather was getting cold, but in Ruston green leaves clung to the trees, and for comfort Rooney drove with the air-conditioner turned on in his car.

Two months before, when the Steelers were in Baton Rouge for an exhibition game, Rooney had taken care of the Tech coaches' ticket needs, and now they received him affably. They set up a movie projector, and in muggy darkness Rooney watched films.

Later, at practice, he saw Bradshaw throw. He was deeply interested. After a while Rooney turned to a nearby student manager who was gathering up footballs and stuffing them into a sack.

"What kind of a guy is Bradshaw?" Rooney asked.

The student manager, tall and dark, paused in his task and straightened up.

"Wonderful guy," he said with a radiant smile.

Rooney kept asking questions about Bradshaw. The student manager's answers grew progressively more lyrical.

"You sound like a relative," Rooney said.

"I'm his brother."

Gary Bradshaw, one year older than Terry, had been a football player until he fell from a tree, breaking his back. Rooney was probing him for "headshrinker stuff." Did Terry respect his father? (Very much, which meant he'd be coachable.) Did he drink? (Whatever Maxie Lambright may have thought, he'd take a beer; and Rooney approved of that, being vaguely mistrustful of ascetics.) Did he like girls? ("He sure does," Gary laughed; once again, Rooney approved.)

Terry Bradshaw was looking better and better. Rooney began to think of him as a player who would be a top draft pick, equating him, for the first time, with Mike Phipps of Purdue, the quarterback most frequently mentioned in newspaper stories about Heisman Trophy candidates. The Steelers, who had won their opening game, were now losing week after week, but there was "no way," Rooney felt, that they could finish with the worst record in professional football and thus be eligible for first choice in the draft. He hoped that by the time their turn came around they would still have a shot at Ronnie Shanklin, an elusive pass receiver from North Texas State.

Art's brother Dan, older and smaller, the Steelers' vice-president and ranking shirt-sleeve executive—Art Rooney, Sr., who is 68, takes no part in the day-to-day, front-office management—was not as starry-eyed. On a frosty Sunday in November, watching the Steelers lose disgracefully to the Chicago Bears, his accustomed good humor slipping away, Dan Rooney knew they'd be 1–13 for the season.

The season would end on December 21. On December 10, the BLESTO-V scouts met in Pittsburgh to arrive at their final evaluations of a thousand college players. From that day on, says Art Rooney, Jr., it was certain that Terry Bradshaw would be the first player chosen in the draft. In the ·BLESTO-V ratings—the lower the rating, the better—Bradshaw scored a 1.3, higher than Norm Bulaich, running back from TCU, or Mike McCoy, defensive tackle from Notre Dame, or Phil Olsen, defensive tackle from Utah State, or Cedric Hardman, defensive end from North Texas, but the ratings are based on a player's probable effectiveness in his rookie year, and because quarterbacks develop at such a leisurely pace, Bradshaw's 1.3 was superior to Bulaich's or McCoy's 1.0. After the BLESTO-V meeting, a scout walked up to Rooney and said, "This guy's like buying Xerox. There might not be another one like him for 20 years."

Dan Rooney's premonition was accurate. The Steelers wound up with a 1–13 record, losing their final game on a touchdown in the last 50 seconds, but the Chicago Bears also were 1–13. In January, at New Orleans, two days before the Super Bowl game, a coin flip would determine whether the Bears or the Steelers drafted first.

The season had been over just a matter of hours when Chuck Noll and his backfield coach, Johnny Bridgers, were flying to Miami, where College All-Star teams from the North and South would be playing on Christmas Day. Noll, 38, compactly built, is a thoughtful and even a cultivated man with a soft, deliberate way of speaking. In the previous three months, though he had tuned in a college game on a television set every Saturday, he had spent little time considering draft choices. In any event, he was not keen on drafting a quarterback, for the Steelers' second-round choice in 1969 had been Terry Hanratty, the Notre Dame cover boy from Butler, Pennsylvania, near Pittsburgh.

Troubled, as most rookies are, by a preoccupation with the

opposing team's rush, Hanratty failed to distinguish himself greatly last year. Noll, the truth is, had not expected him to, sharing in the popular conviction that quarterbacks ripen slowly.

But Noll was extremely impressed by Bradshaw in Miami. "He's an athlete," Noll said to himself when Bradshaw walked onto the practice field. Then he saw Bradshaw throw. "I was startled," Noll said. "I knew from the films that he had a strong arm, but a film doesn't measure intensity."

In the lobby of the South team's hotel, Johnny Bridgers chatted with Bradshaw, subtly recruiting him for the second time. Noll met Bradshaw on the practice field. The meeting was brief, just a handshake and hello after South coach Bill Peterson had introduced them, and Bradshaw seemed distant, absorbed, impatient to resume throwing a football.

That day he had pulled a hamstring muscle. Although practice was over, he intended to stay on the field and throw to several willing receivers. The South's other quarterback, Bill Cappleman, happened to be from Florida State, where Peterson was head coach, and Bradshaw could sense that he was not going to start.

The draft, he would say later, occupied just a nook in the back of his mind. " 'Course, I'd be lying if I said I'd forgotten it completely, but no, sir, I never started thinking I'd be a first choice," he went on. "I heard rumors, but I didn't believe it would ever happen. There was Phipps, there was McCoy."

On Christmas Day, Phipps started at quarterback for the winning North team. Cappleman, sure enough, started for the South. Bradshaw relieved him in the second and fourth quarters, handicapped, everyone took it for granted, by the hamstring. "Bull!" exploded Bradshaw with an absence of charity that was somewhat surprising in a Christian Athlete. "I didn't play more because the coach wanted Cappleman in."

Noll, back in Pittsburgh, saw the game on television and awaited a copy of the films. Running the team and passing, Bradshaw gave a good account of himself, "but we still didn't have that convinced feeling," Noll was to say. A roll-out quarterback from the Air Force Academy, not regarded by Noll as professional material, had played most of the game for the North, upstaging Phipps.

At this point, according to Noll, Dennis Shaw, San Diego State's quarterback, was worthy of serious contemplation. Shaw had been the Most Valuable Player in the East-West game. In the Steeler offices, Noll and his assistants and Art Rooney, Jr., worked from nine in the morning until 10:30 at night, looking at films, reading BLESTO-V reports, "tying information together." They were taken with Mike Reid, Penn State's aggressive defensive tackle. But when defensive line coach Walt Hackett returned from the next all-star game, the All-America Bowl in Tampa, he was trumpeting, "Bradshaw's the guy!"

He wasn't really the guy until Chuck Noll flew to Mobile five days before the Senior Bowl game and stayed for three practice sessions. Bradshaw did not remember having met him in Miami. He accepted an introduction to Noll and shook hands abstractedly. "I went down there to beat out Cappleman," he would say. "I just went there with the feeling that I would win the position, start, and have a good game." In a 40-yard sprint—Bradshaw's time was 4.7 seconds, very fast for a quarterback—he pulled the same hamstring. South coach Don Shula offered to send him home, but Bradshaw refused to hear of it. Watching him set up and pass with an injury, watching him respond to the "topflight competition," Chuck Noll shed the last of his doubts about the quarterback.

So did Art Rooney, Jr. In February, holding up a sheaf of papers, Rooney said, "This might be the thing that swung it." At the request of Jack Butler, BLESTO-V's managing director, Bradshaw had agreed to take a personality test and an IQ test in Mobile. "He came out okay," said Rooney. "Or he wouldn't have been our first draft choice."

There remained the question of whose choice he would be, the Steelers' or the Bears'. On the day before the Senior Bowl game, Noll was in New Orleans for the coin flip. Amid Super Bowl hoopla, while the Bears' man called out "heads," Pete Rozelle flipped a 1921 silver dollar. It bounced on a cloth-covered table and came up tails. "We have no idea who we'll take," said a smiling Dan Rooney, but Chuck Noll talked of Bradshaw with suspicious enthusiasm.

Bradshaw started in the Senior Bowl and was still firing passes with authority at the end of the game, a 27–27 tie. He had ignored, since the third quarter, two broken ribs. The quarterback for the North was Dennis Shaw. Noll, Dan Rooney estimates, made at least 10 exhaustive studies of the film.

From early until late, Noll and his staff continued their evaluations. The Steelers have a history of unfortunate first-round picks, reversed by Chuck Noll with his selection last year of defensive tackle Joe Greene, a Big Daddy Lipscomb reincarnate, but what they now had to decide was whether to trade their first choice for established veteran players who could move them up quickly in the standings.

Even before the coin flip, the offers had started coming in, and they were to hear from every other pro team except three. "All I'm going to tell you is this," said Art Rooney, Sr., to his sons and coaches. "If we trade the guy, if we give away a guy who turns out to be great, just make sure we get front-line ball players." He assumed, as the Steelers' competitors did, that Bradshaw would be the first choice, and because Bradshaw was a quarterback, Rooney felt apprehensive. "We're experts on quarterbacks," Rooney once said. "We've had Sid Luckman, Johnny Unitas, Len Dawson, Jack Kemp, Earl Morrall and Bill Nelsen, and we got rid of them all, every one."

In Dan Rooney's office late on the night of January 26, the night before the draft, Chuck Noll at last said, "Well, let's take this kid." Tacitly, Noll and Dan Rooney had come to an agreement in the 16 days since the Senior Bowl game that "this kid" was Terry Bradshaw. Now they were deciding that there would not be a trade.

Only one deal had tempted them, an offer from the St. Louis Cardinals, who were drafting eight. The Cardinals wanted to trade their first choice for the Steelers' first choice and throw in four regulars. If Mike Reid had been available when the Cardinals' turn arrived, the next day, the Steelers would have thought long and hard, but the Cincinnati Bengals, drafting just ahead of the Cardinals, eliminated the Penn State All-America as a pawn.

On the Wednesday before the draft, Art Rooney, Jr., had telephoned Bradshaw in Ruston and found him to be well disposed toward the Steelers. Terry and his father never had given credence to rumors that Pittsburgh was cheap, for in 1952, when the Steelers played an exhibition game in Shreveport, their bus driver—Bill Bradshaw—received a $20 tip. "The most I ever got from any other team was $5," he said.

Terry Bradshaw, destined for bigger money than $20, heard from Dan Rooney at 9:45 A.M. on January 27. With his mother and father and the neighbors, with sports writers and sportscasters there, with television cameras set up, he was sitting in the kitchen at home. "Well," he said when he put down the phone, "I'm No. 1."

The news that Bradshaw was No. 1 traveled swiftly. In February he made a trip to New York to be photographed for a picture layout in *Harper's Bazaar* that would "show how women's fashions are influenced by sports." Said a *Harper's Bazaar* editor named Gloria Moncouer: "I was looking for a fresh new face. Joe Namath is too old, too overphotographed." Beholding Terry in his Steeler uniform, she exclaimed, "Oh, wow, terrific . . . really terrific." From New York, Terry flew to Dallas, where he modeled slacks for $100 a day. ("I'd wear a dress for $100 a day," Terry said.) Later in the month he visited Pittsburgh, exciting miniskirted chicks and young men in Edwardian clothes on a tour of the Market Square nightclub district with Andy Russell, Steeler linebacker. Terry had a couple of drinks—whiskey, perhaps. Toward the end of the evening, he casually asked Russell how the veterans would accept him. "Oh, you'll get your share of needling," Russell answered. Looking hard at Russell, Terry said, "Listen, I'm a leader. If anyone gives me trouble in the huddle—I don't care *who* they are—I'm going to sting them." He put Russell in mind of Bobby Layne.

PUT YOUR MONEY ON THAT MAN IN THE STRIPED SHIRT

By Stanley Frank

Reprinted with permission from TV Guide

Copyright, ©, 1970 by Triangle Publications, Inc.
Radnor, Pennsylvania

After the final game of the pro football season several years ago, Alex Karras, resident cutup of the Detroit Lions, dropped into the officials' dressing room with a winsome smile on his craggy kisser and rancor seething in his 255-pound carcass. "I hope you guys have a good winter," he said amiably, "because you sure had a lousy fall."

The incident gave players and fans a big yok, uniting them in traditional antipathy to the officials, the blind bums. But that was before the introduction of instant replay, which continually attests to the remarkable job done by the six-man crews who play drop the handkerchief under the most difficult conditions in any sport.

"I was awfully apprehensive about the instant replay at the start," Bernie Ulman, a veteran NFL referee, admits. "Many calls are hairline decisions and you're dead if you hesitate momentarily. Infractions in the scrimmage line and on passes usually are committed in a split second. I was afraid TV would show we'd blown some key plays, but it has piped down gripes by proving how good we are."

Indeed it has. Mark Duncan, director of NFL personnel, claims instant replays support the officials 98 percent of the time. This may be a slight exaggeration, but one thing is certain: the men who run the game make fewer mistakes in judgment than the players. Of course, officials are not subjected to physical beatings that addle their senses, but there is a better explanation. They go through a longer apprenticeship learning the trade and then must meet tougher criteria of competence than the tigers they keep on a short leash. Every year about 150 players fresh out of college win jobs with pro teams. An official must have at least 10 years of experience with the whistle and rule book before he is even considered for the big leagues.

Pat Harder, for example, had to wait 13 years despite his excellent credentials. A former All-America and All-Pro fullback on the champion Chicago Cardinals in 1947, Harder wanted to maintain his association with the game after he retired as a player in 1953. So he put his trophies and scrapbooks on the shelf, went back to Wauwatosa, Wisconsin, his hometown, and started at the bottom—officiating in obscure high-school games for nine years. He also worked in the semi-pro Tri-State League, then put in four more years handling small-college games. Finally, in 1966, Harder broke into the NFL as a 43-year-old rookie umpire.

He didn't have it made though. Every week the work of each member of a crew is rated by an observer, usually a retired official, on two counts: (1) the accuracy of his decisions and (2) his general demeanor under pressure—how he enforces penalties, keeps the game moving and handles disputes on the field.

A more intensive check is made at league headquarters in New York after the game. The game film, provided by the home team, is studied by Art McNally, supervisor of officials in the National Conference, or Mel Hein, his counterpart in the American Conference. Duncan also sits in on these sessions, which take four hours for each game.

The film is run in slow motion and stop-action to see whether infractions were missed and, more important, if the men responsible for covering the plays were in position to spot them. Commissioner Pete Rozelle occasionally is called in to comment on the sideline conduct of the players and the policing of the field. The film and criticisms then are sent to the crew for review before its next game.

Officials who fail to maintain consistently high ratings don't last long. "A number of men have been dropped for incompetence," Duncan confides. "We don't embarrass them by making a formal announcement. If we're asked why someone is off the roster, we say he had to quit because of business pressures. We constantly scout college games for additions to the staff, but the requirements are so tough that only two men were accepted this year from 800 applicants."

The best officials are not exempt from censure when they goof.

Norman Schachter, principal of a Los Angeles high school and author of eight English textbooks, generally is regarded as the No. 1 referee in the business. He handled the first Super Bowl and four of the NFL championship play-offs between 1962 and 1967, but he and his crew were slapped down hard for pulling a boner in a crucial game.

It happened late in the 1968 season when the Los Angeles Rams had a chance to tie Baltimore for the divisional title. The Rams, losing to the Chicago Bears by 17–16, drove within range of a game-winning field goal with 58 seconds to play, then lost the ball on downs and with it a shot at the Super Bowl. Several hours later it was discovered that the officials had deprived the Rams of a fourth down that could have won the game for them.

The strangest part of the whole thing was that no Ram player or coach, no broadcaster or sports writer caught the oversight at the time. Rozelle suspended the entire crew for the rest of the season, costing them fees for two regular assignments and a play-off game.

"The action was taken because the situation was not a mistake in judgment, which may be excused," Rozelle announced. "It was a mechanical error that never should occur."

The reprimand hurt Schachter more than the Achilles tendon he ruptured in a game last September, which put him out of action for the balance of the season. He tried to reverse direction after a fumble, lost his footing and was buried under a pileup. As it happens, officials frequently suffer painful injuries when they are knocked down by players, to the amusement of everyone except the victims. Officials are supposed to get out of the behemoths' way, and if they lose their agility they soon wind up watching games on TV with the rest of us.

Something more than good fees impels the 85 substantial, middle-aged gents on the NFL staff to brave the rigors of violence in the arena, miserable weather and criticism. Five are high-school principals, five teach on the college level and 13 are school administrators. There are 43 business executives, several lawyers, bankers and engineers, a landscape artist, a computer programmer and, appropriately, two police officers. They have only one common characteristic. All of them are football nuts of the first water.

"Before the kickoff I get the same sense of exhilaration as I did when I was playing," Ulman gushes. "That's the big kick of the job for all of us. The money is just a bonus for keeping in the middle of the excitement."

Of course, the pay is not unattractive. The fee per game is $250 at the start, and it increases to $400 after 10 years. Play-offs bring $750, league championships $1,000, and the Super Bowl $1,500. Although the referee is the crew chief, his five colleagues get the same scale. A man who receives a postseason assignment can earn up to $7,000 a year. As a moonlighting proposition, officiating is a good job—but it's a very tough dollar.

The official gives up every weekend from August through December and travels about 25,000 miles a year. He must be on the scene of a game on Saturday night to review the films of the previous week and hear the criticism, often caustic, of the observer and supervisor. After a game he frequently breaks his neck to get back to his regular job on Monday. In addition he must attend a four-day preseason clinic and one in midseason for discussions of rules and new trends that may cause trouble. As a final fillip, his spring is occupied with a written test of 200 questions. It usually takes 25 hours to complete.

Keeping in shape to go at top speed for two hours in a game is a year-round ordeal for some men who, as former players, tend to run to meat and gristle. An official who shows up overweight at the preseason clinic remains on the sidelines until he presents a trimmer appearance. Officials generally do not retain sufficient speed of foot and stamina to work much beyond their early fifties, although Harry Brubaker just retired at 59 after 20 years of service.

Once a crew is formed and there are no personality clashes, it stays together as a unit indefinitely. The jobs are so specialized that a man who comes up as a line judge, let's say, may spend his entire career in that post. The chief responsibilities of each official are:

Referee—Runs the game, enforces penalties, explains the options to team captains. Protects the quarterback by curbing rough stuff designed to dismember him.

Umpire—Stands five yards behind defensive line and keeps mayhem in the interior line within reasonable limits. Calls most holding penalties and, following linesman's directions, marks forward progress of the ball on line bucks.

Head linesman—Watches scrimmage line for offsides from his position near the chain crew. On a pass or a breakaway run, moves downfield to help out as the play develops.

Line judge—Is stationed on opposite side of line. Rules on laterals and legality of forward passes. Also backup timer for official clock.

Back judge—Stands 15 yards behind defensive line and covers all passes and sideline plays.

Field judge—Positioned 25 yards downfield. Rules on field goals, fair catches and monkey business on long passes. Makes certain there are only 30 seconds between plays.

The toughest plays for officials, according to Duncan, are roughing the passer and pass interference. "Deciding whether the passer has been manhandled intentionally is tricky because he can be hit while he has the ball but he may not be clobbered after the ball leaves his hand. A defensive lineman may start to lower the boom on the quarterback a split second before the ball is thrown, and it's difficult to determine whether the contact is a legal attempt to drop him for a loss or a deliberate effort to smear him.

"Calls on pass interference downfield often get the crowd on the officials' necks because fans don't understand the rules. Once the ball is in the air, the defense cannot make contact with the receiver (or vice versa) before it reaches the point of completion or interception. Before the ball is thrown, however, the defense can knock down the receiver on the scrimmage line or bump him all over the place.

"Another situation that gets the fans up in arms comes when a quarterback seems to throw the ball away intentionally to avoid a loss on a pass play. The way the rule reads, intentional grounding can't be called unless the quarterback practically slams the ball into the turf at his feet. What appears to be a throwaway might have been a play that was messed up by the receiver. Until officials are mind readers, it will be impossible to determine the intent on a play."

One headache the league has eliminated is the "homer"—the official who favors the home team to avoid antagonizing a partisan crowd. Officials once were assigned to games near their homes to save on traveling expenses and induce experienced men to take jobs as officials. As a consequence, some men spent the entire season with only a few teams and tended subconsciously to give them the breaks. Now, a crew hits every city in the league during the season and sees no team more than three times.

"This system is much better for us, even though it involves a lot of traveling and inconvenience," Ulman says. "A few years ago I worked a game in Baltimore, where I live and have my business. You know how crazy the town is over the Colts. Late in a tough game with Minnesota, the fans thought the Colts had thrown the quarterback in the end zone for a safety, but I saw he had brought the ball back just over the goal line. I put it on the six-inch line. They tell me people in the stands gagged with rage. I heard about that decision from customers and friends for a month."

Suspicions of prejudice still persist. In the 1969 Super Bowl in Miami when the Jets scored the AFL's first victory, Joe Namath was feeling his oats and all the fruits of victory late in the game. "You guys are doing a pretty good job," he said expansively to referee Tommy Bell, "even though you are NFL officials."

Bell resented the implications of the crack, but he kept his cool. "That's nice of you, Joe," he said, "but my team still is losing." Broadway Joe was speechless—another historic first—until he realized that Bell was putting him on.

Although the instant replay has won grudging respect for the officials from coaches and players, echoes of their age-old feud will be heard until the mongoose and the cobra lie down in harmony. The story is told of a coach who was casting loud doubts on the ancestry and competence of the officials. The referee finally went to the bench and yelled, "You're penalized 10 yards for coaching from the sidelines."

"That's how much you know about the rules," the coach hooted. "There's no 10-yard penalty in football. Coaching from the sidelines is 15 yards."

"Your coaching is worth only 10 yards," the ref snapped.

Basketball

"BATMAN" AND "ROBIN" FALL BEFORE "SUPERMAN"

By Dwight Chapin

From the Los Angeles Times

Copyright, ©, 1970, Los Angeles Times

Get the Bat Car ready for a return trip to Florida.

Artis Gilmore and Rex Morgan, the "Batman" and "Robin" of Jacksonville University, are in reality only wealthy socialite Bruce Wayne and his ward, Dick Grayson.

The UCLA Bruins, again, are the champions of the college basketball world, 80–69 victors over the Dolphins for a record fourth straight NCAA title and sixth in seven seasons.

For many nervous minutes here at the University of Maryland's Cole Fieldhouse Saturday afternoon, however, the Dynamic Duo and their friends were clipping along on the path of a stunning upset. Jacksonville led UCLA by nine points. The dynasty was wavering.

But then along came Superman, a guy who also goes by the name of Sidney Wicks.

UCLA's nine-point deficit was suddenly a 41–36 halftime lead. Superman had removed Batman's mask and exposed him to the country as an uncertain giant who wasn't quite up to what had become the first real challenge he'd faced in a long, long time.

When Gilmore, the Batman, was forced to pack up his cape and get ready to go back to the land of sunshine and palms, the rest of the Jacksonville team, the nation's tallest, had to follow suit.

It might be a little unfair to give all the credit to Sidney.

He had help . . . loads of it.

While Wicks was blocking five—that's right, five—of the 7-foot-2 Gilmore's shots, scoring 17 points and taking down 18 rebounds, John Vallely, the Bruins' only senior starter, was rising again to the excellence he has shown in UCLA's last two tournament years. He held Gilmore's sidekick, Reckless Rex, to only eight points, wheeled and dealed for five assists and scored 15 points.

In UCLA's time of trial, in the first half, Curtis Rowe was more or less conceded the medium-range jump shot by the Dolphins, and he took advantage of it for 14 points. His 19 for the game led UCLA.

Center Steve Patterson scored 17 points in a strong offensive performance and pulled down 11 rebounds.

And Henry Bibby, the fifth UCLA starter, who played 38 minutes of the game, helped out with eight points and four rebounds from his guard position.

But you almost have to concede that Wicks was the key in this title triumph—the big man in UCLA's fourth straight championship and most significant in that string, since it came without Lew Alcindor.

Jacksonville went into the game unawed and ready.

Spurred on by a bunch of uninhibited fans raising a green felt dolphin aloft and yelling, "We beat No. 1 [Kentucky] and we can beat No. 2" and "Go to hell, Bruins," Jacksonville burst into a fast, early lead.

The spread was four points, then six, then eight, then nine, at 24–15 with 9:35 to play in the first half.

What was worse for the Bruins, Gilmore was tearing them apart.

Wicks was playing to the side or in front of Artis and that wasn't working.

"So we had Sidney get behind Gilmore," said coach John Wooden, "and dropped Patterson off the high post to front him . . . and we made a couple of other moves that helped."

Then it happened.

Gilmore received the ball on the low post and went up in the air like an arrow. But Wicks, six inches shorter, was suddenly above him, jamming the ball right back at him.

From that point, Artis was never the same.

In the last portion of the first half and the first part of the second half, he went 16½ minutes without a field goal. He scored only five points in the entire last half.

What was worse for Jacksonville, the intimidation of Super Sidney made Gilmore a confused player in other ways, too—on the boards, handling the ball.

Suddenly, UCLA had the lift it needed. The Bruins, who had

been committing turnover after turnover (14 in the first half), quickly congealed into a team of precision and force.

Despite the fact Jacksonville was substituting freely and UCLA wasn't substituting at all, the Bruins were fresher. In the last nine minutes of the second half, they were running and fast-breaking with as much verve and skill as they had all season, and they outscored Jacksonville, 26–12, during that period.

Vallely was the hero now.

His shooting pulled UCLA to within a point, 36–35, with 2:13 to play in the half. Then he zipped a precision pass to Bibby for the lay-in that put UCLA ahead for the first time, but to stay, 37–36. John came right back with an equally brilliant assist to Patterson for another lay-in basket.

Rowe's two free throws gave UCLA its five-point edge at the intermission, and the momentum it never lost—despite some cool shooting at the start of the second half.

Most of the way in the last 20 minutes, UCLA was a patterned team again, but doing exactly what it wanted to do, expanding its lead to 16 points twice and then stalling away the final minutes before the reserves came in.

With the threat of Gilmore, who hit on just nine of 29 shots from the field, removed and Morgan ineffective, too, there was little Jacksonville could do to catch up. Gilmore finished with 19 points and 16 rebounds.

When it was over, Vallely was wearing one of the basket nets around his neck. Wicks, the player of the tournament, was sticking his finger in the air to signify that UCLA was No. 1, and the rest of the place was buzzing about Sidney.

His buddy, Rowe, was talking about Wicks's work on Gilmore. He grinned and said, "He just ate 'im up."

Patterson added, "I've seen Wicks guard Alcindor before and he never blocked a shot on Lew. Gilmore is great, but he's no Alcindor. Sidney proved he was human."

That was exactly what Wicks had done, and it took all the humor out of a recent comment by coach Arad McCutchan of Evansville, whose team lost to Jacksonville earlier this season.

McCutchan had said that "Jacksonville is very vulnerable. An eight-footer would murder them."

Sorry, Arad. A 6-foot-8-incher murdered them.

The principals themselves said this:

"The ball was on its way down a couple of times when he blocked them," offered Gilmore. "He caught me by surprise. I've had a few shots blocked before—one of them Thursday night by Matt Gantt of St. Bonaventure. But not very many."

"It was like playing last year against Lew," said Wicks, "but no matter what I did against Lew, he could score. Gilmore wasn't the same, but if he could have stuffed the ball there would have been no way I could have stopped him."

Jacksonville coach Joe Williams, the man with the mod outfit and free-and-easy approach to basketball and life, took defeat—only Jacksonville's second of the year—with a smile.

"We were proud of the boys," he said. "They played as hard as they could. But UCLA did a great job defensing us. They are a great team and it was a real honor and thrill for us to meet them in the NCAA championship game."

Then he yielded the press-room microphone to Wooden, a man he greatly admires.

Outside the room, Wooden's wife, Nell, was saying she thought "this might be the most gratifying championship ever for John."

Now he was telling the press that the victory would mean he would finally get a tournament championship watch of his own. The other five, he said, had gone to his son, his son-in-law and his three grandsons.

"I'm awfully glad," he said, "to get one of my own."

It was a milestone of sorts all around.

The Bruins' first national title, in 1964, came on the date that the Woodens' daughter, Nan, turned 30. This one was achieved on the day Nan became 36.

Wooden talked about the fact that he was "worried all the time in the game," about his distress ("gracious sakes") over UCLA's numerous turnovers, about Wicks ("I wouldn't trade him for any other player in the country").

He stayed for a long time, answering all the questions.

Then he went back to the UCLA locker room and opened it up for the press, which streamed in and packed the place like locusts.

Vallely, the only starter that will leave this team, still had the net around his neck and he was stripping off his socks.

"Comparing the championships this year and last year," he said, "I guess I'd have to say I appreciated them both about the same.

"But there was so much more pressure this year because we had to do it without Lew. I can't tell you how it feels, now, to have that pressure gone."

HARLEM PLAYGROUND

By Dave Klein

From the Newark Star-Ledger

Herman the Heliocopter and Funny were doing it one night on the blacktop of a playground in Harlem.

Heliocopter is about 30 years old now and he stands about 6-foot-2 and he lives for the times he can go up against somebody 6-foot-9 or 6-foot-10 and stuff 'em. It does something for him. It turns on the music inside.

Funny is younger but he, too, is past college age, and he is only about 5-foot-11, but the last time they let him play somebody his own size he scored 74 points in just under 30 minutes. Funny has this thing about stuffing the ball, too, like Heliocopter, only he won't do it unless some new kid, some new and very big kid, has been making a pest of himself by showing off.

And that's when they call for Funny. When he shows up, the crowd parts like it says crowds should do in books, and when he walks out on the court, he hunches a little and shuffles a little and introduces himself to the new kid. Funny looks up, way up, when he says hello, and he loves the look of scorn mixed with relief when the big kid stares down. Then he says, "Man, you are one big cat, but I want to see it, so let's play." And the first chance he gets, Funny takes the ball under the basket, makes sure the big cat is covering him close and then Funny jumps.

Only Funny doesn't just jump, you understand. He soars. He sort of gets up in stages, then hangs in the air, almost as if he is waiting for the big cat to get up to him. And then, with a flair that smacks of pure show business, Funny slams the ball backward—"windmilling, man"—into the hoop and the crowd screams and Funny smiles and the big cat gets a funny feeling down where his heart is. Which is why they call Funny, Funny.

Heliocopter and Funny are just two of the neighborhood legends who have sprung up in the Harlem playgrounds, kids who spent most of their teens and twenties playing ball, kids who could never have made it to college, kids who are pure basketball. They are all black kids, and this is their game.

There is Dr. Blackheart and the Elevator Man, and they have come to need basketball the way other folks need money, the way other folks need cars or pools or clothes. Basketball gives these kids status, which is vital to the egos of inner-city kids, who have no status at all the minute they step outside their world. But certain college coaches and recruiters have learned to haunt the playgrounds of Harlem, looking for the ones who can make it to school. And if they can handle the books, there is no way they are going to stay away from the basketball team, and there is no kind of basketball better than Harlem basketball.

Al McGuire, a New Yorker, knows this, and he has begun to register national impact with his Marquette teams, which have the New York kids. Dr. Blackheart, who played for Al, is really Pat Smith, a 6-foot-3 center who did it against the major competition Marquette schedules and never lost a jump. The word is never, and it includes the time he faced Kentucky's Dan Issel (6-foot-10) in Lexington and Issel slapped at the Doctor's wrist when the Doctor was up there controlling the tap. He is called Dr. Blackheart because he wears capes and looks sinister and because that's what he wants to be called. He goes to college games and shows no emotion at all until and unless some cat does a playground thing, and then he smiles, silently.

Ric Cobb, the 6-foot-6 center who played for Marquette's NIT champs this season, is the Elevator Man. Why? Because he just keeps going up when he wants to, because you say, "How high today, 'Vator?" and he just smiles and says, "Call it, man, I'll get there."

And Texas Western's NCAA championship team a few years ago had a kid named Willie Cager, who was 5-foot-6. That's right, 5-foot-6, and Willie was from the city and when he found a big cat on him, Willie just took off and stuffed and the big cat never came back again.

And they say Elevator Man can pick quarters off the top of the backboard, but no one around can jump up there to deposit them, so he has to do both. And the Doctor says they outlawed the stuff shot not because of Lew Alcindor's presence in college arenas, but to avoid embarrassment for "the big kids who couldn't do it the way us playground kids can," which means white kids.

And if you would care to see it in action, hit the trains and the subway and get to Lenox Avenue or Amsterdam Avenue and watch them go. Marquette's Dean Meminger, the NIT's most valuable, said it after his guys beat LSU and Pete Maravich. "He's okay, but I know lots of cats in the parks who are at least as good, man." And he does. He really, truly does.

HOW JACKSONVILLE EARNED ITS CREDIT CARD

By Paul Hemphill

From Sport

Copyright, ©, 1970, MacFadden-Bartell Corp.

It was still early in the season when a Jacksonville television station got carried away and put together a wonderfully hokey 60-second love poem to its Dolphins: film clips of 7-foot-2 Artis (Batman) Gilmore loping downcourt like a giraffe and little Rex (Robin) Morgan spinning toward the basket like a water spout, all of it synchronized in slow motion to the strains of "The Impossible Dream." That had been the Muzak, the music to work miracles by, as the Jacksonville University basketball team kept on winning, kept on moving up in the national rankings, kept on soaring upward on a collision orbit with the great powers like UCLA and Notre Dame and Kentucky.

After all, 15 years ago Jacksonville had been a junior college. Six years ago the team had an annual recruiting budget of $250 and played to crowds of less than 1,000. Two years ago they had been losing to Wilmington College and were the fourth-best team in perhaps the nation's weakest basketball state. *One* week ago they had borrowed cash from their play-by-play announcer so they could pay for dinner after beating Kentucky in the NCAA Mideast Quarter-finals. But here they were in the throne room now, coach Joe Williams and recruiter-assistant coach Tom Wasdin of the Jacksonville Dolphins, sitting in a traditional restaurant down the street from the White House on the eve of the 1970 NCAA finals, ordering brandy milk punch for a gaggle of writers representing big-city dailies and national magazines, giddy and loose and expansive and struck by the wonder of it all themselves.

"Y'all," said Wasdin, "go ahead and order anything you want."

"Sure you can afford it?" a writer said.

"Shoot, we got a credit card now."

Somebody said, "Say it ain't so, Tom."

"Look here, American Ex——"

"No, I mean that story about you dressing up like a member of the booster club so you could recruit Artis. You expect us to believe that stuff?"

"Tell you the truth," Wasdin said, "I'm starting to believe some of those stories myself. The more we win, the better they get. I'll tell you one that *did* happen, though." He is a finely chiseled man with a hint of Kirk Douglas in his bronze face; he is 34, two years younger than Joe Williams. He spread his elbows on the white linen tablecloth and grinned like an old boy about to tell a shady story on the town beauty queen.

"About three years ago we'd kicked off a couple of boys and some others had gotten hurt, and we were down to nine players. Coach Williams wanted to scrimmage one day so he says, 'Why don't you suit up and be the 10th man, Coach?' Well, I did, and after a while one of the kids tried to cut the base line on me and I sort of laid a body check on him, you know, and it—you ready?—well, it broke his back. Then we had eight." When the nervous laughter had died down, Williams told about the time the elevator in an old hotel in Cookeville, Tennessee, broke down between floors with the entire squad on it ("That's when we were driving all day in cars for $200 guarantee"). Then Wasdin said JU's amazing season had brought "one real concrete offer" to him and Williams: "The president of the school called us in the other day and said no matter what happens in the tournament he thought we'd done a real good job." And then somebody offered Wasdin a cigar after dinner and he said, "No, thanks, Artis won't let any of us smoke," and then the evening degenerated into burlesque.

Not everybody was laughing, of course. There was nothing particularly humorous to the NCAA Establishment about the arrival of Jacksonville University in College Park, Maryland, for *their* finale. There is an Establishment in college basketball, just as there is in anything else. The NCAA Establishment includes people like Kentucky's Adolph Rupp, who thinks zone defenses and tall players are Communist threats; UCLA's John Wooden, who has all the sartorial and verbal flair of a funeral director; the anonymous coach who said that a national title for Jacksonville would "set basketball coaching back 20 years," and even the sports writer who wrote from the University of Maryland campus that freewheeling, undisciplined, free-form play was "for playgrounds and Jacksonville University."

The Establishment did not like it that the Jacksonville Dolphins were in the 1970 NCAA championships. "What is this, Rent-a-Goon?" said a writer, pointing at JU's two giant black junior-college transfers, 7-foot-2 Artis Gilmore and 7-foot-0 Pembrook Burrows III. "Just look at them, would you?" said the wife of an NCAA official, nodding toward the entrance to Cole Fieldhouse as Joe Williams and his team came to work, smacking gum and horsing around and wearing bell-bottoms and zippered racing jackets, and what she was really saying was *How tacky, the very idea.* Williams, they had read, had no curfew for his players, scribbled his game plans on the backs of cocktail napkins and wore this God-awful "lucky" outfit to every game: white six-button blazer, blue bell-bottoms, psychedelic tie and watermelon-red shirt. And their followers: route salesmen and hardware-store owners and small-town doctors, many of them still trying to straighten out the difference between charging and hooking, self-conscious and still suspicious about any game that's played indoors. And the players: good old boys from places like Chipley and Jacksonville, who gorged themselves at the "training" table, drank beer in public, pulled pranks like hiding each other's shorts, and had painted green and gold stripes on their shoes when they found out they were going to be on color television at College Park. "Basketball is supposed to be fun," Williams had been quoted, and that was especially disturbing to the Establishment when they realized that Jacksonville University had lost only one of its 27 games and was ranked fourth in the nation.

A lot of this incredulity, this shock, was seen on the Thursday night of the semi-finals, just after UCLA had blown past New Mexico State, and Jacksonville had slopped its way over Bob Lanier-less St. Bonaventure to set up the UCLA-Jacksonville championship game. John Wooden would be going after his sixth NCAA title in seven years Saturday afternoon against JU, and when he entered a dressing room off the floor for the postgame press conference, the writers crowded in to ask him what he thought about Jacksonville and Williams and the Mod Squad and Artis Gilmore. Wooden doesn't normally delight in talking to the press, but it seemed as though they were all in this thing together this time; Wooden and the big-time basketball writers, making the best of it. Inflections and raised eyebrows and dramatic pauses did the job nicely:

Q—Did Jacksonville impress you with anything besides its height, John? (*Laughs*)

A— (After thoughtful pause) Depth. Height and depth.

Q—Have you played anybody as good as Jacksonville this year?

A—Yes. (*Quick, clipped, definite answer, bringing a burst of laughter*) I won't name them, but there are *plenty* of good ball clubs around.

Q—Do you think Jacksonville will outrebound you?

A— (Acid smile, the Jack Benny delivery) *Well,* they *should.*

The Establishment *knew.* Sitting across from each other at dining tables in the bowels of the University of Maryland field house, they were passing silent messages. *Jacksonville will get theirs.* They had seen these instant teams blow in from the boondocks before, the boondocks being anywhere basketball is not king. *UCLA isn't exactly Mercer or Biscayne or Richmond.* Class and discipline and tradition would, they were certain, overcome.

It must have been the fall of 1962 when I first met Joe Williams. Most newspapermen, at one point or another, succumb to the illusion of public relations—thinking it is the rainbow leading to money and class and peace of mind—and I had just quit writing sports to become the sports publicist at Florida State University. It was football season all of a sudden and I was buried in brochures and 8-by-10 glossies and travel arrangements when Bud Kennedy, the FSU basketball coach, walked in one day and introduced Joe Williams as the new freshman basketball coach. Even then Williams was not the kind to make dazzling impressions. He was quiet and pleasant, tall and hunched over, a man in his late twenties, who grinned out of the side of his mouth and looked *up* at you, in spite of being 6-foot-4, through bushy black eyebrows. He was, it seems, sort of a part-time coach while doing graduate study or something. Florida State was just beginning to flex its muscles in football then, and so Bud Kennedy (who died recently) and assistant coach Hugh Durham (now the head basketball coach at FSU) and, by all means, Joe Williams sort of hovered about like extra men at a picnic softball game.

Joe *did* have a beautiful young bride named Dale, whom he had met while he was coaching high-school basketball in Jacksonville. But she was the only outwardly outstanding thing about Joe Williams, and they lived in what sounded like a fishing-camp cabin in the swamps outside Tallahassee, and I suppose I had his picture taken for the basketball brochure and I suppose the freshman team played out its season. I just don't know. I went back to newspapering very shortly, and Joe took an assistant coaching job at Furman University, both of us roughly the same age, both of us just looking for a home, and we went separate ways without looking back.

Jacksonville's basketball program was, in those days during the early sixties, almost nonexistent. I had seen them play, against teams like Tampa and Valdosta State and Mercer, and it was a twilight zone of dark and airy gyms, small crowds, travel-by-car and intramural offenses. There was a line in the papers about Joe Williams leaving Furman in 1964 to become head basketball coach at Jacksonville University, not the most exciting announcement but at least news about an acquaintance. Jacksonville, you could find out if you bought a Jacksonville paper, got progressively worse—from 15–11 to 8–17 in Joe's first three seasons—and people like me who had known him however vaguely were wondering whatever in the world possessed him to take a job like that.

The Jacksonville Dolphins began getting a little ink outside of Jacksonville in 1968–69 when they finished 17–7, but everybody knew they were still playing the same humpties who had once populated a league called the Florida Intercollegiate Athletic Conference. The feeling was the same when the 1969–70 season began and Jacksonville won its first 13 games: sure, they were averaging 105 points a game, but they were beating up on Mercer and Biscayne and Richmond and Miami, and Florida State had ended the streak with an 89–83 victory in Tallahassee ("The prince has turned into a frog," crowed the *Florida Times-Union* the next morning).

They kept coming, though, Jacksonville did, and now they were in the Top Ten and avenging their loss to FSU and whipping NIT-bound Georgia Tech in Atlanta, and suddenly they had advanced through the first two rounds of the NCAA tournament. And then came that Saturday when everybody in the country was watching the Mideast Quarter-finals on television from Columbus, Ohio, and there was Joe Williams wandering up and down the sideline with a hand in his pocket and the camera zooming in on him and his team, the Jacksonville University Dolphins, advancing to the World Series of college basketball by laying it on Adolph Rupp's Kentucky Wildcats, 106–100. "Remember?" my wife said to me. "He had a real pretty wife." *My God,* I thought.

There was plenty enough work to do at home, but I found myself on the phone to Jacksonville and Joe Williams Tuesday morning.

Lucky I had left my name with his secretary, Joe said, because he had just about stopped returning calls. Some starlet wanted to come out and have her picture taken with the team, and the mayor wanted to *work out* with them that afternoon, and he didn't know whether his throat would make it through the next press conference in an hour. Dale was fine, they had two young sons, and the team was flying off to College Park early the next morning.

"It's been a long time since FSU," I said.

"It sure has."

"I didn't believe it, Saturday."

"Nobody did," he said, "but us."

A certain giddiness prevailed at the Interstate Inn, a short mile from the scene of the finals, where Jacksonville's fans and press and players and official family had set up headquarters on Wednesday afternoon. The lobby, restaurant and bar of the motel spilled over with Dolphin fans wearing white straw boaters and oval green and white stickers that said J-U CAN DO. The very idea that this school of 2,700 students that squats across the river from a cigar factory and a paper mill in North Florida might very well be playing UCLA for the national championship within 72 hours was really too much to bear. "The deal is *on*," JU fans would yell, for no apparent reason, sticking thumbs up. "JU can do," would be the reply. "The Big A has come to play," somebody else would yell. And in the midst of all this were Joe Williams and Tom Wasdin, who were back in their rooms tying up the Interstate Inn's three outside lines with calls to some 50 prospects all over the country ("I just wanted to tell you to be sure and watch us on TV this weekend").

The story of Joe Williams is as unlikely as the story of his team. His father was a Methodist preacher, sort of a circuit rider in Oklahoma, and Joe remembers that on more than one occasion Mr. Williams was paid off in maple syrup for preaching. When Joe finished high school, he went to Oklahoma City University and became a so-so basketball player for Abe Lemons, who has been, along with Hank Iba, the biggest influence on Williams' coaching philosophy ("In a way, I was always *against* Adolph Rupp and his coaching, like most kids in Oklahoma were, because he was the enemy"). Two of Williams' brothers also became ministers, but Joe had decided he wanted to coach basketball, and he somehow wound up coaching a junior-high team and then Ribault Senior High in Jacksonville.

In 1962 he coached the Florida State freshmen, in 1963 he was an assistant at Furman University. In 1964 he was offered, and accepted, the head coaching job at Jacksonville. The administration told him they wanted "a nice program that wouldn't lose too much money."

Jacksonville could afford no more. It was founded as a junior college in 1934 and had been changed to four-year Jacksonville University in 1956.

Joe Williams' recruiting budget for his first year totaled $250 ("I wouldn't go visit a boy until about 8 o'clock at night, when I was sure he'd already eaten supper"), and he ran the wheels off his '60 Chevrolet scouring his territory for high-school prospects.

Joe Williams needed 10 hands to keep up—he was the head coach and the recruiter and the publicist and the wet nurse, and in addition to all of that he was teaching five classes at JU and commuting to the University of Florida in the summer for his own studies. "Sometimes it was like trying to climb a greased wall," he has said. He was even arranging for the printing of automobile floor mats with Dolphin schedules on them, and organizing a booster club (which now has 125 members, paying $100 a year each). The 15–11 finish in 1965–65 represented the best record a Jacksonville team had ever had, but then it dipped to 12–11 in 1965–66 and 8–17 the next season. About all Williams had to cling to was something told him by Abe Lemons that first year when Oklahoma City and Jacksonville happened to run into each other on the road in Memphis.

"We had been on the road nearly a week," Joe recalls, "riding cars, playing people like Carson-Newman and Tennessee Tech for small guarantees, not even making the bills, and we'd split the trip. Abe started telling us about the fine restaurant they'd been eating in while they were in town playing Memphis State, and he said, 'If you're going to lose or break even, you might as well do it in style.' I think that's when I made up my mind on the 'Four-Year Plan.'"

The Four-Year Plan is something that evolved soon after Williams hired Tom Wasdin as his assistant coach and recruiter in 1966, the year of the 8–17 disaster. They had known each other since junior-high coaching days in Jacksonville (Wasdin was the Duval County coach of the year twice, but lost two of three games he played against Williams' team). Wasdin, like Williams, had also come out of nowhere: he had been a star quarterback on the six-man football team at Waldo, Florida (pop. 800), and had his Florida basketball career cut short by a sandlot football injury. He and

Williams complemented each other, Wasdin being the more glamorous recruiter type and Williams being the brooding executive,
and at the very beginning of their relationship, they went to the
school administration and said they wanted a chance to build a
major basketball program in four years and if they didn't succeed
they would leave quietly. The Jacksonville administration didn't
necessarily give Williams and Wasdin a carte blanche, but they did
give their blessings.

The next season the Dolphins broke even at 13–13. But things
were happening. Super-recruiter Tom Wasdin had rolled up his
sleeves and gone to work.

Practice time at Cole Fieldhouse on the University of Maryland
campus in College Park, the eve of the semi-final round of the 1970
NCAA championship tournament. A chance for the teams to get
used to the strange floor and the huge coliseum. At 7 o'clock, on
Wednesday night, it is time for the Jacksonville University Dolphins, and a crowd of some 800 Maryland students and sports
writers surges around the glistening floor to watch. They do not
believe Jacksonville. They do not believe that a "pickup" team like
this can be the first NCAA team ever to average 100 points per
game during the regular season, or lead the nation in rebounds.
They want to see this Artis Gilmore, the 7-foot-2 transfer who is the
nation's leading rebounder and 18th scorer; and that 7-foot play-
mate of Gilmore's, Pembrook Burrows III; and the little (6-foot-5)
playmaker, Rex Morgan.

The first thing they see is a little bushy-haired black player, Chip
Dublin, walk to the side of the court and put a home tape recorder
on the floor and turn on the electricity. Dublin has brought a reel
of tape filled with soul music. The Dolphins begin shooting basket-
balls, but then "Sweet Georgia Brown" drifts out of Chip Dublin's
tape recorder and Pembrook Burrows III yells, "Show time!!!" and
now they are all blurring around Rex Morgan, while Morgan goes
through his Harlem Globetrotter drill. Then they line up and eight
straight men dunk the ball, Gilmore ending the show with a twist-
ing, backward, two-handed dunk that sends the crowd up the wall.

Once the 1969–70 season had ended, Tom Wasdin was being
called one of the very strongest recruiters of basketball talent in the
United States. He denies it—"except for Pembrook, we sort of fell
into all of these boys"—but when you see the sort of talent he was

able to recruit in competition with schools that have so much more to offer than Jacksonville, you have to give him a large amount of credit. Jacksonville has a limit of 15 basketball scholarships to give out (the Southeastern Conference has 25, for a comparison), there is no freshman team and it is extremely difficult to lure a hot prospect to a school that plays some of its games in exotic places like Tallahassee and Greenville, North Carolina. It happened this way:

ARTIS GILMORE—Grew up in Chipley, Florida, a depressing little town in the scraggly piney woods of the Florida Panhandle some 250 miles west of Jacksonville. The son of a yardman, he was a good high-school basketball player at the black school in Chipley and—in his senior year, when he became too old to play in Florida—at the black school in Dothan, Alabama. First discovered by George Raveling of Maryland, maybe the premier scout of black talent in the nation, but couldn't get into Maryland and was put under a rock, more or less, at tiny Gardner-Webb Junior College in Boiling Springs, North Carolina. Was averaging 23 points per game at G-W but was unhappy there. Wasdin, who had tried to get him out of high school, received a letter from another unhappy G-W player who wanted to transfer to JU and bring "a friend of mine who is 7–2." Wasdin went after Gilmore, who wanted to be close to his aging parents and liked Williams, and he got him.

REX MORGAN—From Charleston, Illinois, he was also courted by Wasdin when he was graduating from high school, but decided to go to the University of Evansville in Indiana. Unhappy there (according to one story, he didn't like it because the freshman team was given sandwiches in brown paper bags on road trips), he moved to Lake Land Junior College in Illinois. Still unhappy, he called Jacksonville and came running. "Morgan may be the original tramp athlete," says one cynical writer who has covered the Dolphins, but he gave the team go-power and set the style for it.

CHIP DUBLIN—An all-city prep player in New York City, he signed with Loyola of Chicago but didn't like it and left after four months. Wasdin was in New York trying to recruit another player when the player's coach suggested he forget that one and find Dublin. Wasdin found Dublin working as a clerk at Chase Manhattan Bank on Wall Street and easily convinced him that playing basketball would be a lot more fun.

PEMBROOK BURROWS III—Came out of West Palm Beach and was so awkward he didn't make high-school varsity until his senior year, and then scored a grand total of nine points in the two games he played. Started putting it together at Brevard Junior College (in Cocoa, Florida, where Wasdin once coached) and hit 69.4 percent from the field his second year there. This is the one Wasdin had to work on, against stiff competition.

"What's writing all about?" says John Crittenden of the *Miami News*. "It's sticking around and asking one more question and not getting your feelings hurt, and that's Wasdin as a recruiter." Says another writer, on the usual suspicions that arise whenever a small team comes out of nowhere: "Hell, Jacksonville was so broke it couldn't *afford* to cheat." Says Williams: "I just called practice one day and they all showed up." However they got to Jacksonville— these two 7-footers and these transfers—the fever began to rise before the season ever got started. All five of the starters were back from a 17–7 team, and now JU—with Gilmore and Burrows—had the tallest team in the world, probably.

There was a closed-doors practice game against Davidson in Jacksonville before the season started, and the results of it had Gene Pullen writing about a national champion in the *Jacksonville Journal:* "Jacksonville led by 12 points at the half and ate 'em alive. We started going with that game, and everybody was laughing at us." The thing is, the players believed in themselves and in Joe Williams, their hunched-over young coach who listened to jazz and read existentialist authors and visited museums on the road. "What's discipline?" asked Williams. "It's getting them to do what you want them to do."

There were the openers, all of which JU won—East Tennessee State, Morehead State, Mercer, Biscayne. Jax led Georgetown 41–26 and Gilmore had 21 rebounds with 1:23 left in the first half when a fierce fight broke out. Morgan was belted above the eye and bled like a stuck pig. The Dolphins won it on a forfeit.

They were 13–0 when they went to Tallahassee to play Florida State, and as noted above FSU won by 89–83 (Gilmore scoring "only" 21 points), but it was to be the only regular-season loss.

For the first time, Jacksonville was showing up in the national rankings of the wire services. The legend was growing about "the Mod Squad" (at Richmond, 5,000 showed up for Jacksonville a week after another Spiders' game had drawn less than 1,000). JU was making money now, packing the Jacksonville Coliseum with between 6,000 and 10,000 fans a game (they made $10,000 off the

FSU-Jax return match, which drew a state record crowd of 10,500).
The year before Williams had gotten to Jacksonville, gate receipts
for basketball had totaled $3,000 for the year, but if the Dolphins
could make it to the NCAA finals they could gross nearly $100,000
for the season.

They made it. They were 23–1 when they went into the NCAA's
first round at Dayton against Western Kentucky ("Jacksonville
Who?" read a motel marquee back in Bowling Green). Then they
knocked off Big Ten champion Iowa and Southeastern Conference
champ Kentucky in a space of three days at Columbus in the Mideast Quarter-finals, and all that stood between them and a national
title were St. Bonaventure (which had lost star Bob Lanier to injury) and, most likely, powerful UCLA.

Artis Gilmore was sitting all alone in a booth in the Interstate
Inn dining room, working on his fourth Coke and staring through
the rain-spattered plate-glass window, when the writers caught up
with him on Friday afternoon. It had been a long, restless day for
him, and although most of the other Dolphins were already leaving
for the movies, he looked as though he were going to stay there
until he got sleepy. The Jacksonville performance against St. Bonaventure the night before had been listless, even if JU *had* won the
game, 91–83. Artis Gilmore had scored 29 points and taken 21
rebounds, but he had been heckled by the St. Bonaventure fans,
and when 30 sports writers crowded around him in the dressing
room after the game, most of their questions implied that they
thought he had played badly. And in the morning paper, he was
referred to as a giraffe. So it was not a good day for the nation's
leading rebounder.

He is a brooding man, a dusky giant with sad eyes and a trim
goatee. Few white people besides Joe Williams had ever been able
to talk with him. He is courteous to almost everybody, but he
simply doesn't unwind and talk about the weather or girls to anybody who comes along. He is a black man from the Florida Panhandle, and maybe that is why. It is poor country, for black and
white, and in the past two Presidential elections the area has gone
overwhelmingly for Goldwater and for George Wallace. So maybe
Artis Gilmore hasn't had much practice with white men.

There were three or four writers who moved in on the booth with
Gilmore, all of them traveling with Jacksonville, and Gilmore was
reluctant to say much at first. He had had about 15 offers when he

finished at Carver High in Dothan, he said, Florida State not "showing much interest," and when George Raveling had recommended Gardner-Webb Junior College to him he had gone. He didn't like to think about Gardner-Webb, he said.

"Somebody said the coach was always slapping you."

"No slapping," Gilmore said. "Pinching and kicking."

"Did you try to leave?" somebody asked.

"A lot of times I laid in bed and thought about it. But then I thought about losing hours in school and everything. One time I went to the bus station and bought a ticket, but it was late and the coach came and got me and took me back."

"Why did you decide on Jacksonville?" he was asked.

"Because," Artis Gilmore said, "Coach Williams was the first white man I ever trusted."

What happened in the finals was, the best team won. UCLA fell behind quickly to Jacksonville, but when Johnny Wooden made some adjustments to shut off Artis Gilmore, the Bruins closed the first half with nine straight points and went on to win, 80–69.

There was no great joy that night at the Interstate Inn, but neither was there a wake. Of the key players, only Rex Morgan would not be around next season.

"We're in pretty good company," Tom Wasdin was saying. It was almost midnight and he was in the crowded motel bar with the tension off for the first time in months.

"How'd you feel tonight, before?" he was asked.

"I felt like we were a team of destiny."

Throats were cleared and a round of drinks was ordered. Wasdin insisted on buying. "We had a pretty good payday today," he said.

"That's what I understand."

"But don't forget," said Dr. Judson Harris, the crew-cut JU athletic director, "we haven't eaten breakfast yet."

The Sunday after the finals, the city of Jacksonville honored its Dolphins with a huge banquet. On Monday morning Joe Williams went fishing and Tom Wasdin taught four classes. On Tuesday the Boston Celtics drafted Rex Morgan and forward Rod McIntyre, the latter a star two years earlier, but now buried in the shadow of Artis Gilmore. As though they had just discovered the game of basketball, Florida papers that week after the tournament were pouring out thousands of words about Jacksonville. Then it was announced that Joe Williams was leaving to become head coach at Furman

University and would be replaced by Tom Wasdin. The money was one thing, Williams said (he was being boosted from $12,000 to $18,000 a year), but the real reason for the switch was that Furman is a basketball school. "There were too many extra duties at Jacksonville," Williams said, and nobody had to have it explained.

THE SAD PASSING OF AN ERA

By Richard Koster

From The St. Louis Globe-Democrat

Copyright, ©, 1970, The St Louis Globe-Democrat

The obituary was brief and incomplete. It failed to pay the proper respect to the end of a basketball era.

A terse wire story a couple of weeks ago announced:

"The Goodyear Tire and Rubber Co. has discontinued its Akron Goodyear amateur basketball team in an effort to reduce anticipated losses brought about by the United Rubber Workers' strike against the company.

"The team, formed in 1914, won two national AAU championships, three intercontinental world cups and numerous other titles."

That was all there was. It was hardly enough. There should have been a eulogy.

The Goodyears had been the first industrial employee basketball team—and they were the last. Preceding them into oblivion were rivals like Phillips 66, the Wichita Vickers, the Peoria Cats, the Denver-Chicago Truckers, Twentieth Century-Fox, Continental Airlines and the New York Tapes.

In the forties and fifties, basketball fans followed the National Industrial Basketball League just as religiously as they did the colleges and pros.

In 1948, Phillips edged the great Groza-Beard Kentucky team, 53–49, at Madison Square Garden for the right to represent the United States in the Olympics. Four years later, Peoria beat Kansas and Clyde Lovellette for the same honor. And in '56, it was Phillips over Bill Russell, K. C. Jones, Willie Naulls and other collegiate stars.

That was before the professional leagues began making instant millionaires out of college stars. The NIBL members could recruit players with something approaching equality—and they got their share.

Salaries were below those of the NBA, but there were compensations. At Goodyear, for example, the current president—Victor Holt—is an ex-basketball player. And the company's executive structure is full of men who joined the organization as players.

Bob Kurland, the Jennings giant who was college basketball's first towering star, went with Phillips after graduating from Oklahoma A & M in the late forties. His starting salary was a pittance—but today he's president of Phillips Films, a wholly owned subsidiary.

Dick Boushka, holder of St. Louis U.'s career scoring mark, chose the Vickers Petroleum Co. over the NBA. He was president of the company at 29, an office he still holds.

Pete McCaffrey, whose 39 points against Wichita is the St. Louis Billikens' single-game high, is the manager of communications research at Goodyear at age 31.

And remember Ray Steiner, the peppery little Billiken guard in the early fifties? He's currently a Phillips division sales manager in Raleigh, North Carolina—in charge of five states.

Given the inflated pro market of today, coveted collegians like Kurland and Boushka might choose the NBA over the NIBL, but in their days they certainly made correct decisions.

"My only problem," says Boushka, "was deciding whether I wanted to go with a large or small oil company. My degree was in geophysical engineering and both Phillips and Vickers offered me jobs.

"The pros were talking $12,000 to $15,000 and I started at Vickers at $500 a momth. A few years later, the Lakers traded the rights to me to the Hawks and I gave turning professional deep consideration.

"I could have made more money, but I'm fortunate I stuck tight. The only thing I miss is knowing if I could have made it in the NBA."

Boushka says the caliber of the NIBL was "about like the ABA compared to the NBA. We didn't have the superstar. But we drew 6,000 a game at home and you couldn't buy a ticket in Akron, at Phillips or Peoria."

Like Boushka, McCaffrey played on an Olympic team and enjoyed considerable foreign travel. In the sixties alone, the Goodyears played in 20 countries.

"Goodyear recruited me," McCaffrey says. "I started at $536 a month and played basketball three years, while I was in a training program. I worked a regular day and practiced at night. I think we got eight hours a week overtime for practice.

"When I came out of college, the top starting pro salary was about $17,000. I think that's what Jerry West got.

"My salary was less than half that. So there was no immediate payoff. But I'm glad I made the decision I did. At 31, I'm on the way up, not on the way down."

The Boushkas and McCaffreys, of course, regret the demise of employee basketball. "You know I have to be sorry," says the former. "But I know how much it cost. The end was inevitable."

"Around here it was a tradition," McCaffrey observes. "It produced a president and past chairman of the board. Basketball was a way to get in here. I hate to see it go."

But gone it is. And in Akron, the 300-seat gymnasium is being used as an auditorium for meetings—attended and conducted by some of the tallest executives in the country.

THE LADIES WHO LOVE THE KNICKS

By Peter Bonventre

From McCalls, New York

Copyright, ©, The McCall Publishing Company

The New York Knickerbockers are down by one point, and in the smoky haze of Madison Square Garden, the rival team is dribbling with lightning speed toward the basket at the far end of the court. Mrs. Dustin Hoffman is on the edge of her front-row seat, clutching nervously at her husband's arm, straining to watch the players as they desperately jockey for position around the moving ball. Suddenly, the Knicks' Walt Frazier has snatched the ball away and is madly dribbling back up the court, as the crowd screams its delight. Anne Hoffman is on her feet, shouting, cheering, laughing.

Beneath the hoop the players are now scrambling, pivoting, reaching, each Knick seeking an unguarded teammate who can drive for the hoop. Without warning, Willis Reed's large hands shoot up to receive a pass. Majestically he leaps above the gaggle of wildly flailing arms and jostling bodies and rams the ball downward through the hoop.

"You're beautiful, Willis!" screams Anne Hoffman, clapping her hands together wildly. "You're beautiful!"

"There's really nothing like it," Anne babbles enthusiastically as she and her husband file out of the Garden. "There's *nothing* like watching the Knicks win a close one in the last few seconds." A look at the multitude of women crowding out the exits, their faces flushed with excitement, their voices animated, clearly indicates that many other New York women share Anne's enthusiasm.

And in the dressing room, an exhausted Walt Frazier sprawls on a bench and smiles broadly. "When I hear those foxes squealing, I get all jiggly inside," he says. "It makes me feel like I can do anything I want on the court."

"Those foxes" are a growing breed of New York women who have involved themselves in the fortunes of the New York Knicker-bockers—Anne Hoffman is just one of them. The Knicks, considered the finest team in professional basketball today, play with a grace and guile that delights a legion of bright, sophisticated female fans—heretofore a largely untapped source of admiration.

"When we were uptown we got a lot of fat broads who, when they got tired of beating up their husbands, came to the Garden looking for a fight," a Knick official observed recently. "Or we got West Side hookers on the make. No class." He shook his head sadly, then brightened immediately. "But it's a whole new ball game now. There are a lot of great dames who come to the games now from all over the city."

The "Uptown" referred to was Eighth Avenue and 50th Street, where Madison Square Garden once sat in an area of grimy bars and hotdog stands, where gamblers compared notes before the games and ladies of questionable reputation drummed up business.

But two years ago the Garden moved from its crumbling confines to 34th Street and Eighth Avenue. Now an impressive glass-encased polygon perched atop Pennsylvania Station, the shiny new Garden is one of the easiest places in town to reach. With its cushioned seats and unobstructed spaciousness, it is an ideal arena for the spectator.

With New Yorkers seeking new pleasures to fill their ever-increasing leisure time, and with the blossoming of the Knicks as invincibles, the gleaming new Garden became a center of attention. "Let's face it," one female sophisticate said, "attending a Knick game is the In thing to do."

Indeed, any self-respecting male couldn't help but notice the transformation in the decor and clientele of the Garden. "Get a load of these broads," an inveterate gambler was overheard to say. "They're gorgeous."

If a gambler's gaze can be shaken from the action on the court, then you know something is happening. A look around before a Saturday night game proves it. "These broads" come in all shapes and sizes. They wear their hair tumbling in tendrils or swinging long and straight. They come in midi culottes and miniskirts and dungarees, in ski parkas and maxi coats. Some slither in in their Puccis; some in mink and low-cut gowns. They are young swingers, chic career girls and attractive middle-aged suburban housewives. They all became curious about an attraction that could inspire the exuberant loyalty of boy friend or husband—and now they can't stay away.

"I thought basketball was such a crummy sport," said an attractive young *New York Times* reporter. "When I was at Radcliffe I went to a few Harvard basketball games, and I couldn't understand how anybody could enjoy watching a bunch of guys running around in undershirts. But last winter a date asked me to get tickets for him, and I just went crazy over the Knicks. Now I go every chance I get—even if I have to go alone." Ilene Goldman, wife of William Goldman, author and screenwriter of *Butch Cassidy and the Sundance Kid,* puts it even more emphatically: "It's such an exciting game that I'd go even if I were pregnant with triplets."

Betty Friedan, president of the National Organization for Women, feels there's a specific force at work luring women to the games. "This attraction is a symptom of the fantastic unused energy potential of women—it's being expressed vicariously," says Miss Friedan. "Women are beginning to express their own need to be part of the action, since for so long they have been denied their right to participate." (Indeed, only last spring the San Francisco Warriors drafted Denise Long, a 5-foot-11 high-school graduate from Whitten, Iowa. But the National Basketball Association hierarchy said the draft made "a travesty" of the league, so she never got to play.)

Dr. Paul Weiss, a professor of philosophy at Yale and author of *Sport: A Philosophic Inquiry,* has another theory. "Team play does not have much of an appeal to most women," says Dr. Weiss. "Women are evidently more individualistic in temper, more self-contained than men. Women do not normally assume a role that is carried out in the light of the way in which others carry out their roles."

Women, then, seem simply more apt to appreciate the skill of a single player than the exploits of a team that functions as a unit. And even though five men are in action on the court, a basketball team is really sparked by each individual talent.

True enough, when discussing the Knicks, women invariably speak in terms of their favorite players. They marvel at Willis Reed's persistence, Bill Bradley's ingenuity, Dick Barnett's skill, Dave Debusschere's alertness.

And the female mind is charmed by each idiosyncrasy. "It's marvelous the way Dick Barnett curtsies when he shoots," gushes Joan Simon, the girlishly attractive wife of playwright Neil Simon. "Mike Riordan is right out of a ballet class, and Bill Bradley is a great backward runner."

Of all the players, though, the overwhelming favorite is Walt Frazier, a slender, muscular athlete whose presence on the court is dramatized by his quickness and agility. An immensely exciting performer, he has been nicknamed "Clyde" because he wears the wide-brim hats and broad lapels so popular in Clyde Barrow's day—and because he steals a basketball with the same cool, crowd-pleasing flair that Clyde Barrow used to steal a bankroll. Frazier doesn't mind at all—"Clyde was a swinger in pinstripe suits. He had class."

Women frankly comment on the sexuality that Frazier exudes on the court. "He's terribly attractive to watch," says Ellie Azenberg, the articulate wife of Emanuel Azenberg, co-producer of *The Lion in Winter*. "All those men, beautifully developed and coordinated, playing in shorts—it's quite appealing."

To be sure, the Knick players are very aware of such feminine adulation. "When I steal the ball, I can see them cheering for The Man," says Frazier, grinning. "I know the chicks come to see me do my stuff."

Significantly, there are few sports that require the skill and grace which Frazier possesses and basketball demands. Women, according to Dr. Weiss, tend to "emphasize gracefulness and coordination . . . to treat their sports as developments and extensions of the dance. Part of the reason for this, undoubtedly, is our socially inherited view of women's capacity and function, the firm conviction that women should be graceful rather than strong or swift."

On a less aesthetic level, basketball is simply an easy game to understand. There are no fly patterns, sacrifice plays or earned run averages to fathom. "Football is too complex, with all those crazy formations like slot left and split right," a female Knick fan remarked. "And baseball is much too boring. But basketball is so dramatic—and the Knicks are sexier than anything."

Of course, there are still those other ladies at the Garden who could articulate no such reasons for their presence—bitchy Berthas and abusive Gertrudes, shouting their insults at referees, players and coaches. But the fact remains that a vast number of women at the Garden today are theatergoers, museum visitors and discothèque veterans who have discovered that the East Side is not the only chic playground of New York. The newly discovered charm of the Knicks is undeniable, and as Ilene Goldman puts it, "For many of us the game has become a very personal experience."

Golf

THAT INTOXICATING MOMENT

By Shirley Povich

From The Washington Post

Copyright, ©, 1970, The Washington Post

For Eli Marovich, club pro from West Mifflin, Pennsylvania, it was that intoxicating moment. For 12 years he had yearned to qualify for the U.S. Open, and now he was hearing it from the United States Golf Association itself. "Mr. Marovich, to the first tee," the official starter intoned.

It was a frigid 8 A.M. and the winds were ripping and the morning was bleak. They don't select any of the tournament's precious big names for the first threesome to tee off in a U.S. Open. Usually, it is the rabble in the field, like the aging club pro Marovich and the driving range pro Gaylon Simon from Melrose Park, Illinois, and the amateur kid with a golf scholarship at Houston U., Corker DeLoach. The idea is to get that kind out of the way. Quick.

For others, it might not have been a stylish hour, but for Eli Marovich it was nirvana. This was it, the biggest one of them all, and he was in it. A little bit late, perhaps, at the age of 48, but his name was finally in the books as a pro who had teed off in the Open. And then he heard the starter's traditional "Play away, please." It was golf's equivalent of Indianapolis' "Gentlemen, start your engines."

It was a bad day for golf. The course was brutally long, too many tight holes on it and the winds were gusting to 41 miles an hour. The day could have been called Chaska's Revenge and perhaps it was.

Chaska was the Sioux chieftain in these parts in the mid-1800's when the miserable, poaching palefaces finally chased him from his happy hunting grounds. He did not consider it darn white of them to name their settlement Chaska, Minnesota, in his memory. And today it was easy to picture the old chief in his heaven calling down all the evil spirits on his unworthy brothers, and cranking up the wind machines to visit his fury on them.

Eli Marovich was up at five this morning. Had to, if he wanted to get out to the course by 6:30 A.M. and hit a couple of buckets of practice balls before he was called to the first tee. Not even the guards were stirring at that hour. He could have robbed the joint. His hands were cold, and he blew into them, because it was important he get a good feel of his clubs Thursday.

The people at the Duquesne Club near Pittsburgh where he is the home pro had written dunning letters to each other to help get up a $500 pot that would help Marovich get to Chaska and back. This didn't pay the way of his wife, Mary, but he would make out all right, even if he did have to cancel a week of lessons at the club.

His lessons don't cost much, $5 for half a hour, but he gies 10 lessons a day, and, "I guess I passed up $350 lesson money to get out here," he said.

Marovich's locker was not far from Arnie Palmer's. They situate the Open players alphabetically at Chaska. The locker-room area offered contrasts. Marovich came in from his round just as Palmer was nearing his call to the first tee, at a fashionable early afternoon hour. Marovich was talking of lessons he gives at $5 a half hour. Palmer's caddy fees are more than that.

If Marovich ran into any debit in the Open, he could make it up by giving more lessons, he said. At a nearby locker, Lee Trevino was having no such concerns. At the same moment, Trevino was telling a Madison Avenue type, "No, thanks. Sorry. But I don't smoke." In his honesty, Trevino had just turned down an offer of $10,000 for his endorsement of a brand of cigarettes.

Marovich was saying how nice it was he had qualified for the Open. "There are a couple of things that were important to me," he said. "I didn't know how much longer I could take those two 36-hole qualifying rounds at my age, and there were other reasons." One of them, he intimated, was the importance of pleasing his club members, after his 12-year famine as an Open qualifier. "Their eyes lighted up and they slapped me on the back," he said.

For Marovich, the 456-yard first hole, with the wind in his face, leered like the forbidding stretch at Belmont Park, and his drive went into the rough. A bogey five was his beginning. And on the long third hole he sevened, and was out in an awful 43 strokes. The 15th was his horror hole, a daymare eight.

The gruesome eight began with a drive into the fierce wind that caught the left rough on that 592-yard monster. "I had to play out with a five-iron. Then my three-wood caught the trap. I blasted out too far, and didn't get to the green until my sixth shot," said Marovich. "I'll just have to tell the folks back home what happened, I guess, and hope they'll still remember I was one of the 150 qualified in the crowd of 3,450 who tried."

Things were less embarrassing for Marovich later in the day, and his 85 was not looking so ghastly. The big scoreboard was dotted with a seven for Gary Player, and Arnie Palmer needed 40 on the out-nine, and Jack Nicklaus had his troubles, too, and came in with a big 81, and when the folks at home ask Eli Marovich how he did in the Open, he can say, "Well, at the end of the first round I was only four strokes back of Nicklaus."

FLORIDA FATS

By Stan Hochman

From the Philadelphia Daily News

Copyright, ©, 1970, Philadelphia Newspapers Inc.

Okay, all you skinny, hipless guys who stand there on the mound behind the ninth green and snicker as Bob Murphy comes waddling down that hill, jiggling like three dishes of lemon Jell-o. Bob Murphy would like any of you lean, lanky loudmouths to put your money where your loud mouth is.

"Jealousy, personal jealousy," Bob Murphy sneered yesterday, "and you can put that in the paper. If they don't think I'm an athlete, let's arrange a decathlon, and I'll take 'em on.

"Anything. You name it. Shoot baskets, pitch baseballs, shoot pool, I've done all of it. I just happen to be fat. Well, I know a lot of good fat athletes."

Murphy had waddled around Whitemarsh Country Club's steamy landscape in 67 shots. He started out with his mustard-colored shirt plastered to his skin, rambling blotches of sweat staining the back of it before he ever took a swing. He is about 5-foot-9 and he weighs 212 and he left a wake of tsk-tsks behind him, which is a shame because he played splendid golf. The whole world is supposed to love a fat man, but somebody forgot to tell that to the galleries.

He would not list his favorite stout performers, but he rambled on, getting something off his shimmying chest. "I had no idols," he said. "I've always been a doer, not a watcher. When my little brothers would go to Lakeland to watch the Tigers train, I'd go out in my backyard and practice hitting a ball. A baseball, not a golf ball.

"Anybody who does things well is due their credit. Whether it's a guy who plays the piano well, or sings, or writes a good story, they're due their credit. The thing to do is to try to be the best in your field. Just because a guy is fat, doesn't make him automatically lazy or slovenly.

"Chi Chi Rodriguez once told me to get down to 175. I told him the last time I weighed 175, I was in the third grade and I'd been sick for three weeks. Actually, I was up around 228, and I lost 20 pounds. Gave up beer. Gosh, I loved that beer. Nothing tastes like a cold brew after a round. If they could make iced tea taste that way . . ."

Ordinarily, Murphy doesn't get his Irish up that way. All that tsk-tsking has to rankle him, though, because he did get to college on a baseball scholarship, and he didn't turn to golf until a football injury tore up his throwing arm. And he does sharpen his putting touch by shooting pool well enough to be known as "Florida Fats" behind his ample back.

Two years ago he finished second at Westchester and then won the Philadelphia tournament and the Thunderbird Tournament. It added up to $70,000 in three weeks, and how many skinny guys east of Frank Sinatra make that kind of money?

Last year his luck went sour in Philadelphia. Some rascal stole the golf clubs out of his station wagon. "My fault," he admitted. "There was a rainstorm and I got my wife, Gail, and my little girl, Kimberly, out of the car and upstairs and I left the clubs in the car. I didn't go down till the next day and they were gone.

"You have to understand about those clubs. It's like an old pair of shoes, partner. They just feel good. Gosh knows how I've worked and worked and worked to get other clubs to feel the same. I've only had three sets of irons, but I've had 15 to 20 drivers and 15 to 20 wedges and goodness knows how many putters."

It has been win one, lose one in Philly for Murphy, and it may be time for win one again. "I'll get revenge," he said. "I'll win the tournament. For $30,000 I can buy three sets of clubs like the old ones.

"The thing is, I'm putting like Houdini. Everything under 20 feet, if I don't make it, I feel like something went wrong. Funny thing is, on that first hole [he started a 10], I walked up to Homero Blancas and I said, 'This looks like an easy putt.' "

It was a 25-footer, downhill, and Murphy rapped it right into the middle of the cup. "I always think," he said later, "that it's a great way to start a round of golf, get an easy putt and knock it in the bottom of the hole. I call it getting the round in gear. I told Homero I wouldn't have an easier putt all day."

He was four-under-par after 16 holes when he rapped his second shot too hard and it skittered across the green at number eight and into the tough, wiry grass beyond the fringe. Murphy tinkered with a putter, switched to the wedge and flicked the ball into the hole for a birdie three.

"I was going to gamble and try to make the birdie," he confessed, "and then I thought I'd better use the wedge and try to make a par . . . and it went in."

For all his Kewpie doll dimensions, Murphy is a sound player. Not a single bogey marred his card. And he sneers at the critics who would have him challenging places he cannot reach.

"I have to play my own game," he said. "Today I played with Homero Blancas who hooks every shot. I try to fade every shot. If a guy tried to convince Homero or me that the hook or the fade were wrong, then one of us would have to get out of golf, and that's wrong, because we can both earn a good living out here. You've got to go with what you've got.

"It doesn't really matter how you do it. You have to get it on the green and get it in the hole, and it doesn't really matter how you look while you're doing it. If you bounce it off a car, or through some trees, or whatever."

Oh, yes, the social notes from Del Ray Beach indicate that the Bob Murphys will be moving into their $100,000 home in two weeks. Keep that in mind the next time you're about to snicker at Bob Murphy's backside. Sure, it looks large, but every time you see the rascal, he's bending over the cup to pick up a golf ball he's just knocked in for a birdie.

BEN HOGAN TODAY

By Nick Seitz

From Golf Digest

Copyright, ©, 1970, Golf Digest Magazine

The day after the Colonial Tournament, in which he played respectably at the age of 57, Ben Hogan, the blacksmith's son, sat back in a leather-covered chair after a long lunch in the relaxing atmosphere of the men's grill at Shady Oaks Country Club in Fort Worth, where he is the most esteemed member. He wore an expensive gray business suit and handsome striped tie, having come from a morning's work at the Ben Hogan Company. The company, under his direction, is doing so well it cannot produce golf equipment fast enough to fill orders.

He gazed reflectively out a large picture window overlooking the ninth and 18th greens of an exquisitely cared-for course. Beyond, in an exclusive residential area called Westover Hills, Hogan and his lovely wife, Valerie, live in a tastefully sumptuous home, identifiable from this distance by its three chimneys. Contemplating his hard-gained success, Hogan said, "A fella's never satisfied, I guess." His voice halted meaningfully. "But . . ."

For millions of golf followers, it will matter not a shred if Arnold Palmer wins the rest of the schedule, or Raquel Welch becomes a touring caddie, or the price of a hot dog on the course dives to a nickel. The year 1970 was made when William Benjamin Hogan, his swollen left knee squeezed into an elastic brace, limped intently out of retirement to finish ninth in the Houston Champions International and challenge briefly in the Colonial, which he has won five times.

Imagine Joe DiMaggio donning his old uniform and coming off the bench to rip a grand-slam home run before a capacity crowd in Yankee Stadium, and you have some idea of the drama that drenched Hogan's performances on two of the most arduous courses in the sport.

The short return to professional golf of the man widely considered the greatest player ever, a winner of all four major championships, a national hero after he overcame the near-fatal effects of a 1949 car-bus crash, gives rise to fascinating questions. Why did he do it? What is his life like today? Has he, as some reports suggest, "mellowed"? What achievements mean the most to him? Hogan long has been the least understood of great athletes, often summarily characterized as "cold" and "aloof," and the years since he reached his playing zenith in the late 1940's and early 1950's have brought disappointingly little insight into his life-style and outlooks.

Hogan permitted me to follow him for a week in Fort Worth, observing and questioning. I took up with him during the Colonial and spent two days with him afterward, as he reverted to his customary activities, which seldom include complete rounds of golf, let alone tour play. In that time I think I came to know somewhat a Ben Hogan only remotely related to the single-dimensional, distant figure I had been led to expect.

The thing that surprised me most about Hogan was his sense of humor: droll, flavored with an earthy Southwestern spice, often evident. I remember my unsuspecting introduction to it. I accompanied him to Shady Oaks for lunch—he lunches there regularly—and he introduced me to the manager, who personally attends him. "This guy has 15 kids," Hogan said. Expressionless, he added, *"Bleeped* himself right out of a seat in the car."* I had heard dozens of stories about Hogan's dourness, and in no way was prepared for this. I nodded innocuously. After a lengthy silence, I suddenly became aware of what he had said, and burst out laughing. Hogan, who had been watching me closely, joined in the laughter. He was amused not at his own line but at my delayed response. His probing blue-gray eyes suggested, "Didn't expect that from the austere Ben Hogan, eh?"

Later that afternoon, touring the course on Number 53, his private, plastic-topped green golf car, we stopped to watch a foursome teeing off.

"Hey, here's the albatross!" one of the players shouted toward Hogan, making reference to Hogan's lack of success in a local game called The Wheel. A team of two plays against all combinations of several other players. The stakes begin as a $2.50 Nassau but multiply rapidly. Hogan, a plus-2 handicapper, some months ago shot 64–64–65–67–67, and lost all ways. "I checked it to 'em," he says. "I don't play that game anymore."

"You going to watch me swing?" another man asked Hogan.

"Yeah," Hogan replied drily. "It'll give you an excuse."

Of his friend, Jimmy Demaret, who does not have to be coaxed hard to sing, Hogan says, "I love Jimmy's voice . . . but I don't think I can stand 'Deep Purple' again."

Hogan is no raconteur, but he enjoys hearing a good story. Golf temper stories featuring Tommy Bolt and Lefty Stackhouse are his favorites. And he enjoys, even more, spontaneous humor. Paired with Bob Goalby in Houston, Hogan burned a long drive into the wind. "Who do you think you are," Goalby asked, "Ben Hogan?" Hogan liked that.

During the Colonial, Hogan did his warming up at Shady Oaks, 15 minutes away. The practice area at Colonial Country Club is not large, and he always has preferred to practice by himself anyway ("You don't get in anybody's way, and nobody gets in yours, and you can have your own thoughts"). At Shady Oaks he hits balls from a spot between the 14th and 15th holes, across the 14th, 13th and 17th fairways. One morning, some writers covering the Colonial were playing at Shady Oaks, and "played through" Hogan's practice area. Hogan chatted with them and asked one, Kaye Kessler from Columbus, Ohio, about his swing. "It's kind of disjointed," Kessler said. "My boss told me I shouldn't take it out of town because if it broke down I couldn't get parts." Hogan chuckled delightedly. There is plenty of Irish in him.

Hogan spends several hours a day and an occasional evening at Shady Oaks, the club built by his close friend and early backer on the tour, Marvin Leonard. He is comfortable there. It is the poshest club in Fort Worth, but the members treat one another with a congenial irreverence, Hogan included. "Ben gets tired of people gettin' down on their knees when he walks into a room," Tommy Bolt says. "I've had some great name-callin' arguments with him and he loved it."

Hogan plays gin rummy and golf with a regular group. "I'm not a very good gin player," he says. "It passes the time." Those he plays with say he competes as fiercely as he does at golf. Hogan does not play casual golf at Shady Oaks: "I play with friends, but we don't play friendly games." His partners frequently will be bankers John Griffith and O. K. Shannon, precision instrument company owner John Howell, and Irving L. Taggart, a maker of panel boards for such things as television sets and airplanes. Last year Hogan played only about 10 rounds, usually in a golf car. This year, his leg improved, he expects to play once or twice a week. "If cars were legal I could play more tournaments, but I couldn't play as well. You don't have time to compose yourself."

Early every afternoon, his leg and the weather permitting, he will empty an old shag bag and hit balls for 40 to 90 minutes, starting with a nine-iron and working through the set. With each club he will hit basic shots, then, before putting it away, will hit two different types of shots, moving the ball to the right or left, or hitting it low or high. "The basics of the swing remain the same," he says. "But I'm always experimenting, looking for better ways to hit finesse shots. I never hit a shot on the course I haven't practiced." His clear voice, neutral at first, takes on more of the drawling intonations of Texas as he warms to talking. "I'm a curious person. Experimenting is my enjoyment. I won't accept anything until I've worked with it for a week or two, or longer. I bring out new clubs from the plant and try them out, and I get ahold of clubs that we've sold to check them. If something doesn't work, some part of my swing or a club, I throw it out."

The scientific method. Hogan is the Linus Pauling of his field, subjecting any hypothesis to rigorous, impartial testing. If it works, he keeps it, generalizes from it. If it doesn't, into the garbage can it goes. Gardner Dickinson worked for Hogan when Hogan had a club job in Palm Springs in his younger years. Dickinson majored in clinical psychology in college, with a minor in psychometrics—mental testing. Intrigued by Hogan's personality, he would slip IQ test questions into conversations with him. "I knew I'd never get them all past him, so I'd give him only the toughest ones from each section, knowing if he could answer those, he could get the others," Dickinson says. "I calculated that his IQ was in excess of 175. Genius level is about 160. Ben didn't go to college, he regrets that, but he's a brilliant person."

One reason Hogan practices where he does at Shady Oaks is to hit into the prevailing wind. When the wind moves, so does Hogan. "If the wind is at your back, it destroys your game. You tend to try to pull the ball, swinging from the outside in, which is bad. If the temperature is below 60 degrees, you lose me. You can wreck your swing playing in cold weather, bundling all up." Each shot is aimed at a target: a small nursery building near the 18th fairway. He uses no glove. "I never could feel anything wearing a glove." Traffic is light at Shady Oaks. Such is Hogan's eminence, when strangers playing the course interrupt his practice, they often apologize.

If he is not too tired, Hogan will chip and putt for an additional hour or two hours, at the second green, adjoining the clubhouse. For him, two extra holes always are cut in the back of the large green.

Shady Oaks, not as long or difficult as Colonial, where Hogan formerly belonged, is nonetheless challenging, and pretty, if that term may be applied to a golf course. Hogan designed most of the bunkers. They are numerous and imaginatively and variously shaped. They are not difficult to shoot from; they are not deep and do not have high lips. "Bunkers serve two purposes," Hogan says. "They are for framing a green—to give it definition and to give the player an idea of the distance he has in hitting to the green. And for beauty. They are not for trapping people."

Hogan holds decided views on what a golf course should be, and no one knows more about shot values. It is his ambition to build The Perfect Golf Course, a project he has contemplated since his touring days. "I'm very close to buying the property now. The market research looks favorable. You have to know where you'll wind up before you start—otherwise you'll go broke. You have to have the right piece of land. I'm in hopes of getting a nice, rolling site with a lot of trees. That means it won't be in the Fort Worth area. I want a course that both the club member and the pro can play.

"Length isn't necessarily the key. Length has to do with climate. Where it's humid, you can't have too long a course. The greens have to be large to provide multiple pin placements and prevent their wearing out. You have to have heavy play or you're going to lose money. You give the greens character in the contouring. I like a clean course. You could grow rough for a tournament. Champions Golf Club in Houston is my idea of a tremendous course for the locale."

Hogan probably will build his course in or near sprawling, wealthy Houston. The course is sure to place a premium on driving, which Hogan deems the most important area of play. Expect the par-4's to bend slightly left or right (an equal number each way). The par-3's will call for iron shots, even short-iron shots, precisely placed. "I won't design it," Hogan says, inhaling hard on a cigarette. "I'm no architect. A person can have just so much knowledge, and there isn't enough time in the day to absorb very much and be proficient. I'll work with the architect, but not in detail. Everything takes a professional."

Hogan will build only one course.

Hogan and his wife went about the building and appointing of their 10-year-old home on a winding, climbing private road in west Fort Worth with the same attentiveness to detail he is bringing to developing a golf course. From the time they were married in the mid-1930's, while traveling broadly in golf, they compared mental notes on what they wanted in a house. Finally they called in a top contractor, designer and decorator. The results are remarkable.

The one-story house, on a modest acreage, is of off-white brick, in French country style—subtly different from French provincial, which has become *démodé*. Each brick was molded on the spot with a slight irregularity—under Hogan's watchful overseeing—to give texture to the exterior. The inside, predominantly white with blue and touches of yellow, as the decorators say, is mindful of a small manor house. Entrance is through a spacious, marble-floored hall with a striking crystal chandelier. The rest of the floors are of pecan, each board personally picked by the Hogans. The living-room and dining-room rugs were specially designed and made in France by a meticulous process that takes a year.

In the study-library in the evening, in his cozy green lounge chair near the fireplace, Hogan reads newspapers and magazines and an occasional book. The bookcases hold a set of literary classics, a few copies of more recent fiction, golf texts—among them his *Five Lessons: The Modern Fundamentals of Golf* and his *Power Golf,* art and antiques encyclopedias and two editions of *The Making of the President.* The birch paneling is simple and subdued. A distinctive feature is an old regimental drum that serves as a coffee table. "I like antiques that are functional—that aren't falling down," Hogan says. On the top of the drum, covered with glass and scarcely noticeable, are a few of his golf medals—the only indication that the man of the house may well be the greatest golfer in history. "I didn't want a lot of medals and trophies flaunted all over the walls," Hogan says. (A good-sized room just inside the front entrance at Colonial is filled with mementos of his famous victories.) Jimmy Demaret has kidded Hogan that he built a $200,000 home with one bedroom so Demaret wouldn't come to visit him. However, Hogan says, with his even smile, the large study can be converted into a bedroom for guests.

The house is generously endowed with fine art, selected by the

Hogans and smoothly blended with the colors and character of the respective rooms. "Ben loves art," Valerie says. "When we're in New York he goes gallerying. Lately he even goes antiquing with me. He says he's just an amateur—he only knows what he likes. He admired these two paintings in the living room so enthusiastically when we were staying with friends in Palm Springs, they gave them to us." The Hogans' favorite work, done mainly in pastel blues and white, is a semi-Impressionistic study of a woman by a Vietnamese artist who has synthesized French and Asian styles, and was acquired at the Findlay Gallery in Manhattan.

In the bathroom off Ben's large, paneled dressing room hang lighthearted sketches, and over the bar are the only golf pictures, four prints, the originals of which Hogan is seeking throughout the world.

Outside in the back is a paved court and pool. There are plants and a live oak that provides shade. To one side is the garage-cottage and four cars, two driven by the help, a married couple that lives in. Behind the pool is a low brick wall and behind the wall an undisturbed valley. "I own that lot," Hogan says. "I don't want a house built there. You put a two-story house in there, and people are going to be looking right down on you."

We are sitting near the pool, sipping large glasses of Coke over ice brought by the help. I ask Valerie if she plays golf. "No, I never have," she says. She is demurely dressed in a green and white sleeveless summer day dress, the hemline just at the knees (these things are crucial this year). She is scented with a flowery perfume. Her smile and charming manner are faultless. "I followed Ben during the Colonial. He kids me that I never used to follow him when he was playing well, but I did."

The Hogans, who are childless, are not inactive socially. Valerie, who has joined committees for charity, occasionally entertains during the day. Ben will cook steaks outside for a small group, or will, with Valerie, give an infrequent large dinner party. "We go to people's homes, and they come to ours," he says, "but not once a week. We'll go to a couple of charity balls a year. I'm not antisocial, I just don't feel good the next day. I can't work. Ever since my accident, I've had to get a lot of rest. I try to get at least eight hours' sleep, and I'd rather have 10. I like to go to bed early. I have an awful time waking up. If I'm in a tournament and I have a morning tee time, I'll get up three hours before."

It is common for a legendary athlete, no longer very active competitively, to sell his name—to let it be used for promotional purposes or to open doors, as the saying has it. Ben Hogan does not play the game of business that way. "I don't consider myself a businessman," he says crisply. "Once you consider yourself something, you fall flat on your face, you see." He is behind the wide wooden desk in his spacious office, in front of two framed full-color maps. Several neat foothills of mail have accumulated while he was playing the two tournaments.

A high-salaried executive in the employ of AMF, with stock options and the rest, he is in full command of the Ben Hogan affiliate. He does not play golf with customers. He plays company golf once a year, at the principal sales meeting. He makes few speeches, although he is a captivating speaker. "Some people love that sort of thing. I don't like it. If I accept a speaking engagement, I do the best I can, but I'm not comfortable. I wanta be in the background someplace."

The plant and offices are in a nondescript, outlying warehouse district. Fronted by a perfectly-kept expanse of putting grass, they stand out. A visitor is asked to sign in with a receptionist, then is led to Hogan's office by Claribel Kelly, his trusted executive secretary. There are no slick public-relations people around Hogan. He is not easy to see, but Claribel is his only visible shield. She went to grammar school with Hogan, and remembers him and his mother, who still lives in Fort Worth, attending a music recital she had a part in. She has worked for him for 18 years. She calls him "Mr. Hogan" as often as "Ben."

She opens his mail, but does not screen it. He reads it all, scrawling terse notes across the tops of letters for her to amplify. Hogan is sterner in his office. Trying to reach a businessman on the phone, Claribel enters his office to report that he is in a meeting and will call back. "When?" Hogan asks. Gene Sheely, the man who puts together the models for Hogan clubs, comes in with a wedge special-ordered by a tour star. Hogan puts on the glasses he wears for close work. "I found out playing in the Colonial I'm gonna need 'em to play golf, too. I couldn't see the pins. I had to ask the caddie." Hogan asks a couple of pointed questions, soles the club on the carpet. Sheely wonders if the player should be charged for the club. "Well heck, yes," Hogan answers softly but firmly. The player endorses the clubs of another company. "That's one reason we don't have playing pros on our staff," says Hogan. "Just me."

In the Hogan company's early, struggling years, Ben worked 14 and 16 hours a day to set up a system that was just as he wanted it. Walking through the plant, nodding at employees, occasionally stopping to inspect work at a particular station, he says, "I've done all these jobs myself. I like to work with my hands."

Dealing with his help, Hogan relies on direct communication. He does not phone them or send them memoranda; he has them summoned to his office and talks to them. Directly.

Today, Hogan usually will work only in the morning, and is perhaps the only executive in the country who consistently can take off at noon for his golf club and not be second-guessed. He cannot understand modern golfers—or executives—who say they do not have time for golf. "I have other business interests that I find time for. I piddle around in the oil business. I fool around with the stock market quite a bit. I'm in the process of looking for a cattle ranch. I'll find what I want. I want it within 150 miles of Fort Worth. I keep hearing there's no money in it, but if that were true you couldn't buy a steak."

Each year Hogan is offered well-paying peripheral jobs, such as commentating on golf telecasts. Each year he declines. "Television is a different business entirely," he says. "It takes a professional to do a professional job. And I'm fed up with traveling."

He has been approached many times about involving himself in a tour event that would carry his name, but always has refused, in part because he is wary of lending his name to an undertaking if he does not have complete control over the quality, and in part, probably, because he has had it in mind to build his own course, the natural site for a "Ben Hogan Classic."

Hogan is considering writing an exhaustive instruction book. "It would be this thick," he says with thumb and forefinger as far apart as they will stretch. "It would confuse a lot of people, but I can't help that. I get so darn tired of these bromides that don't mean anything. Explain to me the expression 'coming off the ball.' What does that mean? What caused it, that's what I want to know. I never see that explained. Or 'stay behind the ball.' What does that mean?"

Gardner Dickinson says he has seen Hogan turn down $500 for a five-minute lesson. Why doesn't Hogan teach? "You can't find anybody who wants to learn." A silence. "I did teach at one time."

Hogan says the movie about his life, *Follow the Sun,* is going to be reshot to bring it up to modern technical standards, and that he would be a consultant. "I hit all the shots before, and I'll probably do it again." Followers of golf have devoted many hours to trying to guess the identity of the supporting character who was Hogan's friend and rival. Some have guessed Byron Nelson. Others Jimmy Demaret. Others Lloyd Mangrum. "It was a composite," Hogan says with a mischievous smile.

It is a virtual certainty that Hogan will not approve Peter Fonda, or any other long-haired pop actor, to play his part. In areas such as dress and hairstyle, Hogan is staunchly conservative. "Sometimes I'm damn glad there's a generation gap," he says emphatically. "I think it's just ridiculous the way some of these golfers look. Here they're asking important people around the country to put up millions of dollars for tournaments. . . . If it was my tournament I wouldn't let 'em in the front gate." His hands are expressive, gesticulating. Of one pro with whom he has been friendly, but who recently grew heavy muttonchop sideburns, Hogan says, "I don't even speak to him anymore. He looks like his head's on upside down." Hogan's own thinning hair is short and neatly combed when not covered by a straw hat or a golf cap.

Noticing one day that his vinyl-topped new Cadillac, his cuffed golf slacks and the grips on his clubs all were gray, I asked him if gray is his favorite color. "It doesn't offend anybody," he said.

Hogan, like a couple of hundred million others, has sharp opinions on the state of the nation. "I'd like to know where in heck half of my tax dollar goes," he says. "If I were president of a small country, I think I'd start a war against my neighbor, so the United States or Russia would jump in and give me a million dollars. Then the other one would give my neighbor a million. It's darn foolish." Maybe Ben and the kids aren't so far apart after all. Then he says: "The trouble in this country started when I was young, when the vote was extended to people who had no property. A lot of them don't give a darn. Now, I don't know what you can do." The kids wouldn't groove so well on that.

Frank Beard, one of the best of the current players, has a theory about Hogan-the-man. "The uncanny thing was that he seemed able to concentrate and pour it on from the moment he got up until the time he left the course," Beard says. "But it's not true that he is a shy, withdrawn, cold man. I heard him speak at a dinner once, and he was about as warm and witty as can be. I think at one time he was a regular guy. He acted like most pros—chatted and larked around—and was in no way an enigma. But early in his career he decided to dedicate himself to golf. Wholly. To forfeit many family and social pleasures. He did this as a man might take to religion. And this regimen made him detached, the way an obsession with science or medicine might have. By the time I met him he had mellowed. Several of us had some drinks one night after an exhibition in Fort Wayne a few years ago, and from 10 until 2 Hogan told stories about his early days on the tour that regaled us. It was great to see him so relaxed."

I quoted Beard's theory to Hogan and asked him to react to it. "I think he's right," Hogan said. He was silent for a full minute, as he often is when answering a hard question. He will give an almost blunt initial response and then, if the questioner meets his glinting look and does not interrupt his thought processes, he will elaborate, often at near-loquacious length. "I got credit for a lot of things I didn't do, but I did dedicate myself to the game. And I loved every minute of it. And I'm the same person today I was then."

I asked him if his popular reputation as a grim, machinelike person bothers him. "I couldn't care less," he said caustically. "I get along with everybody I know. I know who started those stories and why, and he's sorry, and that's enough. Too many people hear or read something written from uneducated preconceptions, and it takes off. There's a great difference between intelligence and wisdom. You might have a college sheepskin, but that doesn't make you educated. Life's too short for me to go around explaining myself. A lot of people don't understand modesty. Not everybody wants publicity, you know."

Beard is correct about Hogan's ability to reminisce enthrallingly. Hearing him speak about the formative years of the tour is a remarkable experience. "I'll tell you how the tour got started, and I've never read this anywhere," he said one noon as we ate chalupas, a zestful Mexican dish that is perfect by Fort Worth criteria—hot enough to make your eyes water but not hot enough to make you choke. "The wives of a handful of club professionals in the East—Bob Cruickshank, Al Espinosa, Tommy Armour, I believe—took it on themselves to book a tour in the 1930's. Their husbands were off work in the winter. Before that you just had a smattering of tournaments across the country. The wives wrote to chambers of commerce and so forth in California, and convinced several cities to have tournaments. Some of the purses were only a few hundred dollars, and we'd go to civic-club lunches to promote ourselves. The wives kept up all the correspondence and handled the books. Then the manufacturers saw what a great promotional vehicle the tour could be and hired Bob Harlow, Walter Hagen's manager, to conduct it. Later the PGA got in on it. That's how this $7 million business began.

"We'd play five exhibitions apiece to pay our Ryder Cup expenses. We got no money from the PGA. If somebody on the tour died or had troubles, we'd work out an exhibition schedule to help out. I never did make money playing the tour. It cost me more, total, than my purse winnings. I had to do other things.

"We traveled together and ate together and sat around hotel rooms and talked at night. We were a smaller group, and invariably more closely knit. It seems to me like we used to have a more gracious life playing tournaments in those days. In many places we dressed for dinner, in dinner jackets. I cringe when I see fellas today, walking into nice restaurants in golf clothes."

Hogan does not begrudge the modern stars their riches. "The money is fine. It's only a 35-cent dollar anyway. I am a little dubious about the future. Commercial sponsorship for tournaments is shallow. These companies might come in for three years and get out. Civic sponsors are best for the game."

How does he compare the quality of play? "There is so much more of everything today. More players, more tournaments. There are more good players, of course, and the best ones might be better. Competition improves people. Fifteen years from now the level of play will be better still. You have to beat the competition. To do that you have to find a way. You have to have an edge." Hogan's voice hardens, as if he were himself hungering for that edge all over again. "The fundamentals of swinging are the same, but the technique of hitting the ball has improved, and the equipment is slightly better . . . not as much better as the individual and his technique. All golf shots are missed to a degree. Today fewer are missed. These boys think better. They're bigger and stronger, and they practice harder. These fellas putt better—more boldly. That's due to practice. When I started, they used to laugh at me for practicing.

"The fella who starts today has a better chance to be a real good player than I did. The facts are all laid out for him. All you have to do is read and apply what you read through hard work. I had to dig it out for myself. It took me from age 12 to age 35, trying things, proving and disproving." Hogan paused and studied his clasped, permanently calloused hands, then said, "But maybe that made me a better player, a better competitor. Most of the enjoyment in life is

in improving. If I didn't think I could improve right now, why
. . ." He shook his head sideways and stopped, appalled.

Does Hogan expect the emergence of another great player, a man
whose name will stand out in brilliant relief from the rest? "I think
all sports have to have leaders. Golf is getting away from that a
little bit with this multitude of good players. But I suppose it'll
happen. One leader, with half the crowds coming to see him win
and half to see him get beat. It's hard to find that type person." A
pause. "He'll have to be an awful dedicated man."

I asked Hogan which of his 60-some victories, including nine of
the modern major championships, an unequaled three in the same
year (1953), means the most to him. The 1950 United States Open
at Merion was his answer, because there he proved to himself, in a
tense, wearing, 36-hole final only a year after that horrendous car-
bus accident, that he could be the best in spite of his injuries.

The past and the present were joined this spring when Hogan,
away from tournament golf for nearly three years, his last victory 11
years ago, played back-to-back tournaments, and made them quite
special. Each time he walked slowly onto a green with that rolling,
purposeful stride, his younger playing partners often lagging re-
spectfully behind, he was met with an ovation, an ovation very
different from the usual. There was none of the raucous shouting
that welcomes Arnold Palmer. This was loud, prolonged, sincere
applause with an added depth. Bearing himself with customary
dignity, Hogan nonetheless was moved. He frequently tipped the
white cap he special-orders by the dozen. "I'm very grateful," he
said in the locker room after one round. "These people are just
wonderful, and I wish there was some way I could thank them."

He was, of course, thanking them merely by his presence. His
huge galleries were heavily peopled with fathers in their forties and
fifties who had brought youthful sons to see a man who was the best
at his profession, who elevated it to the level of aesthetics. But there
were, not entirely expectedly, thousands of teen-agers on their own
and young couples in their twenties. Yes, there were even a few
dozen hippie types, protesting nothing except that it was damned
difficult to get a look at Hogan.

Bob Goalby counted 31 of his fellow pros following Hogan on a
hot afternoon in Houston, and said they were impressed. The
deeply tanned Hogan's swing appeared superb. His putting stroke,
once a shambles, was smoother. His yogic concentration, a striking
amalgam of intensity and composure that suggests utter transcen-

dence, seemed not to have been impaired by the long layoff; Herb Wind's description of Hogan competing "with the burning frigidity of dry ice" came to mind.

Always his own severest critic, Hogan knew better. He devoted months to modifying his swing in favor of his aching left knee, hurt in the automobile accident but no bother to him until the past couple of years. A tendon transplant last year fixed an ailing shoulder, but doctors were afraid to operate on his knee for what probably is torn cartilage, because he might not be able to walk. Hogan had been taking diathermy treatments three times a week and lifting weights on the edge of his bed at night and sleeping with heat pads. A dull pain always was present, and occasionally when he swung, a sharp pain would pierce the knee. "I wouldn't recommend that anybody swing the way I'm swinging," he said. "I used to go in on my left leg as much as anybody, or more. I've had to take the left leg out of the swing. I opened my stance and moved the ball back toward my right foot, and I lay back on my right leg. I used to play the ball up and go forward to catch it. If I played it up there now, I'd hit back of it every time. I still need a lot of work. I hit one heavy or thin occasionally."

Hogan looks to be putting on a count. It is "one-two-three-hit" from the time he positions the putter behind the ball to the time he initiates his stroke. Hogan says he is not. Speaking of the recent years when he would freeze over the ball, then jerk his stroke, he said: "It was so bad for a while there I didn't know whether I could get the putter back. I moved the ball way forward, and now the only thing I can do is take the putter back."

He gloomily assayed his concentration. "I knew I wasn't ready mentally. It would take six months of playing tournament. I would never expect to go through that process. Golf and tournament golf are as different as baseball and hockey. I can't describe the tournament feel you have to have. . . . Call it toughness."

Hogan always has said he would not compete unless he believed he could win. Possibly he has softened that stance. Why did he play at Champions and Colonial? "I don't know what in the world he is trying to prove," Byron Nelson had said. Claude Harmon said he didn't know if Ben was trying to inspire business for the Ben Hogan Company, but that Winged Foot, where Harmon is the head professional, is selling a lot of Hogan balls to guys who never bought them before.

Hogan says he expects a business residual from his tournament appearances, but that isn't why he played. "I couldn't play until I got better," he says. "Plus I was overweight, and this is a good way to lose it. I used to run in place a lot and exercise. I like to hunt, but had to quit. I was up to 175. Now I'm about 165. In the 1940's I weighed 130 to 135, then after my accident it was 145 to 150. I was curious—I wanted to see if I could walk for four days. I wanted to see if I could play some kinda decent golf hitting off my back foot. The fact it was the 25th anniversary of the Colonial had something to do with it. I've played a lot, but I've missed a lot of years. I missed three years in the service. I missed a year after the wreck. I missed two years because of my shoulder and two years because of my knee. Time's runnin' pretty short if I don't play now. I enjoy practicing and playing in tournaments. Besides, I haven't really done what I wanted to do."

What is that? someone asked.

"I haven't won enough tournaments."

Hogan's tournament plans in June were indefinite. His knee is no worse. His legs, sore through and through for a week after the Colonial, feel better.

Do the doctors give him clearance to play?

"No, I tell myself when I'm ready."

He wants to play more tournament golf, but not in successive weeks. "That's just too much for me," he says. "I was much more tired in the Colonial. . . . I'll have to practice shots around the green. I didn't have time for that before. It's just ridiculous to enter a tournament if you can't hit every shot you have to hit. If I can find a tough, flat course where there's a tournament, I'll go play. Unfortunately there aren't many like that. I'd love to play the Masters, but I can't. If the course isn't flat there's too much pressure on my legs. When I get an uphill, downhill or sidehill lie, I can't hit the ball right. I have no plans to play anyplace at the moment, but I'm not ruling it out."

During the Colonial, a newspaper reporter asked Hogan if he intends to enter any senior tournaments, being over 55 and eligible.

Hogan, the mellowed Hogan, skewered the man with a disbelieving glare. For a long time he said nothing, debating, probably, whether to dignify the question with an answer.

Then he said, not coldly but making himself very clear, "Not until I'm a senior."

FORE PLAY

By William Murray

From Playboy

Copyright, ©, 1970, by William Murray

Chi Chi Rodriguez is a small, compactly built man with an un-smiling face, copper colored from the suns of a thousand golf courses, and he doesn't believe in wasting time. Looking very trim and natty, a small-brimmed white Panama planted like a muffin on his brow, he addresses the ball, brings the club back behind his shoulder in one long, beautifully vicious sweep and whacks the ball on a low, rising line over the uphill fairway of the 10th hole at Indian Wells. Somebody whoops and a couple of hundred other fans crowding around the tee applaud appreciatively. Chi Chi turns to the crowd and says, "I was born poor and here I am, on my first hole, a rich man." The crowd laughs.

The time is 8:28 A.M. on a Wednesday morning in February; and from the first and 10th tees of four different golf courses in Palm Springs, California, many of the best pro golfers in the world are setting out in pursuit of $125,000 in prizes. Chi Chi Rodriguez, as usual, is leading the way. Other guys may outshoot him but nobody outhustles him, and only Lee Trevino can talk in the same league with him. Chi Chi is a very funny man. Here in Palm Springs, during the five-day Bob Hope Desert Classic, one of the major tournaments on the winter tour, a sense of humor is vital.

From a spectator's viewpoint, the place to be at the start of this tournament is somewhere along the back nine at Indian Wells. This is because the pro-am teams scheduled to tee off after Rodriguez include Arnold Palmer, Lee Trevino, Ray Floyd, Julius Boros, Dave Hill, George Archer, Doug Sanders and Billy Casper. And playing with them are Ray Bolger, Lawrence Welk, Hank Stram, Chuck Connors and Danny Thomas, celebrities sprinkled among the horde of eager amateurs indulging themselves in what has become one of their favorite vanities: trying to match strokes with the pros.

The Bob Hope Classic is, in that sense, an idiot's delight. Instead of disappearing after the first day and leaving the serious golf to the professionals, as in most other pro-am tournaments, here the amateurs linger on for four full days. Playing in teams of three, they get to trade shots with a different pro each day, in a 72-hole best-ball contest. Not until the final day, Sunday, do the low-70 pros get to play solely against one another for the prizes that are awarded on the basis of 90 holes. The Hope is a circuslike marathon calculated to put almost unbearable pressure on even cool ones like Billy Casper.

Last February, 544 contestants were on hand, the amateurs all dressed up in the little outfits their wives had bought them; they spent a lot of time that first morning getting their pictures taken with their arms around each other and their pro partners. But then, as Palmer himself said at the end of that first day of the tournament, "It's simply a matter of taking a liberal attitude." "This tournament is unique, that's for sure," says Casper. "But if it weren't for the amateurs, the pros wouldn't be here." A good point. Who else would have put up the prize money and made it possible for this show to contribute well over $1 million to charity during the first 10 years of its existence? The amateurs each coughed up 500 bills to get themselves immortalized standing next to Palmer or Casper, and they obviously think it's worth it; there's smiling and backslapping all over the place. "I love this," says one amateur. "You get to wear all your bright new clothes and you get all these bets going. At night, you get drunk. And the broads! It's a wild turmoil, really fun!"

Just how much fun the pros have is another matter. It takes intense concentration and dedication to win the usual four-day tournament under normal playing conditions, but the Hope lasts five days and is anything but normal. "For one thing, playing on four different courses, you don't get a chance to look at terrain, to get the feel of it," one pro says. "And how can you concentrate for more than four days on your putting without coming down with a bad case of the yips?" In some ways, the Hope is the toughest tournament in which a pro can play. The proof of it is that some of them won't. Quite a few of the famous names were missing this year—Nicklaus, Beard, Player—but then, no pro can play in more than about 30 tournaments a season and expect to keep his game up. High-stakes golf is a sport of frustration, agony, crisis and pressure. But first prize in the Desert Classic this year is $25,000 and a Chrysler Imperial, so you'd have to mind the circumstances a lot to stay away.

Arnold Palmer doesn't mind anything. On the first day of the tournament, he strolls onto the tee to the loudest applause of the day. He has just been voted Athlete of the Decade in a nationwide poll of sports writers and broadcasters, so why should anything bother him? He is 40 now, his hair is thinning noticeably and his powerful arms and shoulders can't entirely disguise the beginnings of a paunch. Back in 1960, when he won the U.S. Open, the golf tour was a $2 million enterprise. Last year, when, after a prolonged slump, he came back to win two major tournaments back to back as the decade ended, the tour had become a $7 million affair, and it was mostly his doing. "We all owe our big paychecks to Arnie—he's made the game what it is," Gary Player has said, and he's right. For sheer charisma, no other golfer even comes close to Palmer, who has already magnetized the vanguard of his famous army around the tee. He clouts a prodigious drive and somebody behind me, applauding wildly, squeals, "He really kissed that shot good-bye!" Arnie's Army rushes off down both sides of the fairway, hurrying ahead to secure the best viewing points. They seem oblivious to the fact that one of Arnie's partners this morning is Lawrence Welk, a symphony in yellow, who hits his shots with awkward, palsied grace, his right thumb twitching wildly over the grip of his club.

Lee Elder, one of the handful of black pros playing on the tour, is next, but he is delayed by an elderly couple casually crossing the fairway ahead of him. Elder and the other blacks have never been invited to play in the Masters at Augusta, Georgia. (This year, Pete Brown, another black who played at the Hope, was excluded from the Masters' invitation list, despite the fact that his earnings for the year were high enough to make the oversight rather obvious.) Elder finally shoots, and one of his amateur partners hooks wildly into what Lee Trevino, up next, calls Marlboro Country.

After Palmer, the big noise with the fans is Lee Trevino, the super-Mex. His army calls itself Lee's Fleas, and its members spend a lot of time laughing at their man's jokes. Trevino, a good-looking, moon-faced Mexican-American from Texas, is full of light banter. But when it's time to tee off, the jokes stop, and under his white golf cap, Trevino's face turns as intensely grim as a carving of an

Aztec god. The ball soars into the air, losing itself against the light-gray sky, and Trevino observes, "I sobered up fast, didn't I? I need the money."

Jimmy Picard, an unsung pro, hooks his first shot way out into the trees; his amateur partners all slice, and somebody in the crowd says they won't be seeing one another for 20 minutes. Other unknown foursomes come and go now, and the chatter around the tee becomes oblique: "I'm not going to take my trousers to London just to get the zippers fixed," an old duffer in a green-visored helmet confides to an equally ancient buddy with a purple nose. You can't help but be struck by how old so many of the people in this crowd are. Palm Springs is full of retired people vegetating elegantly in large, ranch-style houses with pools and cool, green lawns.

Now the names are back: Ray Floyd, a big man with a round, cherubic face and curly hair—a swinger with the ladies; George Archer, tall and thin—a concentrated, deadly putter; Julius Boros, a heavily built, kindly-looking man in his fifties—his big years behind him, but still a tough competitor; Doug Sanders, boyishly handsome, happy-go-lucky—a former winner of the Hope who hasn't been playing well for months, but still with a graceful feathery-looking swing; Billy Casper, the method man, supposedly unflappable, precise, calculating, unexciting to watch—but perhaps the second-best golfer in the world today. They are announced, applauded, step up, tee off and march away, trailing in their wake, like scurrying beetles, the amateurs in their golf carts, fanning out right and left in search of errant balls. The pros, you notice, always walk.

Dave Hill has had the poor luck to draw Danny Thomas for a partner. Thomas is a clown and doesn't know when to quit. "Ladies and gentlemen, the most beautiful golfer in the world," he announced himself and proceeds to swat an orange into smithereens. You wonder how Dave Hill will put up with him, if at all. Hill, who looks like a recent high-school dropout, has a famous temper. Once, during a tournament, he put a club behind his neck and bent it double. Bad, though not quite as bad as Tommy Bolt, who once threw all of his clubs—along with his caddie—into a water trap.

The first day remains determinedly cold and gray. I wander from hole to hole at Indian Wells. Chi Chi Rodriguez is deadly with his irons but can't putt; Ray Floyd must have been partying, because he can't find any part of his game; Palmer blows hot and cold and has drawn an amateur named Tom Jones, a boyish-looking Navy pilot who can drive the ball just as far as Arnie can; Trevino's putts are rimming, but with a little luck he could win it all; Boros is so steady he's sure to pick up a sizable chunk of the money; and Casper is just a little off. The clearest image I retain is that of Palmer, trying for a birdie on the eighth, watching his drive carom off a tree to the left of the fairway and bounce back on and ahead toward the green. He takes advantage of his luck, chooses to pitch and run to within three feet of the pin and, sure enough, birdies the par-4 hole. He ends the day with a 68, one stroke back of the five leaders.

It has been a quiet, pleasant day, full of color and golf—good and bad. All four courses are within a few miles of one another, but the crowd has concentrated itself at Indian Wells. Some people have gone to Eldorado to watch Donald O'Connor and Glen Campbell cut up; and at La Quinta, golfers like Ken Venturi, Gene Littler and Gay Brewer have drawn small, personal galleries. At Bermuda Dunes, where most of the rabbits (young winless pros) are playing, the outlying holes are deserted except for the players. "Of course, there's an A and a B list," a pro tells me off the record, "and that holds true for the amateurs, too. The celebrities and big wheels get to play with the A's; the rabbits draw Joe Blow from Kokomo and nobody sees or hears them right from the start." I find myself beginning to root a little for the rabbits, and the first day's results, posted in the press tent at La Quinta, the host course, are heartening. Somebody named Labron Harris and somebody else named Charles Coody have shot 67's at La Quinta and Eldorado, respectively, to share the lead with Larry Ziegler, Bruce Devlin and Bob Rosburg; and Rod Funseth, Bobby Greenwood, Wayne Vollmer, Mike Reasor, Don Bies, Bill Johnston and Dave Eichelberger are all right up there. Will we ever hear their names again during these five days?

Palm Springs bills itself as the winter golf capital of the world, with a couple of dozen courses already in action and others being built. From the air, they look like rambling green lakes scattered about in a wasteland of white dunes and vast housing tracts peppered with bright-blue swimming pools. At night, in the center of town, a few passersby cluster about a huge scoreboard carrying the day's tournament results. The big weekend crowds have yet to arrive.

There's plenty of off-the-course action, however, even now. Restaurants like Jilly's and Ruby Dunes and night spots like the Howard Manor and Ethel's Hideaway are bulging with celebrants, and private parties are being thrown everywhere. The amateurs come to these functions, but most of the pros are safely home in bed, tucked in long before midnight, either as guests in private homes or in one of the dozens of motels that line the highway. Some of the pros will be seen partying later in the week, especially after it has become clear who will make the cut and who won't. Until then, everyone is concentrating on the money. Especially the rabbits, who, year after year, never haul down a big paycheck but hope at least to survive till the last day and pick up a small piece of the money—enough to pay their motel bills and put gas into the car for the long drive to the next tournament on the tour. The rabbits are also called trunk slammers by the more successful pros, because, after they fail to make the cut, you can see them walk out of the clubhouse to the parking lot, open up the backs of their cars, fling their clubs in and angrily slam the trunk lids down. It's not a good idea, by the way, to call a rabbit that to his face, unless you've developed a fondness for fat lips.

The A list on the second day is playing at Eldorado, the most beautiful of the tournament courses, cradled on three sides by the dark-brown, barren mountains that hem the desert in. At Eldorado, four of the holes—the fourth, ninth, 13th and 18th—finish against the clubhouse's terraces, and it's possible to catch a glimpse, at least, of almost every foursome in action without having to do much walking. Even from there, I am struck, as I always am, by how little of any tournament you can actually see. The fact is that no one can claim ever to have seen a whole tournament; the best you can hope for is to pick your spots, to watch a series of golfers play one particular hole or to follow one golfer through several holes. The faithful year-round members of Arnie's Army never watch anyone but him, which means that they see nothing of a tournament but what their man does in it. A curious way to follow a sport, not unlike watching a one-horse race.

On the second day, the pressure begins to tell. Dave Hill, looking even surlier than yesterday, is having another bad day on top of the one Danny Thomas handed him at Indian Wells—a 73. Ray Floyd, trying to get onto the green of the ninth in two, hooks his drive into the water and spends a gloomy two minutes peering at the ball lying just under the surface. Appropriately, he is dressed entirely in black, while his caddie, a cheerful gnome, sports a pith helmet. Chi Chi Rodriguez hits a beautiful wood straight down to the dogleg of the fairway on the fifth, drops his club and applauds himself. "It couldn't happen to a nicer guy," he says. Later, while tramping after his ball and keeping up a constant, deadpan chatter with a covey of pretty golf groupies who are obviously delighted with him, he observes, "You know, I used to be the funny man of the tour, till Lee Trevino came along. Now you ladies ought to join Trevino's golf school. He'll start you with the irons and work you right into the woods." Lots of laughs, but by the end of the day, Chi Chi will be spouting fewer funny lines. After missing another in a series of short putts, he mutters, "I play golf like a gorilla." What is it the pros say? The man who putts wins.

Trevino is having a fine day, but his luck is still out. On the par-4 11th, for example, he hits a tremendous drive that cuts the corner of the sharp dogleg right and sets himself up for a birdie, but he finds that the ball has rolled into a deep divot. "I don't mind," he tells his Fleas. "I used to mind, but I don't anymore." After hitting his iron beyond the green, he explains how, when Palmer overhits, someone in his army will stop the ball with his chest. "When I do it," Trevino says, "my Fleas shout 'Ole!' and flag it through." But he's playing well today and has confidence in himself. He comes in with a 67 and somebody tells him what Chi Chi's been saying about him. "That little Puerto Rican can walk on water," Trevino says, grinning.

Palmer isn't having a good day. His army has grown noticeably and flows along both sides of the fairway ahead of him like a pair of huge, multicolored snakes. Arnie talks to himself on the tee, urges himself to "find the hole." His drives do just that, but his putting is off, and I remember seeing him early that morning, practicing four-foot putts and missing some of them. He's still missing them, long and short, and he says—after coming in with a 71—"My putter has blood on it."

Most of the crowd at Eldorado remains clustered around the clubhouse, and the knowledgeable types keep an eye on the 18th, a 511-yard par 5 whose green is protected by water on the west side. The choice is to go for it in two and risk a dunking or lay up short and take no chances. A lot of blood flows very freely around that green, but not when Doug Sanders shows up. He had a 75 opening day and is doing no better today, but you get the impression he doesn't care. He has a cigarette dangling from his lips and he's dressed all in lavender. He looks, Trevino tells him, like a frozen daiquiri. Someone to my right says the man obviously plays golf just to show off his clothes. There are a lot of girls following his four-some, and it isn't because Danny Thomas is in it. Thomas is up to his usual stunts, screaming for his momma, and he putts with a trick club bent cutely out of shape.

By the end of the second day, most of the rabbits have disappeared. I find out that Larry Ziegler has blazed around Indian Wells in 65 and taken a three-shot lead, with Bruce Devlin shadowing him. Moon Mullins, a local pro in his second year as the resident at Indian Wells, is two strokes back of Devlin. Of the A-list players, only Trevino is within quick striking distance, five strokes back, and I begin to get the idea that maybe the A-list players, forced to compete in a near-carnival atmosphere, are not going to make NBC happy on Saturday, the day before all the leaders come together in front of the cameras.

If you don't care much about golf, the peripheral action is worth catching—toward the end of the afternoon in the clubhouse at Indian Wells. I discover this after having tried both the Eldorado and the Bermuda Dunes, where a couple of small dance combos begin Welking sprightly fox-trots around 5:30. Here, the average age of the guests is 110 and the lindy is considered a daring innovation. At Indian Wells, however, the scene is pure carnage. Murray Arnold, a bandleader from Las Vegas, has set up shop in the main clubroom, long tables have been jammed together from wall to wall, the bartenders pour whiskey into glasses as if it were iced tea and everyone with a little nonsense in his soul—maybe a couple of thousand people—has swarmed into the joint. Never have I seen so many available girls of all ages, from teenyboppers with bare midriffs and bell-bottoms to swinging grannies in minis. Nobody knows how they've gotten there or where they acquired the passes to get in, but security, thank God, is lax. The adorables are sprinkled along the bar, lined up against the walls, packed together into booths and clustered chirpingly around the tables, and, naturally, there are a lot of Don Juans hustling them. The last thing anybody wants to talk about is golf.

The first familiar face I see, however, belongs to Arnold Palmer. Looking slightly bemused, baton in hand, he is leading the band through a medley from *Hair*. Later, Donald O'Connor takes the floor to do a little mugging and some improvisational dance steps with a variety of volunteers from the audience. Alice Faye (yes, friends, Alice Faye!), looking half her age in form-fitting slacks, has a few songs to sing and some jokes to crack. Other *espontaneos* come and go and, in between, everyone dances, frugging and jerking in a dense, bobbing mass awash in enough noise to drown out a battery of cement mixers.

I get into conversation with a trim little blonde who, it turns out, is a year-round resident. It so happens she has rented her house for two months and is currently living in her car, and where am I staying? she wants to know. A couple of lovelies in see-through frills tell me that they are secretaries and part-time models and they have a slightly blue look around their eyes, because, they confess, they haven't been to bed—to sleep, at least—since the tournament began. I rescue a miniskirted number from a rickety chair she has been standing on to watch the proceedings, and it turns out she is a child psychologist from Long Beach. Her friend, a pixie with a mop of curls and a tiny waist, is a piano teacher from Redondo who's just dying to dance.

One of the lady officials, a handsome redhead in white slacks and blue blazer, laughs at everything I say and tells me, apropos of nothing at all, that she has no dinner plans. A tall, beautiful blonde with sleepless red eyes informs me that she's a television producer from Los Angeles who showed up to follow the fortunes of her favorite rabbit, who, it runs out, has played so badly on his first three rounds that he's already slammed his trunk lid and departed for Tucson to warm up for his next try. In other words, the lady has been stranded and hasn't been able to find a room, but she thinks she can bunk with some pals at the Racquet Club, unless, she says with a smile, I have some other suggestion. The evening becomes a long, bubbly, pink blur of laughs, drinks, music, camaraderie and other pleasures. I can't remember now exactly where our large, unwieldy group of celebrants went, though I do recall other places, other bars, other dance floors and the sunken living room of some oil billionaire's pad out of which we spilled, shrieking like banshees, into the dawn.

There is one other major form of extracurricular activity associated with golf tournaments, and that is gambling—though nobody likes to talk much about it. The pros don't bet—not in tournaments, anyway—but nearly all of the amateurs, as well as most of the spectators, do; and the bets range from a friendly dollar or two to well up in the thousands. The bettors can play parlay cards or bid for a favorite pro in a Calcutta-type pool; but to get in on the big action, you have to have the right underground connections, since, needless to say, betting is not legal and the transfer of large amounts of cash from one pair of hands to another has been known to arouse the curiosity of the Internal Revenue Service. Yet every clubhouse during these major tournaments seems to have its quota of hard-eyed speculators, most of whom look distinctly out of place in the sunshine.

Nor is golf itself the only form of gambling that goes on every day at tournaments and in country clubs. Backgammon and gin rummy are extremely popular. "There's more money won and lost after golf than during," an expert once confided. "You can blow a grand on the course and win five times that amount back in the clubhouse." The pros, however, when they do gamble, stick pretty much to golf, where they know what they're doing and what the traffic will bear. "When I play a guy for $50 or $100," one of them has said, "I'll let the bum hold his own. After a while, of course, he'll want to raise the ante. Usually, he'll find he can't make a shot." Lee Trevino was once asked during a tournament if he minded the pressure, and he is reported to have answered that no one knows anything about pressure who hasn't come up, as he has, from the hustling world of municipal golf courses, where you can find yourself having to sink a 20-foot putt to win $100 and don't have enough money in your jeans to pay off if you don't make it. That, my friends, is pressure.

The mob at La Quinta on Saturday morning is huge, and a lot of the people crowded around the tees and greens have rented little stands that look like inverted wastebaskets, so that they can see over the heads of the early arrivals in the front rows. It's hard to believe that this crowd has come to see the golf, because, of the A-list players, only Trevino and Casper are still in contention, and they are six and seven strokes back, respectively. The leaders continue to be Larry Ziegler and Bruce Devlin, with three strokes separating them, and you would think that the real fans would get over to Bermuda Dunes to watch them play. Arnold Palmer is nine strokes off the pace, but maybe his army expects him to make another of his spectacular late charges—though, of course, it won't desert him even if he doesn't.

Temporary stands have been set up around the greens of the ninth and 18th holes, and already some viewers, armed with picnic baskets, Thermos bottles and six-packs of beer, are encamped there to wait out the long day. Nearly everybody else, however, is surging around the first tee, where the big celebrities and the game's glamorous figures are scheduled to show up. When I get there, Ray Bolger, who is playing in Boros' foursome, is cutting up. After executing a series of little dance steps, he whirls on Boros and waves a club at him. "I'm not going to play with him," Bolger quips. "He cheats." The people love it. They laugh, applaud, banter with the celebrities. Chuck Connors, looking like an emaciated King Kong, is another favorite. "How about a hand?" he exhorts the crowd and gets it. But through all the clowning, there is an undercurrent of anticipation, of excitement, a feeling of something spectacular about to happen. The place is jammed with photographers and reporters, officials in blue blazers, pretty girls in light-blue mini-skirts, dignitaries with big round badges stuck on their lapels, and, overhead, from a tower platform, television cameras are focused on the scene.

Everyone is waiting for Doug Sanders' foursome, which today will include Vice-President Agnew, Senator George Murphy and Mr. America himself, Bob Hope. Agnew's arrival is greeted with a big hand. I glance at the faces around me, which look as if they've been posed for Kodak commercials, and I understand why golf is the silent majority's favorite game—no effete snobs nor supercilious sophisticates here. Sanders, ablaze in orange today, greets the V.P. and tells him he's looking forward to the match, then introduces him to his wife, a perky little brunette. "I'm looking forward to it with great trepidation," says Agnew, who admits he doesn't get to play golf more than once a month. Senator Murphy, a little gray man in a little gray golfing outfit, is hustled up to be posed for the cameras with Sanders and the V.P. A Boy Scout festooned with merit badges is tossed in. Bob Hope, driving a custom-built golf cart hand-sculpted to reproduce his famous profile, suddenly arrives and upstages everybody. A Miss Lorraine Zabowski, one of three so-called Bob Hope Classic Girls whose job it is to wander around in nearly nothing, is now propped up beside the V.P. as cameras click. Miss Zabowski has a round, innocent face, a great cascade of blonde hair and she confesses, blushing prettily, that she'd never even seen a golf club before.

Agnew's trepidation, it turns out, isn't misplaced. The V.P. hooks his drive into the crowd lining the fairway just as an admirer shouts, "You're the greatest!" Murphy slices and Hope ding-a-lings one practically straight up in the air. Agnew's second shot is mildly historic. It's the one that hit Doug Sanders on the head, drawing blood. Who's going to follow this act? I wonder.

Arnold Palmer, that's who. It turns out that the crowd cares less for celebrities and politicians than for the Athlete of the Decade.

Arnie's appearance on the tee brings a full-throated roar and a five-minute ovation. Watching him standing there, waving and smiling and nodding, you understand how he succeeded in making golf as popular as it is; clearly, he is to his sport what Babe Ruth, Johnny Unitas, Bill Russell and Bobby Hull have been to theirs, only more so. Other golfers may now outshoot him—a Casper or a Nicklaus—but no one outranks him. With his go-for-broke style, with that reckless, lunging grace that hammers golf balls into the blue and batters courses into submission, Palmer is it—the man himself.

But following the play at La Quinta today is impossible. Fifteen thousand people are swarming all over the course. The sun is bright and hot and so many fans have brought cameras that the clicking of shutters succeeds in destroying even the normally supercool Casper's game; eight times he is interrupted in midswing and, finally, he drops out of contention with a 74. And play is so slow that Palmer, who comes in with a more than respectable 69, says wearily, "I felt like I was born and raised on that course today." The final day, when the low-70 pros will compete only against one another, promises to be even more of a serious-viewer's nightmare.

The real drama of the day is taking place at Bermuda Dunes, the most remote of the four courses, with broad, gently rolling fairways set down smack in a lunar wilderness of sand dunes and rock formations. When I get there, Ziegler, who started off early that morning from the 10th tee, is just coming in on his last few holes—the seventh, a tough three; the eighth, a 540-yard par 5 with four traps around the green; and the ninth, a 390-yard par 4 that will yield a birdie to anyone who can really blast his drive. The gallery, I'm amazed to discover, consists of about 50 people, true aficionados all.

Ziegler is a big, blond 30-year-old from St. Louis, who looks like an elongated Mickey Mantle and hits monster drives. So far, he has also been putting well; but now, as the fourth day draws to a close, he shows signs of faltering, especially on the greens. He comes in with a 71, and I find myself wondering how he'll respond to the pressure of the final day at La Quinta. Ziegler won $59,000 on the tour last year, but he has yet to nail down any one of the major tournaments.

Seven or eight holes behind him, Bruce Devlin, playing to an even smaller gallery, turns out to be a cool customer. A tall, slender, ruddy-faced Australian, he plays a slow, deliberate, carefully studied game. He spends a lot of time replacing divots, patting the greens into shape and, all concentration, he stays well apart from his amateur companions. He misses a long putt on the par-4 third and mutters, "If I want to make money, I'll make one of those." But he goes on to bogey the fourth by failing to sink another putt, a three-footer this time. Yet not much seems to rattle him. With three birdies, he picks up a stroke on Ziegler, and you get the feeling the pressure won't bother him as much as it will the American, who, after all, has had to set the pace for two full days now. At the end of the afternoon, in the comparative stillness of the Bermuda Dunes locker room, Devlin says calmly that he'd gladly settle for a 67 the last day and take his chances. You get the feeling he doesn't believe Ziegler can recapture his Friday form, when he climaxed a great round by eagling the par-5 13th at Eldorado, reaching the green with a driver and a three-wood and then sinking a 50-foot putt. Devlin is clearly playing tortoise to Ziegler's hare.

The last day, the crowd numbers roughly 15,000, and Devlin's chase after Ziegler provides the excitement. Devlin, with three birdies on the front nine, catches Ziegler at the turn, and then picks up another birdie on the 15th, a good par-3 hole. Then, on the 16th, he wins all the marbles by dropping a 35-foot putt for still another birdie. "I thought we were tied," he explained later, "and I decided to go for broke." I don't think anyone realized until later what a fantastic round of golf the Australian had shot—a six-under-par 66 on the toughest of the tournament courses. He wins by four strokes, with an astonishing total of 339, 21 under par and only one stroke away from Palmer's tournament record.

I have two vivid impressions of the award ceremony. The first is of Arnold Palmer, hands on hips and grinning at Devlin, barking into the television cameras, "Just how in the hell did you do it, Bruce?" The man still is and always will be the champion as long as he's around. The second impression is of Ziegler standing off by himself and staring for a moment at his check for second place, estimating, perhaps, the difference between this and first place, symbolized by the $10,000 less he is receiving for being runner-up.

Agnew is also there, as are the celebrities and the girls, but it's all over now. Long shadows are falling across the fairways, and the stands, littered with refuse, are quickly emptying. Bits of paper blow over the greens, and, in the distance, a long line of cars is crawling slowly out toward the highway. From the clubhouse comes the thump-thump of the dance band playing and, over it, the laughter. In the press tent, a few typewriters are still banging and the NBC technicians are clambering down from their tower like arthritic monkeys. Behind the clubhouse, the caddies are packing up their gear; and from the parking lot you can hear the trunk lids coming down. It's a long drive to Tucson.

I remember Lee Trevino, who tied for fourth, watching his putts rim that first day and whirling to tell his Fleas, "I'm going to become a Mormon, because I ain't sinking any putts as a Catholic!" But where are all the jokes for those who don't come in as high as fourth or even fortieth?

On my way out, I catch up with Chi Chi Rodriguez, still as natty and imperturbable as ever, despite his finish somewhere toward the middle of the pack. "What do I like about all this besides the money?" he asks. He waves a hand around at the empty greens and endlessly rolling fairways, at the trees and the mountains and the sky. "This is my office," he says, "and I love my office."

Boxing

THOSE THREE TERRIBLE LEFT HOOKS

By Bill Lee

From The Hartford Courant

Reprinted by permission

Three terrible left hooks in stunning succession gave Muhammad Ali a 15th-round knockout over tough Oscar Bonavena Monday night after 14 rounds of ineffective brawling in which the crowding South American rubbed a lot of the gloss off Ali's self-declared position as the genius of all fistiana.

The end came at 2:03 of the 15th and final round. Any fight is over when a man has been floored three times in the same round, but the ringman who came into boxing as Cassius Clay didn't need any technical help in winning a fight he might well have won on points even if he hadn't belted Bonavena into a helpless stupor with the three devastating lefts, each of which scored a knockdown in one of the wildest finishes to a bout that, nevertheless, has to record as one of the poorest fights between ranking heavyweights the division has known.

Clay couldn't float like a butterfly and didn't sting like more than an undernourished bee until he unloaded the three sticks of dynamite on Bonavena's chin in the last session.

The unfrocked former world heavyweight champion might have torn Bonavena apart with a right near the finish. He flouted all the knockdown rules of the New York State Athletic Commission by following the reeling Argentine around the ring, standing close enough to destroy his stubborn foe while referee Mark Conn was tolling the counts. Twice Bonavena went down for eight counts. When he was rocked to the canvas a third time, there was no need for any counting.

Clay, in this ringsider's view, fought his worst fight ever but still had it won in rounds seven, three and four even for the 14 dreary rounds that were completed. In the end, the man they said could box but not punch had become the first fighter ever to stop Bonavena. All the rest was academic.

Bonavena came down the stretch when Clay tired after piling up an almost insurmountable lead. The South American's aggression had him winning or tying all but one of the last six rounds through the 14th, but in the final analysis, Bonavena had firepower only in his heart. Clay was the sharper and heavier puncher despite a dreary performance that was bailed right out of the barrel by Clay's sensational finish.

There were times when it looked like Amateur Night at Foot Guard Hall. Neither man could fight up to his reputation. The crowd booed and sang derisively. They turned on Clay with catcalls and derisive shouts and began blowing up a storm of rooting for Bonavena, the man who came through the ropes with the name "Ringo" stenciled on his robe.

There is no telling what the reaction might have been had the fight gone the limit and Clay been handed the decision by a clear margin. All three officials scored for the bragging Louisville fighter, who was racking his 30th straight ring victory.

Referee Mark Conn made it 12–2 for Clay, the biggest of all. Judge Joe Eppy scored the fight 10–3–1 for Ali, and judge Jack Gordon tabbed it 8–5–1 for the eventual knockout victor. Eppy gave Bonavena only the fourth, eighth and 10th and ruled round 13 even. Gordon saw the South American taking only the fourth, fifth and eighth and called the 13th even. Referee Conn gave Bonavena only the fifth and ninth rounds.

All this official viewing was not nearly as decisive as Clay was in taking his man apart at the seams in the final session.

A near sellout crowd of 19,417 that made up a whopping gross gate of $615,401 sat in amazement as Clay floundered through a major portion of the fight.

There were times when Clay sent stabbing left jabs, right crosses and left hooks thudding against Bonavena's jaw, but more often he missed and wilted under the persistent, wild charges of the gallant South American. Bonavena started some punches from the third row of the ringside press section and never really hurt the flustered Clay. The old champion's feelings may have been hurting more than his jaw and ribs.

Never was Clay able to float smoothly on the wide perimeter that has made him a target almost impossible to reach. As early as the third round, the man who calls himself the greatest appeared either tired or playing possum in a bid to draw the charging Argentine into a trap.

As round after round went by with Clay piling up impressive points but never coming close to landing the punches it would take to stop Bonavena's bull-like assaults, it was evident that Clay was trying his best and doing the worst he has done since winning the heavyweight championship.

Three and a half years ago, after Muhammad had refused to accept military service, boxing commissions deprived him of his heavyweight championship. He had not fought since, except less than three heats against Jerry Quarry six weeks ago. It became crystal clear last night that Clay has not come back all the way or even half the way.

The dreadful performance of the unbeaten former heavyweight champion left all hands with the conviction that he would not have survived had Joe Frazier been his opponent last night instead of Oscar Bonavena, whose record is now 45–6–1, with the first knockout defeat of his life finally in his ring record.

Clay was trying to prove last night that he would be ready to meet Frazier in February, if the impending judgment of the United States Supreme Court allows Ali to continue his ring career instead of possibly starting a five-year prison sentence.

Despite the jumpy counts started by knockdown timekeeper Zack Clayton, on obvious slips and wrestling maneuvers by which Muhammad put his opponent on the canvas, there was nothing like a knockdown until Clay suddenly found the power to destroy the rugged but easy-to-hit man from Buenos Aires.

At 212 pounds against Bonavena's 204, Clay put his four inches of height advantage and his reach superiority of six and one half inches to good use without ever reminding his fondest rooters of the Clay they knew prior to his long suspension.

For both men, it was a debut in the new Madison Square Garden and Clay's first New York appearance since March 22, 1967, when he starched Zorra Folley in seven. Clay has not been inside the ropes since that fight save for the abbreviated bout with Quarry.

The astonishing and disappointing match was telecast around the world except in the United States and beamed on closed-circuit outlets to 175 outlets in this country, including Hartford and Springfield.

Clay was given roof-raising cheers for his tremendous finish after being booed lustily for his inconclusive efforts prior to the 15th.

The winner proved he could go 15 rounds under pressure if nothing else, and also that he may be able to punch harder than most think when he really cuts loose.

"Ringo," the granite man from Argentina, hung with the controversial Ali, alias Cassius Clay, right to the end, but a left-hand shot that rattled every bone in the South American's body finally turned the gallent heavyweight off for the night, and turned the screaming crowd on.

The gathering, which had roared delightedly at Ali's antics in the early going, when his every gesture was contemptuous toward his rival, cut it loose in the end, an end which they had come not to expect after the showing the Argentine put up over the first 14.

Ali advocates stomped, screamed, pounded each other on the back and mounted their wooden chairs, erected in the cavernous drill shed when Oscar went down once, twice, three times. The last crashing fall to the deck signaled the end of the fight, conducted under the three-knockdown rule.

It was as if a smashed and scattered hope had been magically resurrected, with one touch. It had, and the touch was not a light one.

The early crowd, which came to watch Johnny Duke's Boys Club battlers square off against counterparts from the Manchester Boys Club, grabbed the best vantage points on either side of the small 9 by 12 screen and in the balcony.

They saw the young fighters and then watched appreciatively as lightweight king Ken Buchanan of Scotland went the distance (10) with Canadian welterweight champion Donato Paduano, Buchanan's skill and speed proving too much for the Canadian, a native of Italy.

When Ali and Bonavena entered the ring, each received an ovation from the Broad Street customers. Ringo's was louder than expected, but short. Ali's was long and clear, interspersed with war cries and whistles.

When Ali scolded his man during the referee's instructions, the atmosphere took on its expected mood. The Louisville boxer who had made light work of Jerry Quarry six weeks ago, coming back from his three-and-a-half-year layoff, had promised to taunt the Argentine, punish him and then knock him out.

The taunting had begun. The roar that went up at the warning returned when Bonavena went down on a push and reverberated through the armory again when Ali went into his famous shuffle.

When Ali waved a scornful glove at his opponent at the second round's end, it set off the crowd again, for the ex-champion so far had been making the Argentine miss continuously, and caused him to appear an ungainly fighter indeed.

The armory audience loved it when Ali called Oscar to him repeatedly in the third round, made the bullish South American miss with wild swings time and again and snapped the shorter man's face with whiplike jabs.

But in the fourth, the scene changed. Bonavena threw a leaping roundhouse left at his tall foe and the crowd moaned in disbelief. The 6-foot-1 underdog appeared to have stunned the favorite. Ali appeared hurt again at the end of the fifth. The mood changed dramatically. There was no more shuffle, no more taunting and no more levity from the Louisville man.

At the armory, there was concern. The always well-behaved throng huddled in small knots between rounds now. The buzzing of their excited conversation filled the drill shed.

The fight progressed. Ali appeared to have the edge on the strength of his superior speed and agility, but Bonavena appeared fresher. Round nine, the round Ali had promised to chill Bonavena, came and went. So did round 11, the round in which Bonavena had promised to dispatch Ali.

Oscar's strength had made the audience feel that Ali would be forced to settle for a victory by decision, and a close decision at that.

. . . but he had a left-hand blockbuster left and he used it in No. 15. It drained the starch, every bit of it, out of the Argentine and sent the Hartford crowd into near hysteria at the armory. In the TV rerun, they relived it, and went home—most of them happy.

8-9-10 AND OUT

By Furman Bisher

From The Atlanta Journal

Copyright, ©, 1970, The Atlanta Journal

Stormy Winters died in Macon the other day, but the flags didn't fly at half-mast and the post office stayed open. The mayor didn't declare a day of mourning. Even the garbage trucks went on collecting garbage.

You had to look all over town to find anybody who really cared, and she was in jail. She was charged with the shooting.

It was all right for Stormy to beat up people in a prizefight ring. That was his game. But she wasn't going to take any more of it. That was the story—the drab, sordid, real-life story that you find under the fictional title of *Fat City*.

Fat City is the grimy, sweat-stained, seamy account of the prizefight life at its lowest level. Basement training quarters with exposed plumbing, plodding stiffs who try to make it in tank-town prelims, anything to have a dressing robe with their name stitched on the back. Any kind of booking for 40 bucks a night—before the manager's cut.

It was written by a young writer named Leonard Gardner out of California, and it may be as fine a novel of sport as I have ever read. One of its characters is a Stormy Winters, but only because there is a Stormy Winters in every town where boxing still survives, trying to make it out of the basement to Madison Square Garden. Or even the Miami Beach Auditorium.

This was where Stormy Winters made it, the Miami Beach Auditorium. He reached Miami on a bus from Georgia at three o'clock in the morning, and, as Edwin Pope tells it in his column in the *Miami Herald,* he arrived wearing blue jeans, a T-shirt and a "pair of round-toed farmer's shoes."

He wasn't "Stormy" yet. His name was Melvin Eugene. I think the fighting name of "Stormy" came from that industrious promoter of world renown, Chris Dundee. Chris liked his style and called him the meanest fighter he'd seen since Jake LaMotta.

Dundee had never seen Stormy until he got off that bus and came to the 5th Street Gym in Miami Beach. Stormy wanted to be a prizefight champion, and that was why he was in Miami, recommended by a former heavyweight who was a friend of the Dundees.

I stood in the 5th Street Gym with Dundee one day and watched the kid work out. He was still in the prelim stage, but his time was coming. The question, as it inevitably does, came up—why a kid from a small town wants to be a boxer.

"I asked him that," Dundee said, "and he gave me a classic answer.

"He said, 'Mr. Dundee, have you ever poured tar on a roof in Macon, Georgia, in the summertime?' "

Stormy was a roofer by trade, and back to the rooftops he had gone when the bullet caught up with him in Macon.

There was a time when it seemed he was on his way. He fought, Pope says, about 35 times. He lost only four, and when he won, it was almost always by a knockout, for Stormy was a man of dispatch when set loose in the ring.

Apparently, Stormy was somewhat less diligent between fights, giving off in his search for thrills and sensual pleasures the kind of dull, brown, alcoholic, morning-after odor of the debauchery of Billy Tully, the middleweight of *Fat City*.

Tully was a promising scrapper, a term lifted directly from the handbills. He was on his way, unquestionably to the top, when women intercepted him, followed in swift order by booze. The opening of *Fat City* finds him on his way to hell, downhill on a handcar. It's just a question of which upstairs dump of a hotel he'll find it in.

He works intermittently, long enough to keep in a supply of booze, in the walnut fields, and on the truck farms in northern California. Always in his mind is the plan—ultimately he will find the wife who divorced him, and his world will be glued back together again, and he will straighten out, and the ring lights will come on again, and they will be introducing, in this corner, Billy Tully, "worthy adversary going for the championship of the world."

But the plan is only a mental mirage. He is finally found sleeping in a trash burner in the end, broke, hungry, penniless, with only the clothes he has on his back. Victim of a vagrant dream, alive but not living.

Stormy Winters never hit such depths. He worked the fourth-rate hotel circuit. Worked in amusement arcades between fights, obviously denying himself little of life's lust.

His weight went from 130 to 150, and some of his condition went with it. Pope says that Stormy's dream blacked out the night he fought a junior middleweight named Art Hernandez in 1965. Stormy was 24-for-25 until that bout. That was his big one. The ring lights came up and there he stood in his robe—with his name stitched on the back—ready to revise the history of prizefighting.

Hernandez took him easily. Everything else after that was downgrade. Life in a print shop, a halfhearted attempt at a comeback, a few matches, but his heart wasn't in it, and, eventually, back to Macon, close to the farm where he grew up, and where his daddy had tried to scratch a few crops out of barren ground.

He was only 26 years old, too young for a kid to die. That's still young enough for dreams, and Stormy had one as he went out. He dreamed of being a country music singer. Some friends gave him a guitar last Christmas, but he never got around to lessons. He'd played that dream game before and lost.

Tennis

OH, PANCHO

By Gene Roswell

From the New York Post

There ought to be a law against Pancho Gonzales. If that doesn't work, they ought to try a riot or a tennis-in or something to stop him from further humiliating the youth of this nation.

The kids obviously knew the score when they said they couldn't trust a guy over 30. Pancho, a supposedly creaking 41-year-old, has made their generation look sick. Some creak. When Pancho bends, you hear the riffle of thousand-dollar bills.

First, Pancho did the impossible in tennis. He knocked off Rod Laver, the world champion and top money earner in 1969, in a five-set winner-take-all $10,000 match in the Garden last month.

Then he did the improbable. He knocked off John Newcombe in the same deal in Detroit, taking only three sets to do his thing. And now he's getting ready to give Roy Emerson similar treatment for a similar $10,000 prize in Miami Beach, February 15.

It's all part of the $200,000 Champions Classic Series in which the pros go at each other in a sort of challenge leader arrangement—in $10,000 chunks—until the loot is exhausted. The way it works, a winner keeps going until he is beaten. The way it looks, Pancho can go on forever.

The man is gaunt, almost thin in the arms and legs, his face taking on lines, the black hair streaked with gray. He is past his prime. He has no business on the same court with agile young men. His muscles stiffen. He tires. His beautiful strokes turn awkward at times. Long tournaments, grinding day-to-day play betray him.

But give him a little time to recuperate, space his matches and put important money on them, and Pancho responds. It has changed his image, made him a hero with the public, particularly with the middle-aged who need whatever triumphs they can obtain over the irreverent new generation.

The image disconcerts Pancho a bit. He isn't used to love from the crowds. He likes it but it leaves him weary.

"It's very helpful," he suggests, talking from his home in Malibu, anxious to get off the phone and clear his car from the driveway so his wife can drive out.

"It's so different now. Ten, 15 years ago when I was the champion, well, I was more or less the villain. Now they've changed horses and are on my side. I appreciate it, but at times I feel a little bit sorry for my opponents because I guess it has its effects on them.

"I know how it was when I played in Australia. It was the other way around then and I used to wonder how you get the crowd on your side. I suppose there's nothing special you can do. The crowd makes up its own mind.

"It goes for the underdog or the youngster coming up or the oldster on his way out. It could be any number of reasons. I never could figure it out. With me, it's probably the fact I can still struggle along with those young guys at my age. Probably, it's their way of showing they appreciate and respect me."

Probably. But it doesn't sell Pancho on the idea that it's a miracle for him to be winning money and matches against the Lavers, the Newcombes and all those powerful young racquet-swingers. Pancho always was a rebel, though.

"I don't consider it extraordinary to be playing [in such company] at my age," he says, "but most other people seem to think so. I can't speak for other people."

All Pancho can do is speak for himself. His explanation for his own tennis longevity is continued competition and condition.

No fairy godmother touching him with a magic wand. No Faustus deal with the devil in exchange for everlasting ability on the court. For Pancho it has been hard work.

"I play a lot of tennis," he says, "and run a bit. How much? A mile or two after I finish my tennis. Practice has no special pattern. I just play sets, usually with the kids from UCLA."

With time to recuperate from his rather quick win over Newcombe last Sunday, Pancho won't leave for Miami and the Emerson match until next Monday or Tuesday.

"I like to be there five or six days before a match," he says.

How far Pancho can carry his campaign in the Classic on pride, sputtering skills and aging legs remains to be seen. The remaining challengers include Tom Okker, Tony Roche, Ken Rosewall, Fred Stolle and Andres Gimeno.

Somewhere along the line he may stumble, although the suspicion now is that Pancho has it made. If so, he'll win 10 matches and $300,000, then go into the semi-finals and the final. Should he carry the Classic to a fitting conclusion, Pancho will pocket $147,500. Not bad for a 41-year-old tennis player, is it?

"I WIN WITH MY OVERALL GAME"

By Phil Elderkin

From The Christian Science Monitor

For years, whenever Australia's Rod Laver was part of a tennis tournament, it was like throwing a cork into the water. Laver, regardless of the competition, simply bobbed to the top and stayed there.

His earnings for the past two years, not counting endorsements, are somewhere in the neighborhood of a quarter of a million dollars.

Rod's two tennis Grand Slams, in which he won the championships of Australia, France, England and the United States in 1962 and again in '69, belong in the Louvre. The master's touch is all over them.

It was almost as though Rodney baled his opponents, like hay, and then left them in neat piles along the tennis circuit. If the top spin on his ground strokes could be bottled and sold, there would be no need for the further development of atomic energy. At one point in his career, Laver had a Wimbledon record streak of 31-straight match wins.

When he lost, which wasn't often, it was treated no more seriously than an 0–4 day at the plate for Willie Mays or a missed putt by Billy Casper. Rodney the "Rocket" was a loser only until the start of the next tournament.

Laver is more machine than man. The tension never shows. Only his eyes give away his inner toughness as he walks from clubhouse to court. They seem to be made of steel, and they rivet on an opponent until he either breaks himself or has the job done by Rodney.

Laver's game is like the pump-pump-pump of the needle in a sewing machine. His strokes are radarlike drives which wear out the corners of the court, tear up the sidelines and angle speedily away from whoever is chasing them.

His serve is really the only part of his game that doesn't belong with the great ones. While his first serve is often strong, and usually consistently in, it cannot destroy an opponent the way a missile off the racket of Pancho Gonzalez could. But a man can win without a great serve if the rest of his game is superb, and this certainly describes Rodney.

If there is one thing that surfaces consistently in an interview with Laver, it's his natural indifference to publicity. While he is polite and courteous to newsmen, he seems insensitive to their needs. His yes-no answers to questions drive reporters up a wall. No one would fight the issue if Laver were suddenly credited with writing the line: "Me Jane, you Tarzan."

The fact is all Rod wants to do, or ever wanted to do, is play tennis. He started in Australia at age eight. Three years later he was taking lessons from a pro, who was a friend of his father's.

But his two older brothers, who also played tennis, seldom allowed him on the same court with them because of their differences in age. Rod was the kid, the little fellow who followed on behind—to be avoided unless parental instruction ruled otherwise.

"But there were plenty of other kids my age to hit with, so that's what I did," Laver said. "When I was real little, I played tennis all day. When my group got older, we found a way to get some lights on the court and then we played all night, too."

For Rodney, that last statement might not be an exaggeration.

For most pros, practice is a necessary but boring chore. Once they're established, the idea of hitting a tennis ball for three or four hours a day has little appeal. They like the matches—yes. But the preparation, like the traveling, is a grind. Laver thrives on it.

At 32, Rod is still in racehorse physical condition. He does not tire easily, nor are his best strokes any less crisp in a fifth pro set, if it comes to that, than they were in the first.

"You might say I'm a bug on physical fitness, but I wouldn't say so," Laver explained. "I was always smaller than everyone else as a kid, so naturally I was looking for an equalizer. But all I ever did were body exercises. I never lifted weights or did anything unusual."

This statement contrasts sharply with Rod's book, which tells about him squeezing a rubber ball to strengthen his wrists and also doing finger push-ups. Asked to explain, Rod answered with a shrug of the shoulders.

Laver also seems to have a blind spot when it comes to specific dates and places. For example, he says he can't remember when he won his first tournament or whom he beat. Getting him to talk about Harry Hopman, who was captain of Australia's Davis Cup team during Laver's amateur days, is like trying to get gum off your shoe.

"I didn't discover Harry Hopman," Laver said. "He discovered me. I was 15 and he saw me in a coaching class and then talked to me afterward." If you press Rod on what the Hopman teaching magic did specifically for his game, his reply is that it was Harry who taught him fundamentals and their value.

One gets the impression that he'd like to add, "But I won my own matches."

Laver seems to relax just a little when he talks about his game. You can't have good strokes he says without good rhythm, so that's what he worked on the most—his rhythm.

"It is also important," he continued, "to know how much of a game you've got. In other words, you have to learn not to force your game beyond a certain point. Otherwise, you lose control.

"I'll never be a great server because I'm not tall enough. In order to develop a great serve, you've got to be able to arch the ball by hitting down on it. A man 5-foot-8 and 150 pounds, like myself, always has too much of the net in front of him to do that. I do not win matches with my serve, but with my overall game."

Asked what makes a winner, Rodney replied: "I think it has to be inborn. That's the first part. The second part is how much a man is willing to practice and polish his talents. I feel I'm lucky because I've never lost my desire to train."

While Laver has no close friends among his fellow pros and, in fact, keeps pretty much to himself, the amount of respect they hold for his game is tremendous.

"You really have to be around Rod for a long time before you know him and then you find you don't really know him," said fellow Australian John Newcombe, who was this year's winner at Wimbledon.

"I say the man is a great athlete and very proud of what he has become. Look, I don't care how often he wins, he's still human. He's subject to the same problems and pressures we all are, only he doesn't show it. But I think he works harder than anyone on the tour.

"You know, when Laver first turned pro, he wasn't all that great," Newcombe continued. "He had the usual weakness most left-handers have in their backhand, and his forehand wasn't much better. But he made them both great by going out and practicing and practicing. That's the story of his whole game—work and practice.

"When Rod has a poor day, and even pros have them once in a while, it's usually because his serve is off. If he doesn't get it back under control right away, the rest of his game starts to go and you can beat him. He is also susceptible to a slow game, where his opponent is hitting at his feet, lobbing and jerking him around. But when he's right, he really has no weakness."

Laver, who grew up on his father's cattle ranch in Australia, has since married an American girl and now lives in California.

"I feel I reached my peak last year at 31," Rod said. "But I don't think that's any one-time thing. I feel I can hold that peak for three or four more years. I don't agree with people who say I'm not playing as well as I did last year.

"I'm living in the United States because that's where the pro-tennis business is best right now—where I'm closest to the big money. When I get tired of it all or can't play anymore, I'll take my family and go back to Australia."

Hockey

THE STANLEY CUP AT LAST

By Jack Chevalier

From The Philadelphia Inquirer

John Wayne wiped out an army of renegades to preserve law and order in Boone County. Rock Hudson drove off into the sunset with Doris Day by his side. And Bobby Orr's goal in overtime won the Stanley Cup for the Boston Bruins.

Yes, movie lovers, it was more like Hollywood than Boston Garden here Sunday, as the Bruins wrote a perfectly appropriate ending to a perfectly splendid National Hockey League season.

Orr, the fair-haired prince of skatedom, jammed in a goal after 40 seconds of sudden-death overtime, giving the hungry Bruins a 4–3 victory and a four-game series sweep over the dead-game St. Louis Blues.

It was fitting that Orr climaxed his storybook season by giving Boston its first Stanley Cup in 29 years.

It was appropriate that the clincher came in the old magical Garden, so 14,835 fans could join the Bruins in a tumultuous post-game celebration.

It was convenient to win at home so that Derek Sanderson, hockey's king of swingers, who set up Orr's goal, could host a long, noisy party at his Bachelors III hangout.

And it was a relief to see the season end on Mother's Day, just as the mercury approached 90 degrees and threatened to melt the rink.

"Oh, what a feeling!" shouted Boston coach Harry Sinden in the locker room, where it was actually raining champagne. "I'll never forget this as long as I live. I want to thank my mother for buying me my first pair of skates."

"It was (censored) super to see Bobby get the goal, that's all I can say," Sanderson hollered. "And you know what? I just said (censored) super on television."

Captain Johnny Bucyk saved the Bruins from an agonizing 3–2 defeat by tipping home John McKenzie's pass to tie the score with 6:32 left in the third period.

Shortly after the overtime began, the puck was dumped into St. Louis' zone, and Orr rushed up from the right point to prevent a clearing pass by the Blues' Larry Keenan. Orr shoveled the disc to Sanderson, broke for the net and drove the return pass through goalie Glenn Hall to touch off an incredible scene of joy on the ice.

The Bruins mobbed and tackled each other, and soon about 100 youngsters were sliding across the ice to jump on their heroes and grab souvenir pieces of equipment. Crepe paper streamers flew down from the cheering gallery and smudged the ice with a blue and yellow tint.

Someone rolled out a golden carpet and NHL president Clarence Campbell strolled out to present the Stanley Cup to captain Bucyk. As it was placed on a stand, Ted Green, the Bruins' brawling defenseman who missed the season because of a skull fracture, touched the cup and wept.

Then, as the 10-minute ovation continued, Bucyk skated completely around the rink with the cup raised over his head. It was an emotional moment for long-suffering Boston hockey fans and Bucyk, who played here for eight seasons (1960–67) when the Bruins didn't even make the play-offs.

And the locker room was a perfect madhouse.

It was obvious that these rowdy celebrants, whose ecstasy was unrestrained, were not the Celtics or Montreal Canadiens or New York Yankees. This championship carried true meaning in addition to $7,500 per player.

St. Louis coach Scotty Bowman, whose team is 0–12 in three Stanley Cup final series, didn't think the Blues disgraced the West Division.

"Others think they might have done better, but they had their chance and missed it," he said. "We're happy to come this far and if we ever win it, we'll be happier.

"Our club was hurting through the whole series. But Bobby Plager gave us some courage today."

Plager ignored his aching shoulder and body-checked Sanderson in the opening minute. That gave St. Louis a lift, and it went on to play its best offensive game of the series.

Boston defenseman Rick Smith took a clever Sanderson pass and ripped home a 45-footer at 5:28 of the first period.

The Blues answered back as Red Berenson converted a Plager rebound at 19:17 and went ahead at 3:22 of the second period when Gary Sabourin beat Boston goalie Gerry Cheevers from 35 feet. Frank St. Marseille's check along the right boards set up that score.

Boston's Phil Esposito set a record with his 13th play-off goal that tied the game, 2–2, at 14:22. He overpowered Andre Boudrias on a face-off and whipped a high shot past 39-year-old goalie Hall.

The Blues were still plugging in the third period, and Keenan rammed home a Phil Goyette pass at the 19-second mark. It looked like St. Louis' familiar tight checking defense would force a fifth game unti Bucyk and Orr came through.

Horse Racing

A TORPEDO NAMED DUST COMMANDER

By Bob Barnet

From The Muncie Star

Copyright, ©, 1970, The Muncie Star

A tiny torpedo named Dust Commander sped through the Churchill Downs stretch Saturday to win the 96th Kentucky Derby and provide an answer to the biggest mystery since the world set out to learn who killed Cock Robin.

Dust Commander, long-shot victor in the Bluegrass Stakes at Keeneland, astounded onlookers again, winning at odds of 15–1 in one of the most unpredictable derby races of them all.

Smallest horse in the race, the son of Bold Commander arrived at the finish line five lengths before the favored My Dad George. Finishing third, a half-length behind the place horse, was High Echelon.

Dust Commander ran the mile and one quarter in 2:03–2/5 over a track officially designated as good. The winner paid $32.60, $12.60, $7.00 across the board, with My Dad George returning $5.00 and $3.20, and High Echelon, who ran as an entry with personality, paying $4.40. A total of $2,383,972 was wagered on the derby, and $5,811,127 passed through the mutuel machines during the 10-race program.

The winner was ridden by Mike Manganello, a 29-year-old native of Hartford, Connecticut, who was appearing in the derby for only the second time. Manganello guided Te Vega to a 10th place finish in 1968.

The Derby victor is owned by Robert E. Lehmann, a Paris, Kentucky, breeder who returned from a hunting safari in Nepal to watch his horse run. He arrived in Louisville only a few hours before the race.

Dust Commander's trainer is Don Combs, who told newsmen

after the race that the colt is "somewhere between 15 and 15.2 hands," extremely small for a thoroughbred capable of whipping the nation's best at a mile and a quarter. Dust Commander was not nominated for either the Preakness or the Belmont Stakes.

Purchased for only $6,500 at the Lexington Yearling Sales in 1968, Dust Commander became one of the great bargains of thoroughbred racing when he won his smashing derby victory. First money was $128,000 and the total purse was a record $171,300.

Dust Commander was given little attention as a derby candidate until he won the Bluegrass Stakes on a sloppy track at 35–1. He was the longest shot on the board that day. The Churchill Downs track was sloppy when racing started Saturday but had dried considerably by the time the derby was run.

The agile little Dust Commander was no better than seventh when the field reached the mile post. Silent Screen was in the lead at that point, with George Lewis second and Corn off the Cob third. When they straightened in the stretch, Manganello hurled Dust Commander through a gap between horses, and suddenly the onrushing Dust Commander, an eighth of a mile from home, was in the lead and drawing away. He increased his advantage with every stride as they neared the wire and My Dad George and High Echelon, who had run with the trailers through much of the race, moved up to duel for second and third.

My Dad George, winner of the Flamingo Stakes, Florida Derby and Stepping Stone Purse, and a solid 5–2 favorite with the crowd of more than 100,000, was 14th at the three-quarters but moved up quickly to be fifth at the mile and finished strongly, although he did not menace the winner. High Echelon's late drive was even more spectacular, with Larry Adams bringing this campaigner from 17th place at the three-quarter pole.

Dust Commander's victory was all the more remarkable because he was bumped hard by George Lewis as the field left the starting gate.

Corn off the Cob, who had been a strong factor from the start and who appeared to be ready to move to the front at the top of the stretch, faltered abruptly and faded to seventh, beaten by nine lengths.

Naskra, also far back through much of the race, closed willingly to take fourth under the handling of Braulio Baeza.

Personality finished eighth and another well-backed performer, Terlago, was 11th with Bill Shoemaker in the saddle. Fathom, ridden by Diane Crump, only woman ever to ride in the derby, finished 15th.

Hector Pilar, rider of Holy Land, suffered back injuries when the horse fell as the massive field swung around the turn leaving the backstretch. He was taken to a Louisville hospital. Admiral's Shield, ridden by Jimmy Nichols, was forced to leap over the fallen Holy Land, and Action Getter, ridden by Mike Venezia, also narrowly missed a collision. Pilar was thrown to the outside, a stroke of fate that might have saved his life.

Owner Robert Lehmann, who rode jetliners for 72 hours in order to watch his horse win the run for the roses, told newsmen in the press box after the race that he had killed a near-record tiger in Nepal during his safari. He is a native of the Fremont, Ohio, area and has been engaged in banking and construction. He is now, he insists, in the process of retiring. It was the first derby starter for Lehmann and also for trainer Don Combs, a 31-year-old Lexington native who studied political science at the University of Kentucky in a prelaw course but dropped out of school to become a trainer.

The Derby was run in bright sunshine, and veteran observers called the crowd one of the all-time largest, only slightly smaller than the record throng that watched Majestic Prince win in 1969.

A happy Mike Manganello said after the race that he was "more or less pleased" to see rain and a sloppy track Saturday morning. "I had confidence in this horse on a fast track, too," he said. "He won in Florida and at Keeneland on a fast track.

"I made the rail around the first turn and stayed there until I had to come around a couple of horses at the top of the stretch," Manganello said. "I stayed inside as the others bore out. There were a few mud spots around the turn but they didn't bother us."

Ray Broussard made no excuses for My Dad George. "The horse handled okay," he said. "He ran his race. I had no trouble at any stage. I had all the breaks I wanted until I turned for home, then we just got outrun."

Angel Cordero, Jr., who rode Corn off the Cob, who broke from the 17th and outside position, said, "Post position didn't bother me, as he got a good position before the first turn."

Jimmy Nichols and Mike Venezia both gave close-up, eyewitness accounts of Holy Land's mishap. Nichols, who rode Admiral's Shield, said, "My horse jumped four or five feet high over that horse that fell down. Oh, what a jam! I knew somebody had to go down. It cost us any real chance of winning."

Venezia, who was aboard Action Getter, had this to say: "All I was looking for was a hole along the fence, looking for room just like everybody else. I went right over Pilar's horse. If the jock [Pilar] falls to the inside, I would have run right over him."

Bill Shoemaker said Terlago just couldn't handle the track. John L. Rotz, who rode Silent Screen, said, "He just fell apart at the eighth pole."

Diane Crump, who made racing history aboard Fathom, said her horse ran out of gas. "He handled the track pretty good, no complaint there." Asked if the excitement moved her at all, the 21-year-old Diane said, "It gave me a pretty good feeling. The closer it got to race time, the more I felt it, but I wasn't nervous."

Miss Crump narrowly missed the accident on the second turn. "It was right next to me that it happened," she said. "Holy Land ran up on the heels of a horse, I don't know which one, but when he fell, he fell away from me and I wasn't affected."

Skiing

THE SKI PATROL

By Jeff Prugh

From the Los Angeles Times

Copyright, ©, 1970, Los Angeles Times

At least, nobody could say my first visit to a ski resort didn't get off to a smashing start.

While carrying a suitcase from the car to my quarters, I slalomed down a snowbank and smashed into the porch.

The impact split a toenail, turning it three shades of purple, and I spent the predawn hours soaking it in a pan of hot water.

That was only the beginning. After all, I had never worn a pair of skis yet. Two afternoons and two dozen spills later, I witnessed a first-aid demonstration and rescue operation by the Mammoth Ski Patrol. I was the victim.

The accident happened shortly before dusk, when the snow is slick and hard and when the legs begin responding sluggishly to what the brain tells them to do.

The scene was a crowded slope called Thunder Mountain. All afternoon the hill had been littered with a smorgasbord of injuries—fractured ankles, sprained knees, bruised elbows and wounded pride—and the Ski Patrol was so overworked it could have used reinforcements.

No way I'm going to get hurt, I thought, as I rode up chair lift No. 4, surveying the rescue operations below.

But, it did happen—about 300 yards from the lodge and not very far from a sign that read: "Go slowly."

Well, I was going slowly, all right. I was performing a maneuver called a "snowplow," but it looked more like an avalanche. Suddenly my skis crossed, one of them wedging deeply under a mound of snow. I was airborne.

The only trouble was, neither ski released itself. I pitched head-first into the snow, and my right knee sounded like somebody twisted the tops off a bunch of carrots.

The Ski Patrol immediately swung into action. Within 30 seconds, two patrolmen arrived and began removing my skis.

"Where are you hurt?" one of them asked.

"My right knee," I answered. "But I think I can limp down the hill all right."

"Lie on your back," they said. "Your leg might be broken."

"We better move fast," said one. "There's gonna be a lot of traffic down there at the hospital tonight."

Within minutes, another ski patrolman was towing a long red toboggan to the scene, while somebody placed my leg in a cardboard splint, wrapping it securely in gauze.

I was hoisted onto the toboggan, and dozens of curious skiers began crowding around me, in much the same way motorists slow down on the freeway to gawk at the scene of a collision.

It all seemed like a lot of unnecessary precaution, but this was the method of the Ski Patrol—cordial, competent and cool.

The Ski Patrol is Mammoth Mountain's "cavalry"—rugged skiers in blue and orange jackets who perform the same function as lifeguards at the beach. Some of them are paid, others are volunteers—but they are highly skilled in both skiing and first aid.

One of them covered me from head to toe in brown canvas. "Cover your face with your hands," he said. "This thing kicks up a lot of snow when we start going fast."

Now I was on my back, in total darkness, being dragged down the hill on a sled by a skier. The ride down the slope was swift and bumpy. A roller coaster would have seemed safer. I'll get a concussion for sure, I thought, as my head pounded against the metal shell of the sled.

At the bottom, somebody removed enough canvas to expose my face, and the next thing I knew there were long rows of skiers giving me sympathetic glances.

"Don't worry," a ski patrolman said soothingly. "I had the same thing happen to me. I was laid up only a matter of weeks."

Four patrolmen carried me into the First Aid Station. It looked like a garage and was filled with so many casualties it resembled a hospital in a combat zone.

Other victims studied me as I was placed on a stretcher.

An attendant was asking me questions. "How many hours of

sleep did you get last night?" and, "Was this your first time on skis?"

Then I was transported to a hospital about three miles away. The hospital in Mammoth Village was as busy as International Airport. So many injured skiers were being carted in and out of the place it looked like an assembly line.

I was X-rayed and wheeled into a room occupied by a boy from Anaheim who had a broken leg. A doctor told me, "Your X rays show no fracture but you have a very bad sprain."

The prognosis, he said, was good. He prescribed some pills to relieve the pain and left to tend some more serious cases. I would live, thanks to the Mammoth Ski Patrol, the Good Samaritans of the slopes, the guys who keep their heads while people about them are losing theirs.

Automobile Racing

HELL WEEK AT INDY

By Joe Scalzo

From Car Life

Copyright, ©, 1970, Petersen Publishing Company

To be a hunter at the Indianapolis Motor Speedway during the last desperate week of practice and qualifying before the 500-mile race requires a keen eye (for staking out the right car), some gray hair or baldness (for convincing the car owner that you have lots of experience) and, most of all, a heavy foot (for gunning said car around the speedway at 165 mph-plus without much practice).

It is easy to spot a hunter. I spotted Al Miller, his helmet and goggles tucked under his arm, my first day at the speedway, May 15. It was a Monday. Twenty-seven cars had already qualified, with Al Unser leading the parade at 170:221 mph and rookie Steve Krisiloff (162.448 mph) bringing up the rear. Six starting berths still were open for the 500 and its $1 million purse. One qualifying weekend remained.

Miller, notorious hunter that he is, expected to grab one of those berths for himself.

But first he would have to find a car. And since all the remaining cars already had assigned drivers, the only way he was going to get one was if one of the drivers quit—or was fired.

Indy is a roaring battleground during May. Car owners and sponsors spend thousands readying a car for the 500. They hire a driver well in advance, then give him two weeks to get up to qualifying speed. If he can't get up to speed, he is easily canned. There are lots of aging hunters like Miller looking for rides.

Miller and the other hunters like Bob Veith, Bobby Grim and Bud Tinglestad no longer have big enough reputations to have cars assigned to them before the 500, but during this final week, when everyone is scratching to get up to speed, they suddenly become very popular. The hunters have the courage, and the flair, to cram themselves into a strange car and with virtually no practice qualify it for the 500. In the race itself, they may do nothing more than cruise around, counting on a safe finish and on banking a few thousand at the end. But they will put the car in the show; and with the final weekend staring them in the face, that is all the beleaguered car owners and mechanics are worried about. (Sometimes the hunters overextend themselves. Bob Veith jumped into a strange car on the first qualifying weekend and promptly cracked it up.)

All this makes life hard on the assigned driver still trying to work up to speed. He is driving as hard as he can, but his car won't respond. Time is running out. He is nervous and fast growing scared. Indy is the biggest race of all.

If Al Miller is the hunter, he is the hunted.

For the hunted the final week here is literally a week of hell.

But only for the individuals involved. For the observer it is the best time of all at Indianapolis, far better than the race itself. It is the opportunity to watch the hunter and the hunted struggling under pressure. The pressure crushed some, brought out the best in others. This week is what Indy is all about.

From the garages in Gasoline Alley, the drivers and mechanics push the cars, using small tractors, down a narrow corridor between two grandstands to the pits themselves. Whenever a car is pushed through this corridor, milling fans engulf the drivers, begging for autographs. Guards, determined to keep the wall clear, blow whistles and elbow the crowds out of the way. It is bedlam. In the pits themselves it is quieter. The cars are parked along a strip of pavement in front of a short wall. Behind the wall are more grandstands. Separating the pit road from the front straightaway is a strip of green lawn, then another short wall, then the smooth black front straight itself.

During the last week those poor drivers like John Cannon, who had been unable to get up to speed, sprawled in the grass, passing around cigarettes, sipping iced tea and complaining about the heat. Occasionally a car bellowed past at 190 mph and Cannon got very busy with a stopwatch.

Of Cannon's exact problem, no one was sure. Early in the month he had been lapping easily at 163 mph. Then, tailgating another driver into the first turn, Cannon had closed up sharply. Fearing that he was going to ram the fellow, Cannon jammed on his brakes. All four wheels locked up and he started spinning. He spun for nearly 500 feet. Right in the middle of the spin, Cannon recalled that someone had warned him not to use his brakes in a spin. He released his brakes and his skidding car looped straight into the wall.

So much for advice.

Cannon wasn't hurt and insisted he still wanted to drive; his car owner gave him a backup machine to practice with while the other car was rebuilt.

Now after two weeks of practicing in the backup car, Cannon was unable to top 160 mph.

Indy can be a strange and horrible place. It seems so easy: a 2.5-mile rectangle with four corners. But split seconds mean a lot. If you are driving a lap, as Al Unser was, in 52.9 seconds, you are lapping at 170 mph and on the pole. If you are lapping in 56 seconds, as John Cannon was, then you are averaging only 160, too slow to win a starting place.

There is a real barrier here. Invisible, but real. Veteran Lloyd Ruby explained: "Any driver here can lap Indy at 160. But to get over that is something else. Once you get over 160 your chassis starts working entirely differently and everything changes." Ruby was having no trouble with the barrier (he had earlier been clocked in excess of 171 mph), but was having trouble with the engine; six had so far blown up under him and he still hadn't qualified. As for Cannon, he was having plenty of trouble crashing through the barrier. He would accelerate madly onto the track, drive a dozen flat-out laps, then come screeching to a halt in the pits again, his face expectant. When mechanics told him his speed he looked stunned; he could not believe he was going so slowly.

But where Cannon was perplexed, his face grave, Al Miller was confident. I asked Miller how he planned to lap at 165 mph without benefit of practice.

"By standing on the gas," he declared curtly. "It's do or die."

Do or die. He actually said that.

At 46, Miller is the oldest registered Indy driver. He has raced in four 500's, finishing fourth in 1965. Besides his disconcerting ability to drive so tough on the final weekend, the most noticeable thing about Al Miller is that he is completely bald. But during the week he wore a cap that partially disguised this.

But if one could marvel at Miller's personal courage, one could also sympathize with Cannon and with what he was trying so hard to do.

By Monday afternoon, Miller's first day at the track, he had already secured the ride in the turbo Offy that veteran stock car racer Charlie Glotzbach had tried, but been unable, to work up to speed. After a handful of laps, Miller was roaring around at 163 mph, three mph faster than Cannon.

Cannon wasn't the only hunted driver, not by a long shot.

Another one was Carlos Alberto Pairetti, an Argentine whose sponsors, a television station in Buenos Aires, had paid a reported $20,000 to buy Pairetti a ride in the 500. Pairetti had quickly passed his rookie test. But he could not speak a single word of English. He just strolled through the pits, chatting in Spanish to a few friends, and always grinning. He could not get above 160 mph and his car, not a fast one anyway, kept breaking up under him. Pairetti was still grinning when qualifying finished, and he had not earned a place in the race.

Ronnie Bucknum was chain smoking. A nonsmoker, he had begun to smoke as soon as he discovered that for some reason his speed had dropped four mph—from 166 to 162. Bucknum did not know why. The car or him? Where before he had been confident that he would qualify for the 500, he now was visibly worried.

Larry Dickson, the hard-faced sprint car champion, sat on the pit wall morosely.

"What's the matter, Dickson?"

"Aw, I'm stuck at 161. Can't go any faster."

"Hell, that's not so bad. Vukovich is stuck at 160."

The problems young Bill Vukovich was encountering seemed the strangest of all. In 1968 Vukovich had placed seventh and had been named Rookie of the Year. He seemed assured a brilliant future. Now, chauffering a brand-new car, a turbo Offy, he could not top 160 mph. The car did not feel stable in the turns, he reported. "I can't make myself get my foot back on the gas coming off the corners," he said, "and that should be the easiest part of driving here." His unease increased on Tuesday. As he was rocketing down the backstraight in excess of 200 mph, a bolt in the suspension worked loose and fell off. Vukovich was able to brake to a safe stop. A mechanic apparently had forgotten to tighten the bolt.

Vukovich was not about to berate his mechanics. He was well aware they had been working like beasts to sort out the unwieldy machine. This was true not only of Vukovich's mechanics, but of all the other teams still trying to get their cars in the race. By now the face of the average mechanic was gray from lack of sleep. His finger-nails and clothes were grimy. Like the drivers, his diet had been reduced to cigarettes and iced tea.

The week dragged on. Despair grew.

Many of the slower drivers were no longer rational. They tried everything. They even asked rival drivers for advice, as when Jerry Grant, breaking in a new turbo Offy, asked Lloyd Ruby how much throttle he should apply when accelerating off the corner.

A conference between Bobby Unser, safely qualified for the race at 168 mph-plus and Bill Puterbaugh, a rookie trying to work up to speed, but stuck at 164, was typical.

"Puterbaugh," Bobby told him, "if you want to go 165 you're going to have to poke it down in the corners deeper. And when you bail off the backstraight into that turn at the end, you have to have the gas and the brake on at the same time . . ." As if suddenly realizing the gravity of what he was suggesting, Unser quickly added, "But I don't want to be responsible for getting you hurt."

Puterbaugh snorted: "Responsible, hell. I just want to get in the show. I've got to do it."

But grim determination was not enough and Puterbaugh, flailing round the track lap after lap, could not increase his speed.

By Thursday, relationships between mechanics and drivers de-teriorated. Some of the drivers were convinced that something was the matter with the car, not them. The mechanics, naturally enough, believed the opposite.

With time running out, some mechanics began lying to their drivers, telling them they were going faster than they really were, possibly believing this would increase their desire to go fast.

Other mechanics simply believed it was time for a driver change. Time to hire someone like Al Miller.

Al was ready. On Thursday afternoon he quit the ex-Glotzbach car and went looking for something better.

Friday was the hottest day so far. Track surface temperature was a searing 141 degrees. It was hardly a day to expect great speed. But John Cannon suddenly was up to 164.9, and Ronnie Bucknum and Bentley Warren both clocked 166. Others like Kevin Bartlett, Greg Weld, Sam Sessions and Dick Simon also were nudging 165.

Where did they find it?

But a driver who was not running any faster was Vukovich. His best lap was only 162.7. His pals Gary Bettenhausen and Bruce Walkup, both safely qualified for the race, took shakedown rides in his car and could not go fast either. "Well, I'm not letting it bother me," Vukovich snapped. "If I don't qualify, I don't qualify."

On Saturday morning he was the first driver to take to the track during the one-hour practice session that preceded the qualifying runs. He braked to a stop after a single nerve-wracking lap. The handling of the car was even worse than before, Vukovich reported; he could not so much as hold it in a straight line on the straightaways.

"Better look for another car, Bill," a friend suggested.

"I think you're right," Vukovich agreed.

Later a rookie named Denny Zimmerman tried the car, but he did not like it either. Mechanics had made so many changes in the chassis by now that it was difficult to determine whether the car itself was bad, or simply way out of adjustment. In the end when it became apparent no driver at the track would touch it (word spreads fast about such cars), one of the mechanics who had been working on it all month slumped down beside it, let out a sigh and immediately fell asleep.

The four-lap official qualifying runs finally began. The pits were jammed full of drivers and cars. John Cannon, unable to top 163 mph, was flagged off the track by his crew. Bill Puterbaugh, still stuck at 164, also was flagged in.

For the lucky ones, the newly confident ones, speed seemed no problem at all. Bentley Warren (164:805 mph), Sam Sessions (165.373 mph), Ronnie Bucknum (166.136 mph), Greg Weld (166.121 mph), Lloyd Ruby (168.895 mph) and Kevin Bartlett (165.259 mph) grabbed off the six remaining starting places in less than an hour and a half. Drivers under pressure, they came through admirably.

But the filling of the field of 33 did not lessen the pressure, it amplified it. Now came the cruelest of all the rites at Indy, the "bumping" of slower cars from the race. The first to be bumped was Steve Krisiloff, whose average of 162.448 mph, achieved on the first weekend, had not seemed fast enough at the time. It wasn't.

The driver bumping Krisiloff was Jerry Grant. Grant had not topped 158 mph all month; yet he qualified at a mighty 165.983 mph. He had all his own money tied up in the car, Grant explained, and had been purposely babying it and breaking it in carefully during practice. He always knew he could get up to speed when it counted. But another observer said that Grant went so fast because his friend Dan Gurney had checked out Grant's car that morning. After Gurney had proclaimed Grant's car to be okay (the car was a Gurney-built Eagle), Grant had no trouble going fast. Grant is an admirer of Gurney.

Then Jack Brabham, who had arrived at the speedway on Monday and had little practice, blazed into the starting field with a four-lap average of 166.397 mph. This bumped Jim McElreath, the burly 43-year-old Texas bricklayer who had driven every 500 since 1962. McElreath qualified on the first weekend at a mere 163 mph. McElreath looked stunned, unable to believe what had happened to him. When asked if he would go hunting for another car he mumbled, "I dunno." Now Bentley Warren, the rookie who had qualified for the race only an hour before, was the slowest man in the field. The next driver out, Dick Simon, sped around the oval at 165.548 mph and bumped him.

The last driver to qualify Saturday was Vukovich. Minutes after he had quit his original car, Vukovich was approached by driver Sonny Ates. Ates had piled his Brabham Offy into the wall the weekend before, the car had since been completely rebuilt, but the accident had spooked Ates; he had temporarily lost his appetite for speed. Would Vuky drive it? In only a few laps Vukovich had the car, the Sugaripe Prune Special, hitting 166 mph, and his qualifying average of 165.7 bumped Tony Adamowicz. Just as Vukovich nosed across the line he ran out of fuel.

Those who had crashed through the barrier into the race celebrated in different ways. Lloyd Ruby, drinking a can of beer in the track cafeteria, rushed over and poured half the can in a surprised Bobby Unser's soup. Ruby was in a state of euphoria; he had already blown up six engines and during morning practice had nearly rammed broadside into a car that had spun directly in front of him. Ruby found it incredible that he had finally qualified.

Sam Sessions was relieved. "The car didn't feel safe to me in the corners," he said, "but I would have carried it around if I'd had to."

Ronnie Bucknum, explaining his sudden jump in speed, said, "We made a few adjustments to the chassis. And we found that the turbocharger blades were grinding on the metal. That was why we couldn't run any faster than 197 on the backstraight while everyone else was running 215."

And Vukovich, hearing false rumors that his qualifying run would be thrown out on a technicality (the car's roll-over bar supposedly was too short) muttered, "Let 'em kick me out of the race if they want to. If they do, I'll just get me another car and get back in." But as he remembered the agony he had put up with all month, he added softly, "Like hell I will."

During that last night before the final day of qualifying, some important, last-minute deals were put together by some of the drivers still trying to make the race. McElreath pleaded with fellow Texan A. J. Foyt to give him a car to qualify. With three cars already in the field, Foyt agreed, and his crew started bolting together a fourth for McElreath. Steve Krisiloff lined up the ride in the turbo Ford John Cannon had crashed a few weeks earlier. It had finally been rebuilt and was ready to go back on the track. Only 23 years old, Krisiloff has been racing since he was 13. He had never piloted a car as fast as a turbo Ford before, and he dashed around Gasoline Alley all that night, begging advice from other drivers. John Cannon watched his mechanics tear his car apart a final time. Bill Puterbaugh, stocky as a bull, looked mightily determined. Al Miller was still looking, still hunting.

McElreath wasted no time qualifying for the 500. Sunday morning Foyt broke the new car in for him and literally broke the engine after four laps. A new one was installed in a couple of hours, and McElreath climbed into the machine for the first time at noon. After six laps, his burly tattooed arms easily working the steering wheel, he qualified at 166.821 mph, winning the 33rd starting place. This bumped Kevin Bartlett.

Sam Sessions now was the slowest driver in the field. But no one bumped Sessions. No one could go fast enough. Never before have so many tried to go so fast to such little effect. Not even Al Miller, whose bald skull was gleaming with sweat by the end of the afternoon, could exceed 163 mph. For him, the hunting had been lousy. Tony Adamowicz hit the wall gently and Sam Posey smacked it hard, but neither was injured.

The day's mad mood was eloquently capsuled by Al Unser, the pole sitter, a relaxed spectator to the bizarre proceedings. "Those guys are really trying hard," Unser grinned, gesturing toward the first turn with his thumb where the sound of squalling rubber was all too obvious. "I can hear their voices."

Some of the pressure finally seemed to lift at five o'clock. With but one hour left for qualifying, it was obvious that no one was going to be able to get in the race at this late date. The remaining cars were the turkeys, the worn-out ones. When it was their turn to qualify, some of them were so tired that they refused to start at all.

Only 15 minutes remained when Arnie Knepper accelerated onto the track.

Like Al Miller, Arnie Knepper is a hunter. His hair is laced with gray, he is a veteran of several 500's. Knepper had spent much of the month hunting for a decent car. He had been unsuccessful. Even the car he was attempting to qualify now, he had gotten through default: Al Miller himself had spent much of the day in it, but finally had quit in frustrated disgust.

But Knepper is a hunter with a difference. He scornfully told me that none of the car owners would give him a tumble in the early weeks. But on this last day he had suddenly become most popular, and many of the car owners who had ignored him before now approached him with open arms. Arnie said it had given him great satisfaction to turn them all down. "I'm the same driver now I was at the first of the month," he snapped. "Why didn't you give me a chance then?"

Finally, in the late afternoon, Knepper had wearily climbed into the turbo Offy that Miller had rejected. Arnie knew nothing about the car, not even its age. It was obviously far from new. He drove a couple of laps, pulled in, and asked the mechanics to change the gear ratio so that the engine would not be revving so high coming off the corners and would have more torque. And he had the mechanics bolt on a different, more powerful, intake manifold.

By the time all these changes had been made it was 5:45 and Arnie had no opportunity to test them to see if they worked. But he believed they would make the car faster and he desperately wanted to qualify. One mechanic must have sensed this because as he belted Arnie into the cockpit he told him, "I know how much you want to get into the race. But don't hurt yourself."

Now Arnie roared down the pit lane, grinding the transmission gears in his haste. Few people even bothered to time him. Everyone was waiting for the clock to run out and qualifications to end. But one who did time him was Al Miller.

Knepper stormed past, completing his warm-up lap. Miller clicked his stopwatch. He stared at it incredulously.

"My God," he stammered, "he's close; 164.7 mph!"

Suddenly everyone was watching Knepper charge around the track. On his next lap he signaled the starter he was qualifying and the official clocks were switched on. Sam Sessions, the slowest qualifier, had a pained, nervous expression—would he be bumped now, with only 15 minutes to go? Sessions was so nervous he forgot to engage his stopwatch.

No one in the pits could see how Arnie was driving the corners; the grandstands blocked the view. But later he admitted he was sliding them, careening through them, driving flat out. All four qualifying laps were over 165 mph. And by the final turn of his fourth lap, the crowd of 50,000, previously lethargic, came to their feet, cheering and waving him on.

Then came the announcement: Knepper had just missed quali- fying—his speed average of 165.320 mph was 0.053, the blink of an eye, slower than Sessions. The crowd groaned. Sessions sighed with relief. And a moment later the gun roared and hell week was over.

Knepper had been unable to hear the announcement over the roar of his engine. He still believed he had qualified for the 500. You could see a grin splitting his face as he killed his engine and coasted into the pits to accept the (he thought) tumultuous re- ception.

Abruptly one figure disengaged himself from the crowd. It was the other hunter, Al Miller, his face impassive. There was no mis- taking the curt, heartless gesture he flashed to Knepper with his right hand, the gesture that plunged Knepper into gloom and made him realize he had failed.

Thumbs down, Miller signaled.

You lose, Arnie.

Or, from one hunter to another: Better hunting next time.

Yachting

THE AMERICA'S CUP: AN INCREDIBLE SERIES

By Bill Robinson

From Yachting

Copyright, ©, 1970, Yachting Publishing Co.

It started in driving rain and a lump of sea on September 15 and ended in the cool gray twilight of autumn on the 28th, and into this record duration for an America's Cup series, the New York YC's 21st defense of yachting's major trophy packed more drama, controversy, oddball "firsts" and just plain exciting competition than all the other 12-Meter challenges combined.

It killed all the old clichés about the dullness of match racing, it emblazoned a whole new set of legends into the annals of the sport, and it carried violently heated discussions of sailing into such strange milieus as parliaments, meetings of college athletic directors, and bars, taxicabs, dining rooms and TV dens that had never before heard a word of nautical argument. Press coverage, both knowledgeable and hysterically ignorant, was the heaviest in history.

After the finale, as *Intrepid* proudly bore her 4–1 win into Newport, Rhode Island, on the last tow home, with skipper Bill Ficker a focus of champagne toasts from his tension-drained crew while his bald head gleamed under the watery slant of a late sun and a big "Ficker is Quicker" banner flew from the truck, one would have to hark back to 1934 to approach the wealth of dramatic incident in this series. As in that *Rainbow-Endeavour* match, a seemingly slower boat used superior tactics to fight off a potentially faster one, protests and legal bickering threatened to take the play away from the actual sailing, and the race committee became the center of a storm of controversy reaching far beyond sailing circles.

In fact the 1970 series was even more incident- and controversy-fraught, and it seemed almost too much of a coincidence that the committee boat for this wild series had been named *Incredible* in tribute to the late Willis Slane, cofounder of Hatteras Yacht, who built her. When unable to use saltier expletives in polite surroundings, it was his custom to substitute "incredible" for his original choice of word.

Perhaps as never before in 100 years of challenges had a series been fought so directly on the water, rather than having already been settled at the designer's board, towing tank or sail loft. The technology gap had been completely closed with Alan Payne's creation, *Gretel II*. The Royal Sydney YS challenger was not an underdog in design, sails or rig, and the way the boats were handled in combat determined the outcome. Except for the period after a man overboard, one of many bizarre "firsts" in the series, took *Gretel* out of contention in the opener, there wasn't a minute of any race when a single lapse couldn't have made the difference between victory and defeat. This means match racing at its best, and sailing buffs enjoyed their fill of thrills from it.

Sir Frank Packer's second challenger named *Gretel* showed better speed over the range of winds most frequently met—12 knots and under. (This must have seemed ironic to the Aussies who campaigned *Dame Pattie,* intended for this range, in heavier winds in 1967.) There wasn't much to choose between them in the 12–18 range, also encountered fairly often, and *Intrepid* had the edge in winds over that. *Gretel* had the best foreign-made sails on any 12-Meter challenger. (In 1962 the first *Gretel* was allowed to use United States-made Hoods.) Her distinctive hull accommodated beautifully to the peculiar chop-over-ground-swells sea conditions off Newport that have been the downfall of so many "tank-test champions" among the Twelves, and she accelerated out of tacks with startling speed, especially in light air. Sailmaker Peter Cole put a great mainsail together for her out of Ratsey-made Vectis cloth from England, a peculiar pale lavender reminiscent of *Columbia's* "Purple People Eater" of 1958, and his headsails and spinnakers of Australian Kadron cloth left little to be desired against *Intrepid's* flawless Hood creations, except perhaps in a headsail or two. Payne had designed a very sophisticated mast and rig for *Gretel* that was not ready until she arrived in the United States early in August, accounting in part for her unexciting showing in tests at home. Despite the short shakedown time before the August 21 start of the first 1970 "first," the elimination series in which she defeated *France* 4–0, this rig fell into shape almost immediately and was the catalyst that brought the whole picture together for her.

All the above factors had hampered the previous 12-Meter challengers, but the Aussies licked them this time, so that perhaps the most telling background statistic to account for *Intrepid*'s victory is this: in previous races under the tension of all-out competition, *Intrepid* had a 22–5 record, while *Gretel II* was 4–0. Her brushes at home against *Gretel I* meant nothing in preparing her crew for the pressures of the real thing, and all she had behind her was the far-from-normal series against *France*'s eccentric threat. With 27 tough races under their belts, *Intrepid*'s crew knew almost automatically what the right move at the right time had to be. They knew every sail and exactly what it could do, and match racing could hold few surprises for them.

Against this wealth of pressure-hardened experience, *Gretel*'s gang had to learn as they sailed, and it was interesting to watch them improve her potential with each race and lay day. Their spinnaker technique on reaches left a great deal to be desired the first two times the boats met, as they were overtrimming and starving the sail and often used too big a kite for the circumstances. *Intrepid* breezed by easily at first, but, by the end, the boats were sailing the reaches as though tied together with one line, so close was their boat speed.

It was interesting to watch Ficker go against "the book" on match race orthodoxy to make the most of *Intrepid*'s good features and negate some of *Gretel*'s advantages. When allowed to settle into a long tack and pick her own slants and shifts, *Intrepid* could build up impressive boat speed, but she was much slower through a tack, and in accelerating out of it, than *Gretel*. Until there was no choice, the tall Californian, a former world Star Class champion from Newport Harbor YC who knows what it is to mix it at close quarters when he has to, avoided tacking duels and close infighting. On reaches he went for all-out speed rather than a "stay with 'em" tactic, picking his own best sail instead of matching the other boat's choice. Some of it was unorthodox, once it backfired, and it caused a great deal of wonderment in the spectator fleet, but it paid off in the overall victory.

There was naturally a great deal of discussion, considering *Intrepid*'s narrow squeak over *Gretel II* after the manner in which she whomped all American boats and challenger *Dame Pattie* so decisively in 1967, as to whether she was actually improved over the way she was when Olin Stephens originally designed her. As the first

(and only other) boat to repeat as a defender since the second
Columbia in 1899–1901, she had undergone drastic alterations to
her after underbody under the ministrations of Britton Chance, Jr.
He got the job of readying her for 1970 from William Strawbridge,
J. Burr Bartram, Briggs Dalzell and the other Intrepid Syndicate
members, when Stephens turned his exclusive attention to *Valiant,
Intrepid*'s 6–1 victim in the final United States selection series.
However, since there were no good yardsticks available—*Weatherly*
was not really campaigned in 1967—this is like wondering whether
Joe Louis could have beaten Jack Dempsey.

In any event, she did the job, and this is the chronology of how
she did it.

First Race, Tuesday, September 15

There was a nasty, raw easterly blowing over Rhode Island Sound
to greet the opening day, and Newport's chandleries and Army-
Navy stores did a land-office business in foul-weather gear before the
good-sized spectator fleet headed out into the slop blowing out of
Buzzards Bay. *Intrepid*'s crew was all in natty white foul-weather
suits and *Gretel*'s wore conventional yellow as they towed out, the
rain shining slickly on the defender's pale green deck and the
varnish-hued Aussie one.

The best place to be in the spectator fleet was on one of the lofty
excursion steamers, or as a guest on a Navy destroyer or large Coast
Guard cutter, as it was wet and bouncy on the private boats in a
fleet of perhaps 600. Tenders, syndicate heads, press and club
officers had the best view from an inner circle of boats allowed to
follow along directly behind the Twelves, while the rest of the fleet
steamed around a huge diamond encompassing the 24.3-mile Olym-
pic-type course, consisting of a triangle, followed by beat, run, beat.
Although there was some difficulty the first day due to poor boat-
handling conditions, the Coast Guard added to its luster with a fine
patrol job throughout the series.

Tension was naturally high as the Twelves dropped their tows
and began to feel their way around the starting area under main-
sails. With the breeze near 20 knots at the start, there was no need
for any delay, and the procedure leading to a 12:10 start began on
time. Most of the spectators were still adjusting to the rain and
poor visibility the first time the boats crossed on opposite reaches
along the line, with about seven minutes to go. There was a brief

flurry as both were seen to change headings, but they sped on, *Intrepid* on port and *Gretel* on starboard, and didn't tangle again until after the five-minute gun.

Then there was general consternation when protest flags could be seen on each boat. They circled for a while and *Gretel,* with skipper Jim Hardy at the wheel, gained the advantageous tailing position with about a minute and a half to go, hard on *Intrepid*'s stern as they broad-reached away from the line on port tack. With 38 seconds to go, Hardy tacked away and headed back for the line, and *Intrepid* jibed around as soon as Ficker saw he had been released. As it turned out, Hardy's move was about 8–10 seconds too soon. As he approached the line, he had to drive off to leeward, while *Intrepid,* timing it perfectly from farther back, charged up close-hauled with a split-second start and had the windward gauge by perhaps 75 yards, as Hardy mistimed again, hardening up a few seconds late.

On the first leg, *Intrepid* was lifted a bit and seemed stiffer and abler in the chop, but *Gretel* did not faint away the way every previous challenger (except *Gretel I*) had done on the first leg. Gradually pulling things together, Hardy got her going better and only trailed at the mark by 1:03, most of which he had given away early on the leg.

This was close enough to make it interesting on the spinnaker leg if she could bring up a fresher gust from astern, but Aussie hopes for this were sadly wrenched when a horrendous spinnaker wrap developed. For more than six embarrassing minutes, the unsightly mess stayed up there before it was finally cleared and a second sail set.

Despite this, the boats were going so fast that *Intrepid* only added five seconds in time—but more in distance, at the next mark, and there were still prospects of a battle developing, perhaps a slambang tacking duel on the next beat. There was even greater consternation, then, when *Gretel,* soon after clearing the mark and changing from spinnaker to genoa, was suddenly seen to come about and head back along her track. There in the welter of wind chop and boat wakes was a bobbing head. Paul Salmon, the foredeck man who had just secured the spinnaker pole, had been caught by green water with his back to the bow when she put her nose through a big one, and his feet were swept out from under him. *Gretel* missed him on the first pass, tacked again, and got him the next time, her sails shaking wildly, her lines a mess of spaghetti. In all, she lost about three minutes, and that was the end of any contest. *Intrepid* took it by 5:52 in 3:26:03.

Gretel called a lay day, and the protest, startling at the time but later overshadowed by the second one, was heard the next morning. *Gretel* had protested *Intrepid* for a basic port-starboard situation, and *Intrepid*'s counterprotest under IYRU Rule 34 was that *Gretel* had attempted to obstruct her in the act of keeping clear by luffing up sharply at the last minute. The race committee, which doubled *in toto* as the protest committee, disallowed both protests because there had been no contact, but it was obvious that the Aussies, by initiating this maneuver at first meeting, had introduced an element lacking since the Vanderbilt-Sopwith legal tangles of 1934. There had been no protest in America's Cup competition since then.

The Second Race, September 17–20

Seldom has a race taken so long to get into the record books, and this one will no doubt be talked about for years to come as one of the most famous incidents in America's Cup history. After the September 16 lay day, the boats towed out on a calm, sunny Thursday before a large spectator fleet, waited until 1350, and were sent home because of no wind. Friday brought a misty, rainy day and a moderate southerly, with a mile visibility at starting time. It also brought the announcement that cohelmsman Martin Visser would handle *Gretel* at the start, and a good move it seemed when he broke out of the usual circling into a neat safe leeward at the buoy end of the line.

Hardy was on the other twin steering wheel and took over from there, keeping *Gretel* in front with a loose cover, but obviously holding better boat speed. However, her lead of well over a minute evaporated in the rapidly closing fog right after the second mark, when *Intrepid* simply marched on by under spinnaker without any kind of response from *Gretel*. The defender was still ahead on the windward leg when the fog came down to zero, and, in another "first," the race was abandoned. The wind soon died, too, as the boats towed home in the murk, but *Gretel* had served notice that this would indeed be a real series.

Again a lay day was called by *Gretel* and the next appearance on the course was yet another first, a Sunday race. A spectator fleet of well over 1,000 came out on a day of flat sea and very little wind, the largest fleet since the 1962 opener, and, while waiting for the wind, witnessed two more unprecedented events. First, at the start of the tow out, Steve Van Dyck, *Intrepid's* tactician and a key man in her crew, suffered a severe reaction after having been stung on the lip by a yellow jacket that happened to be on a soft drink can when he sipped from it. Transferred to the tender, he eventually had to be airlifted by Coast Guard helicopter to the Naval Hospital in Newport, where emergency measures cleared up his condition in a couple of hours. Toby Tobin, a recruit from *Valiant's* crew, filled in as navigator, and Pete Wilson moved from navigator to tactician. Next, a supposed mine was discovered floating in the fleet, but it eventually proved to be a float for a fishing net.

Just in time before another postponement would have been necessary, a light southwester riffled in over the sunny seascape, and the 1400 start developed into the famous foul. *Intrepid* came in from a barging situation, headed for the stern of the committee boat, with *Gretel* luffing slowly up from a position to leeward and slightly ahead in an attempt to close out the opening at the committee boat. She was within her rights in doing this before the starting gun, but as soon as the gun went off, the governing rule changed and, under IYRU Rule 42.1 (e) *Gretel* could no longer sail above close hauled. This is the only rule that applies in this situation, but Visser continued to luff, with crew members still shouting "Up, up, up!" for 14 seconds after the gun, until *Gretel's* bow hit *Intrepid* aft of the mast. When contact is made in a sailboat race, someone must be thrown out, and *Gretel* had lost her right to continue luffing when the gun sounded. It is interesting that, with Visser at the helm, *Gretel* again sought a fouling situation, initiating the moves to set it up. Had he not been intent on forcing the foul, the irony is that she could have borne off and gathered way in a fine safe leeward position, and Visser could have turned her back to Hardy so that she probably never would have been headed in the entire race.

It was just her weather, 6–8 knots, and, despite her slow recovery from her lack of forward way and from being shunted to leeward by the collision, she almost broke through on the first leg. Just as she seemed about to climax a continual closing pattern in a tacking duel, Ficker broke off and let *Gretel* tack away, standing *Intrepid* into a fresh puff that was also a lift, and this put her back to a 42-second lead. Through the two reaches and the second beat she slowly built on it with fine sail handling and started the run leading by 1:12.

Then, with *Gretel* bringing up each stronger puff from astern, and with slackened backstays letting her limber rig lean way forward, she closed with good speed, while *Intrepid* failed to jibe at wide enough angles to fight *Gretel* off. Gradually the challenger ghosted by to a 50-second lead at the fifth mark, as Aussie rooters went wild. Few even knew that a protest had been lodged at that time, and when she slipped easily upwind to finish 1:07 ahead in twilight glow at 1837, bedlam broke loose in the fleet and rockets burst into the darkening sky.

The cheers turned to shouts of anger and tempers went off like the rockets of the day before when race committee chairman Dev Barker announced to a packed, tensely hushed press conference the next afternoon that *Gretel* had been disqualified for infraction of Rule 42.1 (e) and that *Intrepid* was therefore the winner. Everything hit the fan from then on, and the reaction reached to the Australian Parliament, to a statement by the United States Ambassador to Australia "apologizing" for the action, and to one Australian politician's suggestion that Australian troops be withdrawn from Vietnam. Packer refused to let the matter die, fighting it in the press for days and twice, with no new evidence, trying to get a reruling out of the committee. It wasn't until the final press conference that any Australian had anything but criticism in public for a clear-cut application of the rules, and it was Jim Hardy who then made the statement that "The New York YC Committee acted with complete integrity."

The Third Race, September 22

In a sobered atmosphere, Tuesday saw the boats on the course again before a much smaller spectator fleet, enjoying a sunny southwester that built from 10 to 18 knots from the 1210 start. The start was it in this race. Ficker gained a leeward position out of some circling with Visser, and the boats headed for the line far too early with about two minutes to go. Visser had nowhere to go but up as Ficker kept forcing him there, and they were at least 200 feet over 30 seconds before the gun. The buoy end was favored, but Visser had to tack away to port and got back to the line far to leeward, while Ficker dipped back, just cleared the buoy on starboard and tacked to port with a tremendous advantage as Hardy took over *Gretel*. Without much variation it remained at just under one minute around the first four marks. On the run, *Gretel* again began to close in the freshening breeze, but this time Van Dyck, back on board, gave Ficker the exact moment to make his last jibe and head for the mark, while *Gretel* continued on the opposite jibe at a wide angle to the rhumb line. Both boats were almost at hull speed, and *Gretel* merely added distance to her leg, so that the margin went from 53 seconds at the fourth mark to 1:16 at the fifth and 1:18 at the finish in 3:24:43.

It was the only race without "fireworks," but one bad move on *Intrepid*'s part after the masterful start could have blown it. Once more the Aussies called a lay day.

The Fourth Race, September 24

This race proved just how easily one bad move could change things. In a virtual carbon copy of the previous start, in a 10–12 knot clear easterly, Ficker again forced Visser to tack away to port, though behind the line this time. *Intrepid* carried on on starboard to the favored buoy end, flipped to port and had the lead nicely established at the gun. Hardy had *Gretel* in close pursuit all the way thereafter, and this was where Ficker gave his fans fits by sailing his own race without covering. For two windward legs, and for the third leg, when he used a ballooner despite *Gretel*'s spinnaker, it worked, but the gamble caught up with him on the final leg, which *Intrepid* began with a 1:02 lead and the Cup all but won. It was almost a fetch, in fact looked like one after just one tack, but this didn't last, and the boats sagged off on starboard tack with *Gretel* well up on the windward quarter. Suddenly, and too late, *Intrepid*'s afterguard realized that *Gretel* had better air and was being lifted. *Intrepid* had to tack over into a bad header to cover, but she couldn't clear by the time she got there, tacked on *Gretel*'s lee bow, and had lost it. Hardy came on with great boat speed and waited until he had one little hitch at the finish, playing it coolly for a 1:02 margin in 3:23:59. It was one of the most amazing comebacks in sailing history, and the closest America's Cup finish in distance since handicaps were used, only about 60–75 yards of *Intrepid*'s painful wallowing to windward in the fading air while the Aussies were already whooping it up in their cockpit.

The Fifth Race, September 28

A lay day Friday at the request of the shaken *Intrepid* crew, a fog cancellation Saturday, spoiling live TV arrangements by ABC-TV's "Wide World of Sports" for the second Saturday, and a fortunate lay day Sunday, when a vicious front whipped through, intervened before the series finally dragged out its record-breaking duration.

In a faint and shifty 8–10 knot northerly under cool, gray skies and before a tiny fleet of diehards, the boats staged one of the all-time great shows of match racing, a cliff-hanger from gun to gun that had just about every classic move of this special genre of sailing competition. The wind was freshest right at the start, and, with Hardy at the helm, *Gretel* got her best start of the official races. It was a windward advantage that made *Intrepid* tack under her in five minutes, but Hardy's hesitation in covering in the next few tacks finally let *Intrepid* break through, with the clincher an encounter when *Intrepid* was on starboard. Hardy tacked under her bow when he probably could have crossed, got caught under a good lift for *Intrepid* and saw the defender ease by into command. *Gretel* had to take two extra tacks to make the mark which gave Ficker a 44-second margin to play with, and he used every trick in the book to fight off the continuously surging, threatening *Gretel* from then on.

They seemed glued together on the reaches, and the second beat then produced one of the tensest tacking duels in Cup history. Ficker almost let the same thing happen that lost the fourth race, but he came back in time to a close cover when *Gretel* started to get a lift. He applied a stifling blanket from then on while inching toward the lay line, where the duel would have to end. Ficker kept his cover on so that they were both on port tack as they carried well beyond the lay line, with *Gretel* too close aboard under his lee bow to tack.

Choosing his time carefully, Ficker tacked away on a good puff, while Hardy held on port for a precious few seconds more that meant lost distance. On her good point of close reaching, *Intrepid* drove for the mark with slightly started sheets and had a 51-second lead in the bank as they squared away for the direct run in the dying breeze. In an agonizingly long, suspense-filled leg that took an hour, the boats tacked downwind at radical angles, with *Intrepid* never letting *Gretel* get on her air, and she still had 20 seconds of the lead left on her last rounding of the familiar orange and white America's Cup buoy.

By then the wind had shifted to the eastward, making a virtual fetch out of the final leg. *Intrepid* tacked immediately after rounding, but *Gretel*'s crew hadn't cleared from dousing the spinnaker quite as quickly, and she had to stand on port for wasted distance while *Intrepid* was chomping away for home. Hardy tried desperately to lure *Intrepid* into some mistake on this last leg, but Ficker would have none of it this time, staying between the challenger and the line all the way, to build a 1:44 margin in 4:29:03. So great had been the tension of this truly fine race that it seemed to escape like air out of a punctured tire when the gun finally went off to mark the end of a fascinating, long-to-be-remembered series.

Outdoors

A SPORTSMAN'S DAYDREAM

By Nelson Bryant

From The New York Times

Once I wanted to write a great lyric poem, make a million dollars and own the island of Naushon.

Now I will settle for a decent sonnet, something less than a million and an occasional stroll on Naushon's beaches.

This is not defeatism, just logic. Most lyric poets are running downhill after 30. Admittedly, making a million, or millions, can come late in life. Colonel Sanders and his chickens have proved that, but after more than a quarter of a century of working for wages, I have learned that I have no nose for money, and Naushon has remained lovely and unspoiled without my help.

One of my lesser goals, to create a classic trout fly, is still within reach, however.

Anyone can tie a fly and name it after himself, but the trick is to create one that will be used consistently by other fishermen. For this reason, it should also be attractive to fish.

Over the years I have labored at my fly-tying labors long after the rest of the house is asleep, to find that one classic fly. Many of my inventions were little more than variations on existing patterns and all of them took fish. Only one of my own patterns failed utterly. It was made from fibers stolen from a cherished whisk broom that belonged to my mother's grandmother. I cannot take a fish with it, nor can I lose it. It rests secure in my fly book, a constant reminder of my youthful indiscretion.

Ten years ago, I developed an interesting little nymph that may be the answer. It is made from hairs clipped from my chest and I've had fair success with it. I shall try tying a few more of these soon, for some of the hair is gray now, and the new color scheme may make the difference between mediocrity and brilliance.

I could call it 46–47 (46 for chest inches, 47 for years) . The next step would be to give a few to some of my trout-fishing friends, preferably those who talk a great deal or who write for newspapers or outdoor publications.

Just a few mentions here and there could turn the tide. Something like, "My day on the Battenkill was a disaster until I tied on Bryant's exquisite little nymph, the 46–47," or "the 10-pound brown in Balderdash Pool, a fish that had refused all offerings throughout the summer, took my 46–47 with a tremendous rush, his gold sides gleaming in the last light of evening."

These flies would, for obvious reasons, be limited in numbers, ideal gifts for close friends or heads of state. I would, if my calculations are correct, be able to produce six dozen a year without venturing off prime territory, and would, of course, always set aside a tuft or two for emergencies and gallant gestures.

Picture Lady Lightcreel distraught in her coracle, trout rising all about her, and her gillie wringing his hands because she has just snapped off her last 46–47 on a big Loch Leven. Picture me tearing open my windbreaker, wrenching the necessary materials from my bosom and fashioning a fly on the spot.

That's the stuff from which legends are made.

General

THE JOE NAMATH SYSTEM

By Dick Young

From the New York Daily News

Copyright, ©, 1970, New York Daily News

Hello, stupid. You reading this while hanging by one arm in a D train? You going to work, stupid? What's the matter, ain't you got no problems? Don't you know if you got problems you ain't supposed to work?

It's the latest thing, stupid. You got problems, you don't go to work. You stay home and mope. This is very good for problems, moping. Turn around and go home. Go ahead. Right now. Nobody with problems goes to work today. Everybody uses the Joe Namath system.

The Joe Namath system is that if you got problems, you don't go to work. You don't stay home, either, but you don't go to work. You go to Bachelors III and some of the other joints on the East Side that are conducive to ironing out problems, but one important thing, if anybody says how come you're not working today, you say to him, I got problems.

Right away, he feels sorry for you. He says, poor Max got problems. This explains everything. It explains everything till he thinks about it for a minute and remembers that he has problems, too; and what kind of stuff is this that you can say you got problems which explains why you ain't going to work?

It helps most if you got a boss who can feel sorry for you. If you got a boss like Phil Iselin, it's great to have problems. You go see him, the way Joe Namath does, or maybe, if you're really hung up by your problems, and they're such gross problems that you can't travel, your boss will come to see you. You tell him that most of your problems would go away if you had some money. Chances are, if he's like Phil Iselin, he'll try to arrange something.

That's if you're working for Phil Iselin's football team, the New

York Jets, he'll arrange something. If you're working for Phil Iselin's dressmaking company, Korell, your problems may not impress him that much. I've heard of some guys in the garment business who went to their boss with problems and what do you suppose he told them? Get the hell out, he told them, I got problems myself. One of my problems, he told them, is you guys with problems, and he hired somebody else.

Some people have suggested that Phil Iselin try running the New York Jets the way he runs his dress company. They say he would not put up with this sort of thing for one minute if his No. 1 fabric cutter stayed home to worry about personal problems, and just when they're going in with the new winter line. They say he would simply get himself another cutter, somebody who wants to work, problems or no. The new man may not be as good as the other guy, not right away, but it can't hurt too much because Phil Iselin can't fill the orders he has now.

Of course, there are other people who think Phil Iselin should run his dress company the way he runs the Jets. But if he did that he probably couldn't afford the football team, because it's very difficult to make dresses if your employees stay home when they have problems.

We got a place here in New York where lots of people with problems never go to work. It's called the Bowery. They used the Joe Namath system on the Bowery long before Joe Namath was born. They refined the system to the ultimate. They blamed the whole world and got off. They moped about their problems for a few days, a few weeks, a few years, and eventually the problems went away.

Joe Namath has an advantage over most people with problems. He has lots of help. It's surprising, really, that he needs Phil Iselin to bail him out. After all, Joe Namath has all those beautiful people hanging around, hanging on, telling him how wonderful he is, how stimulating he is, how right he is, telling him how wrong are all those dreadful people who disagreed with him, who tried to repress his blithe spirit.

"Atta boy, Joey Baby. You show 'em, Joey Baby. You tell it like it is, Joey Baby. You do your thing, the way you want. What's the diff, Joey Baby? Long as you aren't hurting anybody."

That is the copout phrase of our time, of all times. "I'm not hurting anyone else." One day you wake up and say I'm sorry. I'm sorry, I didn't know. I didn't realize.

One day, the bravado oozes out, and there you stand, all alone, needing help, and where do you go for that help? To those beautiful hangers-on, the ones who patted you on the back and said you tell 'em, Joey Baby? Do they come up with the answers? Do you turn to them, or do you mope and not go to work, and finally turn to the people you wouldn't listen to before, the people who weren't kissing your feet, the people who tried to tell you what was best for you, but you couldn't hear them over the chorus shouting, Atta boy, Joey Baby!

"He's a pathetic figure," said a man close to Phil Iselin who has watched the mess develop.

The other day, I saw Roy Campanella. He was going to work. I guess he doesn't have any problems.

THE LIFE AND HARD TIMES OF JIM BOUTON

By Roger Kahn

From Esquire

Copyright, ©, 1970, by Esquire, Inc.

At about the time petrifaction laid an icy hand on his pitching arm, James Alan Bouton appeared at the Methodist Office for the United Nations, as the short reliever in a sorrowful little game. In front of an audience of one hundred, a black soccer player from South Africa was proposing that the United States boycott the 1968 Olympics, unless the Boers were expelled, "in protest against apartheid and in the name of morality." If I read history correctly, morality is central neither to the modern Olympics nor to American policy. (Quickly now, what city with a gauleiter named Joseph Goebbels was awarded the Olympics of 1936?)

To demonstrate support, the meeting's sponsors had recruited a black basketball player from Columbia who sat silently at the South African's right. To the left sat Bouton, white, then a Yankee and crew cut.

"I have a question for Jim Bouton," called Howard Cosell, the Torquemada of the American Broadcasting Company, when the soccer player finished speaking. "If South Africa is banned, what would you say to black American athletes who want to boycott the Olympics anyway because of alleged American racism?"

Bouton rose, looked evenly at Cosell and said, "Howard, in view of what has happened in America, I can't condemn any protest black people make, as long as it isn't violent." Bouton's mind was quicker than his slider. That June the Yankees had to send him to the minor leagues, because he could no longer throw hard.

Like almost every athlete, Bouton rejected the verdict of fate and time. He decided to master the knuckle ball, a complicated pitch, which enables one man a generation to reach his middle forties as a successful major leaguer. The knuckler is held with the fingertips and thrown with a locked wrist so that the ball sails almost without rotation. For reasons of aerodynamics, a good knuckle ball celebrates its arrival at home plate with a giddy, unpredictable lunge: up, down, sideways or at any of the intervening angles. It is difficult for hitters, humiliating for catchers and almost impossible to control. Anyone with a fair arm can experiment with a knuckler. It is a rare man who finds the combination of touch, velocity, assurance and control that makes it a viable pitching weapon. Among those whose fingertips missed the combination was Jim Bouton.

This predictable and ordinary failure provides the platform for *Ball Four,* a four-hundred-page diary which is described in the subtitle as "My Life and Hard Times Throwing the Knuckleball in the Big Leagues." Bouton, the diarist, chips at tradition, ridicules stupidity and makes jokes. When he learns that a teammate starred at Black Earth, Wisconsin, he composed a mock school song. "Black Earth, we love you. Hurrah for the rocks and the dirt." When he spots Bob Smith of the old Howdy Doody show in a drugstore, he sings the complete Howdy Doody theme aloud. He laughs harshly at greenies—green amphetamine pills—on which some ball players depend. A quiet infielder named John Kennedy suddenly shrieks at an umpire and explains in the dugout, according to Bouton, "I guess my greenie kicked in."

In addition, Bouton is conventionally and comfortably liberal, in contrast to the conventional, comfortable conservatism of his teammates. He dislikes bigotry and cruelty to children. He also has little use for discretion and there is the arrowhead of controversy. Bouton feels free to describe and laugh at the sexual habits of others, whom he names. This has delighted many young sports writers, to whom the standard portrait of the athlete as monk must be buried at any cost. To Dick Young, the best of newspaper baseball reporters, such tattling makes Bouton a "social leper." As Christmas approaches, the controversy endures, and sales of *Ball Four* climb over the magic number of 200,000.

The genus of books by American athletes dates from at least 1912, when Grosset and Dunlap published Christy Mathewson's *Pitching in a Pinch.* Mathewson, a Bucknell graduate before the baccalaureate pandemic, worked with a ghost named John N. Wheeler and the resulting book is remarkably funny.

"A friend [wrote Mathewson cum ghost in 1912] who took a different fork when we left college was walking down Broadway in

New York with me one morning after I had joined the Giants, and we passed a cross-eyed man. I grabbed off my hat and spat in it. It was a new hat, too. 'What's the matter with you, Matty?' he asked, surprised.

" 'Spit in your hat quick and kill that jinx,' I answered, not thinking for the minute, and he followed my example. I forgot to mention, when I said he took another fork, that he had become a pitcher, too, but of a different kind. He was a minister, and as luck would have it, he was wearing a silk hat.

" 'What's the idea?' he asked.

" 'Worst jinx in the world to see a cross-eyed man,' I replied. 'But I hope I didn't hurt your silk hat.'

" 'Not at all. But how about these ballplayers who masticate the weed? Do they kill jinxes, too?' I had to admit that they were the main exterminators of the jinx.

" 'Then,' the minister went on, 'I'm glad the percentage of wearers of cross-eyes is small.' "

The style is addictive. Once you adjust, you admire Mathewson-Wheeler for their mixture of irreverence and dignity and, if you come to the book with the right spirit, the past and Great Matty's Ghost embrace you, and McGraw and Cobb and Wagner live by your side.

Is *Pitching in a Pinch* accurate, or even close? Mathewson was gassed during World War I and died in 1925. Although few survive who knew him in his prime, and the evidence is incomplete, Mathewson in real life appears to have been so fiercely competitive and so caustic that gentle people are said to have fled his company. If verity were all, his book could be forgotten, but it is a perfect period piece and the original of an entire genre, and so a landmark.

After *Pitching in a Pinch,* the star's by-line above the handiwork of a ghost became an institution. Editors consistently promised the public inside tips from the secret life of Babe Ruth, Dizzy Dean and Warren Spahn. This was (and is) a questionable business. Ball players are unlikely to tell on themselves, even for cash advances, and ghosting does not always bring out the artist in a collaborator. The result is a chrestomathy with climactic paragraphs that always seem to read about like this:

"The bases were loaded now, and there I was, facing the best hitter in the business. With the count three and two, the manager came out and wanted to know if I was tired. Sure I was. I'm human. But this was no time to be thinking of myself. I thought of Luella and our lovely clapboard house six miles east of Bradford, Pa., and our three daughters who go to Sunday school and how the whole team was counting on me. I told the skipper I could do the job.

"He looked at me and must have thought of all our years together. It kind of looked like mist got in his eyes. I maybe prayed a little and the Big Guy Upstairs must have heard me because I threw a curve that broke three feet. That was it. I had my strikeout. We had the Series. I want publicly to thank the Big Guy for giving me the strength to throw that curve and to add that those stories about me throwing an illegal spitball are being spread by agents of the devil."

The principal preserver of this form was *The Saturday Evening Post* during the disastrous late years of its old regime. At almost every World Series during the 1950's, a diffident *Post* editor appeared and signed a star to compose exclusive memoirs with a writer of the star's choice. Catastrophe came when Casey Stengel offered his reminiscences for sale. Stengel, once called Dutch, was a free spirit, and the idea of a blunt book, sweeping from Dutch Stengel, Kansas City roughneck, to Charles Dillon Stengel, California bank executive and national shrine, had true appeal. In a sense, Casey and the United States had run certain parallel courses. As the agent who handled the bidding recalls, "*Look* quit early, at about $60,000 or so. But I had *The Post* going against *Life,* with book publishers as backup, and it wasn't until we hit $125,000 that I got a little scared. These things can blow up. So I said one more bid each. *Life* offered $150,000. *The Post* won with $155,000."

The judgment of years is that only the agent won. Stengel's memoirs were pale as beer foam and just about as substantial. The old man appreciated the money, but he was damned if he was going to tell about drink, cash and the other hard elements in his epochal life. He settled for tedium, which helped kill *The Post* and which I keep close to the bed in book form because it is safer than Seconal and just as effective.

One clean blow for literacy was struck in 1960 by Jim Brosnan, a tall, thorny, bespectacled intellectual, who made a living by throwing sliders for the Cincinnati Reds. Brosnan recorded the year 1959, when the Cardinals traded him to Cincinnati, in a diary called *The Long Season.* It is candid, sometimes moving and unpretentious. Brosnan likes martinis, needling and semantics. (His friend, Dr. S. I. Hayakawa, then a semanticist of uncertain politics, plays a walk-on, and displays self-confidence and no knowledge of baseball.)

Brosnan recounts the end of the great Sal Maglie with chilling economy. He makes a deal with a rival to throw fast balls to one another, is betrayed and describes the other pitcher with a racial epithet. He misses his wife, who calls him "Meat." He is given to grouches. He gets drunk. He relishes the smile of his manager. He wishes he were a better pitcher.

The diary form eliminated problems of organization and enabled Brosnan to concentrate on content rather than on form. His writing has little slickness and not much lyricism, but carries an irresistible sense of truth.

"The last day of the season comes [he writes].

"The last time to pack the duffel bag with gloves and shoes, jock straps and jackets, souvenirs and clippings.

"The last hours of a team.

"The last moment to say good-bye . . . to say good luck.

"But it's also time to say, 'See you in the spring, buddy.' Every ballplayer thinks he can come back again. On the last day, baseball is a game professionals really do *play;* it no longer seems like work.

"I stuffed my glove into a duffel bag and picked up the last shirt from my locker. The empty locker symbolizes the cold blue sadness of the last day. . . ."

Sweeping afterward, the 1960's provided a kind of graft, combining the hand of the ghost, as in Mathewson, with the form of the diary, as in Brosnan. It is no longer possible to define obscenity, which is probably a good thing, but in lieu of definition, I can present an example. A two-man diary is obscene. A genuine diary, like Brosnan's, is an individual personal record. By the late 1960's sport was infested with gabby athletes and hungry ghosts, holding hands and microphones into which they murmured in infinite intimacy, "Dear Diary and others." This form of collaboration produces readability and sometimes sales, but it is built on a gimmick, and that is a dangerous way to start a book. If the form is false, are we about to spend the winter tramping snows for the grail of honesty?

Among forceful critics of pseudo-diaries was Leonard Shecter who complained that they did not really tell as much as they pretended. Now Shecter appears as Bouton's partner in *Ball Four,* but, he indicates in the foreword, he is a shade of difference. The basic conceit of pseudo-diaries is that they are really the work of the athletes and that the hungry ghosts have helped with only commas,

spelling and typing. Describing *Ball Four,* Shecter concedes that he
and Bouton "had disagreements and suffered frayed nerves" as they
labored together. Score one point for Len Shecter and reality.

Like Bouton, Shecter is a man of unusual gifts. He appeared
during the 1950's on a train bearing the Brooklyn Dodgers, saying,
"They don't want me to write about the games." He meant that Ike
Gellis or Paul Sann, his bosses at the *New York Post,* had told him
to write about people, which he did, extremely well. He moved
from the Dodgers to the Yankees, a journalist of intelligence and
drive, and in time he tried a general column. When the project
soured, he quit the *Post* to free-lance. Four years ago, he called to
ask if I'd write for a new weekly. "Pete Hamill and I are starting it.
It'll be like a *Village Voice,* only well-written." I said that as an
unsuccessful reader of Nat Hentoff I would be pleased to do what I
could. But this plan died, too, for lack of funds.

In the role inflicted on him—free-lance sports writer—Shecter
developed an interesting, skeptical style. "A professional curmud-
geon-in-residence," Bob Lipsyte has written earnestly in *The New
York Times.* One did not have to accept Shecter's view of Vince
Lombardi as a native fascist any more than one had to accept Bart
Starr's sense of Lombardi as The Second Coming.

But sports writing badly needs skeptics. The world is wide and
there is room in it for both Shecter and Starr to be wrong.

When *Ball Four* is at its very best, as in a description of Ted
Williams' batting, an echo of Shecter's cold realism resounds.

"He'd go to the cage [wrote Bouton-Shecter], wave his bat at the
pitcher and start screaming at the top of his voice, 'My name is Ted
f——— Williams and I'm the greatest hitter in baseball.'

"He'd swing and hit a line drive.

" 'Jesus H. Christ Himself couldn't get me out.' "

"And he'd hit another.

"Then he'd say, 'Here comes Jim Banning, Jim f——— Banning,
and that little shit slider of his.'

"Wham!

" 'He doesn't really think he's gonna get me out with that shit.'

"Blam!

" 'I'm Ted f——— Williams.'

"Sock!"

That's it. That's Williams exactly. Shocking. Loud. And all those
astonishing line drives. Where Bouton's notes feed Shecter's skill,

one forgets that *Ball Four* is a pseudo-diary. One is simply swept along. But *Ball Four* is a pseudo-diary and ultimately shallowness and artificiality are its undoing.

Throughout the book, Bouton-Shecter want to tell us about the lonely chaos of the road. That is an excellent goal, but instead of approaching the silver of, say, Willy Loman's fall, they adopt a superior and almost leering viewpoint. Quite literally, they laugh at other men's erections, as though immune.

One infielder announces on a team bus: "Boys, I had all the ingredients of a great piece of ass last night—plenty of time, and a hard-on. All I lacked was the broad." Taste is subjective. What troubles me is that Bouton-Shecter elect to name the infielder and a dozen other people who make similar observations. The issue here is not Puritanism, Women's Liberation or The Playboy Philosophy. Rather it is intrusion from an outsider on tenuous human relationships. Ball players, and even their wives, are people; prick them and they bleed. Men ought to think extremely carefully before capitalizing on the gaucherie of someone else.

In the absence of rules, and there are none, the best test is to reverse roles. How would Bouton-Schecter like to read a smug account of their own wild road evenings, if any? "But I'm as rough on myself as on anyone," Bouton has protested. "Don't I put myself in a Hollywood pool, stripped to undershorts, treading water and holding a martini in each hand." He does, and that is irrelevant. A Hollywood pool is not the road. It's the American dream. *I haven't been one hundred percent faithful to the little woman myself. I've slipped at least three times. Let's see, there was Marilyn and Jackie and Liz.* The road, and Bouton-Shecter know it better than I, is a dirty coffee shop at 2:20 A.M. with a brassy, buck-toothed waitress as the only game in town and, to your own horror, a certain rising interest.

The Puritanism of sport is dangerous nonsense. Whole generations of Americans reach biological maturity still equating chastity with victory and virginity with no-hitters, after which they develop problems. Down with all scarlet letters. But Bouton-Shecter, by calculated, commercial finger-pointing in *Ball Four,* give anti-Puritanism a bad name.

My other reservations are more abstract. In *Ball Four,* Bouton is too often the unobserved observer, supplying facts (his salary), opinion (he likes Father Groppi) and nice incidentals (he is excellent at the game of trivia). But in serious books, the central figure

For the Record

ARCHERY

World Champions

Men (Free-Style) —Stephen Lieberman, Reading, Pa.
Women (Free-Style) —Mrs. Eunice Schewe, Rockford, Ill.
Men (Barebow) —Elmer Moore, Newport News.
Women (Barebow) —Mrs. Sonja Johansson, Sweden.

National Archery Association Champions

Men—Joe Thornton, Tahlequah, Okla.
Women—Mrs. Nancy Myrick, Pompano Beach, Fla.

U.S. Professional Champions

Men—Vic Berger, Springfield, Ohio.
Women—Ann Butz, Suffern, N.Y.

National Field Archery Champions

Open Free-Style—Frank Ketchum, Manton, Calif.
Amateur Free-Style—Joe Young, Medane, N.C.
Women's Open Free-Style—Ann Butz, Suffern.
Women's Amateur Free-Style—Barbara Ann Brown, Ledyard, Conn.

AUTOMOBILE RACING

World Road Racing—Jochen Rindt, Austria (killed Sept. 5) (Lotus Ford).
World Manufacturers—Porsche.
Canadian-American Cup—Denis Hulme, New Zealand (McLaren-Chevrolet).
USAC—Al Unser, Albuquerque, N.M. (Johnny Lightning Ford).
Indianapolis 500—Al Unser.
NASCAR—Bob Isaac, Catawba, N.C. (Dodge).
Le Mans—Hans Herrman, West Germany, and Richard Attwood, England (Porsche).
Grand Prix of U.S.—Emerson Fittipaldi, Brazil (Lotus-Ford).

BADMINTON

Men—Junji Honma, Japan.
Women—Etsuko Takenaka, Japan.
Men's Doubles—Junji Honma and Ippei Kojima.
Women's Doubles—Etsuko Takenaka and Machiko Aizawa, Japan.
Mixed Doubles—Paul Whetnall and Margaret Boxall, England.

BASEBALL

World Series—Baltimore Orioles.
National League—Pittsburgh (East), Cincinnati (West), Cincinnati (play-offs).
American League—Baltimore (East), Minnesota (West), Baltimore (play-offs).
All-Star Game—National League.
Leading Batter (N.) —Rico Carty, Atlanta.
Leading Batter (A.) —Alex Johnson, California.
Pacific Coast League—Spokane (North), Hawaii (South), Spokane (play-offs).
American Association—Omaha (East), Denver (West), Omaha (play-offs).
International League—Syracuse.
Eastern League—Waterbury.
National Collegiate—Southern California.
Eastern Intercollegiate—Dartmouth.

BASKETBALL

National Association—Knickerbockers.
American Association—Indiana Pacers.
National Collegiate—UCLA.
NCAA (College Division) —Philadelphia Textile.
National Invitation—Marquette.
Ivy League—Pennsylvania.
Yankee Conference—Massachusetts and Connecticut.
Knickerbocker   Conference—Stony Brook.
West Coast A.C.—Santa Clara and Pacific U.
Southern Conference—Davidson.
Southeastern Conference—Kentucky.
Big Ten—Iowa.
Ohio Valley—Western Kentucky.
Western Athletic—Texas (El Paso) .
Pacific Eight—UCLA.
Missouri Valley—Drake.
Big Eight—Kansas State.
North-East League—Southern Connecticut.
Mid-American Conference—Ohio U.
Southwest Conference—Rice.
Atlantic Coast—South Carolina.
NAIA—Kentucky State.
Middle Atlantic (University) —Temple.
Middle Atlantic (Coll. North) —Philadelphia Textile.
Middle Atlantic (Coll. South) —Muhlenberg.

BIATHLON

World Champions

Team—Soviet Union.
Individual—Aleksandr   Tikhonov, U.S.S.R.

United States Champion

Individual—Sgt. Peter Karns, U.S. Army.

BILLIARDS

U.S. Open (Pocket) —Steve Mizerak, Perth Amboy, N.J.

BOBSLEDDING

World Champions

Two-Man—West Germany.
Four-Man—Italy.

North American Champions

Two-Man—Paul Lamey and Robert Huscher, Navy.
Four-Man—Lake Placid Bobsled Club.

National AAU Champions

Two-Man—Paul Lamey and Robert Huscher.
Four-Man—U.S. Navy.

LUGE

World Champions

Singles—Josef Fendt, West Germany.
Women's Singles—Barbara Piecha, Poland.
Doubles—Austria.

BOWLING

American Bowling Congress Champions

All-Events (Classic) —Bob Strampe, Detroit.
All-Events (Regular) —Mike Berlin, Muscatina, Iowa.
Singles (Classic) —Glenn Allison, Whittier, Calif.
Singles (Regular) —J. Yoder, Fort Wayne, Ind.
Doubles (Classic) —Dave Soutar, Gilroy, Calif. and Nelson Burton, St. Louis.
Doubles (Regular) —Dick Selgo and Don Bredehoft, Toledo, Ohio.
Team (Classic) —Merchant Enterprises, N.Y.
Team (Regular) —Hamm's Beer, Minneapolis.

Other Champions

All-Star Men—Bobby Cooper, Houston, Tex.
All-Star Women—Mary Baker, Central Islip, L.I., N.Y.
ABC Masters—Don Glover, Bakersfield, Calif.
PBA—Mike McGrath, El Cerrito, Calif.
Tournament Earnings—Mike McGrath.

Women's International Bowling Congress Champions
OPEN DIVISION

Singles—Dorothy Fothergill, North Attleboro, Mass.

Doubles—Gloria Bouvia and Judy Cook, Portland, Oreg.

All-Events—Dorothy Fothergill.

Team—Parker-Fothergill Pro Shop, Cranston, R.I.

BOXING

World Professional Champions

Flyweight—Erbito Salvarria, Philippines.

Bantamweight—Chucho Castillo, Mexico.

Featherweight—Kuniaki Shibata, Japan.

Junior Lightweight—Hiroshi Kobayashi, Japan.

Lightweight—Ken Buchanan, Scotland.

Junior Welterweight—N. Loche, Argentina.

Welterweight—Billy Backus, Syracuse.

Middleweight—Carlos Monzon, Argentina.

Light-Heavyweight—Bob Foster, Washington.

Heavyweight—Joe Frazier, Philadelphia.

National AAU Champions

106-Pound—Elijah Cooper, Paterson, N.J.

112-Pound—Eduardo Santiago, New York.

119-Pound—Robert Mullins, Spartanburg, S.C.

125-Pound—Ray Lunny, Redwood, Calif.

132-Pound—James Parks, Paterson, N.J.

139-Pound—Quiencelan Daniel, Detroit.

147-Pound—Armando Muniz, Los Angeles.

156-Pound—Jesse Valdez, Houston, Tex.

165-Pound—John Mangum, Detroit.

178-Pound—Nathaniel Jackson, Memphis.

Heavyweight—Ronnie Lyle, Denver.

Team—U.S. Air Force.

CANOEING

United States Champions

Kayak Singles (1,000 Meters) Henry Krawczyk, New York.

Women's Kayak Singles (500 Meters) — Mrs. Marcia Smoke, Niles, Mich.

Kayak Tandem (1,000 Meters) —Henry and Eugene Krawczyk, New York.

Women's Kayak Tandem—Mrs. Marcia Smoke and Mrs. Sperry Rademaker, Niles, Mich.

Kayak Fours—New York.

Women's Kayak Fours—Niles, Mich.

Canoe Singles (1,000 Meters) —Andy Weigand, New York A.C.

Canoe Tandem (1,000 Meters) —Andy Toro and Dick Soules, Lincoln Park, Mich.

Kayak Singles (10,000 Meters) —Peter Weigand, New York, A.C.

Kayak Tandem (10,000 Meters) — Henry and Eugene Krawczyk.

Canoe Singles (10,000 Meters) —Andy Weigand.

Canoe Tandem (10,000 Meters) —Andy Toro and Dick Soules.

CASTING

United States Champions

INLAND

Anglers All-Round—Steve Rajeff, San Francisco.

Grand All-Round—Zack Willson, Powell, Ohio.

Distance—Zack Willson.

Accuracy—Steve Rajeff.

Women's Accuracy—Mollie Schneider, Jeffersonville, Ind.

Distance (Baits) —Zack Willson.

Distance (Flies) —Zack Willson.

Accuracy (Baits) —Zack Willson.

Accuracy (Flies) —Steve Rajeff.

SURF

All Distance—Marion Hutson, Chesapeake, Virginia.

Level Line Distance—Marion Hutson and Jim White, Jr., Virginia Beach, Va.

Unrestricted Distance—Marion Hutson.

All Accuracy—Harry Aiken, Georgetown, Del.

COURT TENNIS

World Open—Pete Bostwick, Locust Valley.

U.S. Open—Jim Bostwick, Old Brookville, L.I., N.Y.
U.S. Open Doubles—Jim and Pete Bostwick, Jr., Old Brookville, L.I., N.Y.
Van Alen Cup—England.

CROSS-COUNTRY

National AAU—Frank Shorter, Florida. T.C.
National AAU Team—Pacific Coast Club.
NCAA—Steve Prefontaine, Oregon.
NCAA Team—Villanova.
IC 4-A—Donal Walsh, Villanova.
IC 4-A Team—Villanova.
Heptagonal—Jon Anderson, Cornell.
Heptagonal Team—Harvard.

CURLING

World—Canada.
U.S.—Grafton (N. Dak.) C.C.
Women's U.S.—Duluth, Minn.
Gordon International Medal—Canada
Dykes Memorial Medal—St. Andrews
Gordon Champion Rink—Schenectady, N.Y.
Gordon Bowl—Heather, Montreal.
Caledonia Medal—Bayview, Montreal.
Empire State (Women)—Winchester, Mass.

CYCLING

World Champions

1,000-Meter Time Trial—Fredborg, Denmark.
Sprints (Match)—Morelon, France.
Tandem—Barth and Muller, West Germany.
4,000-Meter Ind. Pursuit—Kurmann, Switzerland.
100-Kilometer Road Time Trial—U.S.S.R.
112.5-Mile Road Race—J. Schmidt, Denmark.
Women's Road (372 Miles)—Konkina, U.S.S.R.
Women's Sprint—Tsarevs, U.S.S.R.
Women's 3,000-Meter Pursuit—Garkuschina, U.S.S.R.

United States Champions

Match Sprint—Harry Cutting, Riverside, Calif.
4,000-Meter Pursuit—John Van de Velde, Glen Ellyn, Ill.

Ten-Mile Open—Bobby Phillips, Baltimore.
112-Mile Road Race—Mike Carnahan, Rochester, N.Y.
Women's 3,000-Meter Pursuit—Mrs. Audrey McElmury, Del Mar, Calif.
Women's 29.30-Mile Road Race—Mrs. McElmury.
Women's ½-Mile—Jeanne Kloska, Massapequa, L.I., N.Y.

DOGS

Major Best-in-Show Winners

Westminister (New York)—Ch. Arriba's Prima Donna, boxer, owned by Dr. and Mrs. P. J. Pagano, Pelham Manor, N.Y., and Dr. Theodore S. Fickes, Marblehead, Mass.; 2,611 dogs entered.
International (Chicago)—Ch. Special Edition, Lakeland terrier, owned by Mr. and Mrs. James A. Farrell, Jr., Darien, Conn.; 3,642.
Trenton—Special Edition; 3,613.
Santa Barbara (Calif.)—Ch. Vin-Melca's Vagabond, Norwegian elkhound, owned by Mrs. Patricia V. Craige, Monterey, Calif.; 3,658.
Boardwalk (Atlantic City)—Ch. Chen Korum Ti, Lhasa Apso, owned by Pat Chenoweth, Saratoga, Calif.; 3,004.
Westchester—Ch. Major O'Shannon, Irish setter, owned by Albert M. Greenfield, Jr., Glen Moore, Pa.; 2,507.
Beverly Hills (Calif.)—Ch. Special Edition; 2,845.

Field Trial National Champions

Bird Dogs (Pointers and Setters)—Johnny Crockett, English setter, owned by H. P. Sheehy, Denton, Tex.
Grouse—Grouse Ridge Will, English setter, owned by Dr. Thomas M. Flanagan, Norwich, N.Y.
Open Pheasant—Handicap Mike, English setter, owned by Santo de Spirt, Southwick, Mass.
Amateur Pheasant—Mr. Thor, English setter, owned by John O'Neall, Sr., and Jr., Hatchechubbee, Ala.
Pheasant Shooting—Andy Capp,

pointer, owned by Mrs. Bazy Tankersley, Barnesville, Md.

Retriever—Creole Sister, Labrador, owned by Donald P. Weiss, Shreveport, La.

Amateur English Springer Spaniel—Misty Muffett, owned by Dr. and Mrs. C. A. Christensen, Cornelius, Oreg.

Open English Springer Spaniel—Saighton Sizzler, owned by John M. Olin, St. Louis.

Brittany Spaniel—Jac Pierre's Pride, owned by James E. Cohen, Hudson, Ohio.

Amateur German Short-Haired Pointer—Schling von Shinback, owned by Don Nicely, Namper, Idaho.

FENCING

World Champions

Foil—Friedrich Wessel, West Germany.
Epée—A. Nikanchikov, U.S.S.R.
Saber—T. Pezsa, Hungary.
Women's Foil—G. Gorokhova, U.S.S.R.
Foil Team—U.S.S.R.
Epée Team—Hungary.
Saber Team—U.S.S.R.
Women's Foil Team—U.S.S.R.

United States Champions

Foil—Albert Axelrod, New York.
Epée—Joseph Elliot, Beverly Hills, Calif.
Saber—Alex Orban, New York.
Women's Foil—Harriet King, San Francisco.
Foil Team—Salle Santelli, New York.
Epée Team—New York A.C.
Saber Team—New York A.C.
Women's Foil Team—N.Y. Fencers Club.

National Collegiate Champions

Foil—Walter Krause, NYU.
Epée—John Nadas, Case Western Reserve.
Saber—Bruce Soriano, Columbia.
Team—NYU

Intercollegiate Association Champions

Foil—Walter Krause.
Epée—Wayne Krause, NYU.
Saber—Bruce Soriano.

Foil Team—NYU.
Epée Team—Pennsylvania.
Saber Team—NYU.
Three-Weapon Team—NYU

FOOTBALL

Intercollegiate Champions

National—Texas.
Eastern (Lambert Trophy)—Dartmouth.
Eastern (Lambert Cup)—Delaware.
Eastern (Lambert Bowl)—Edinboro State.
Ivy League—Dartmouth.
Big Ten—Ohio State.
Yankee Conference—Connecticut.
Middle Atlantic (College, North)—Susquehanna.
Middle Atlantic (College, South)—Moravian.
Southeastern Conference—LSU
Atlantic Coast Conference—Wake Forest.
Southern Conference—William and Mary.
Mid-American Conference—Toledo.
Big Eight—Nebraska.
Missouri Valley Conference—Louisville.
Pacific Eight—Stanford.
Ohio Valley—Western Kentucky.
Southwest Conference—Texas.
Big Sky—Montana.
Pacific Coast A.A.—Long Beach State and San Diego State.
Western Athletic—Arizona State.

National League

NATIONAL CONFERENCE

Eastern Division—Dallas Cowboys.
Central Division—Minnesota Vikings.
Western Division—San Francisco 49ers.
Conference—Dallas Cowboys.

AMERICAN CONFERENCE

Eastern Division—Baltimore Colts.
Central Division—Cincinnati Bengals.
Western Division—Oakland Raiders.
Conference—Baltimore Colts.

Super Bowl

Baltimore Colts.

Canadian Professional

Grey Cup—Montreal Alouettes.

GOLF

Men

National Open—Tony Jacklin.
National Amateur—Lanny Wadkins.
PGA—Dave Stockton.
British Open—Jack Nicklaus.
British Amateur—Michael Bonallack.
Masters—Billy Casper.
Canadian Open—Kermit Zarley.
Canadian Amateur—Allen Miller.
NCAA Individual—John Mahaffey.
NCAA Team—Houston.
World Cup Professional—Australia.
World Cup Individual—Roberto de Vicenzo.
World Series of Golf—Jack Nicklaus.
USGA Senior—Gene Andrews.
U.S. Senior—David Goldman.
Walker Cup—United States.
USGA Public Links—Robert Risch.
World Amateur Team—United States.
USGA Junior—Gary Koch.
U.S. Senior (Pro) —Sam Snead.
Dow Jones Open—Bobby Nichols.

Women

National Amateur—Martha Wilkinson.
National Open—Donna Caponi.
British Amateur—Dinah Oxley.
Canadian Amateur—Mrs. Gail Harvey Moore.
Eastern Amateur—Delancy Smith.
USGA Junior—Hollis Stacy.
USGA Senior—Mrs. Philip Cudone.
U.S. Senior—Mrs. E. C. K. Finch.
Intercollegiate—Cathy Gaughan.
Western—Jane Bastanchury.
Southern—Kathy Hite.
Ladies PGA—Shirley Englehorn.
Curtis Cup—United States.
World Amateur Team—United States.

GYMNASTICS

National AAU Champions

All-Round—Yoshiaki Takei, Georgia Southern G.C.
Floor Exercises—Toby Towson, Michigan State.
Side Horse—Charles Morse, Michigan State.
Still Rings—Yoshiaki Takei.
Parallel Bars—Yoshiaki Takei.

Horizontal Bar—Yoshiaki Takei.
Long Horse—John Crosby, New York A.C.
Team—New York A.C.

Women

All-Round—Linda Metheny, McKinley Y.M.C.A.
Floor Exercises—Linda Metheny.
Balance Beam—Linda Metheny.
Uneven Parallel Bars—Linda Metheny.
Side Horse Vault—Adele Gleaves, Louisville Y.M.C.A.
Team—Southern California Acrobatic Teams.

National Collegiate Champions

All-Round—Yoshi Hayasaki, Washington.
Floor Exercises—Tom Prouix, Colorado State.
Still Rings—Dave Seal, Indiana State.
Side Horse—John Russo, Wisconsin, and Russ Hoffman, Iowa State.
Long Horse—Doug Boger, Arizona.
Parallel Bars—Ron Rapper, Michigan.
Team—Michigan.

HANDBALL

United States Handball Association Champions

4-Wall Singles—Paul Haber, Chicago.
4-Wall Doubles—Karl and Ruby Obert, New York.
4-Wall Masters Singles—Tom Ciasulli, Scotch Plains, N.J.
4-Wall Masters Doubles—Bob Brady and Bill Keays, San Francisco.

National AAU Champions

1-Wall Singles—Mark Levine, Brooklyn.
1-Wall Doubles—Marty Decatur and Artie Reyer, New York.
1-Wall Masters Doubles—Sal Chiovari and Jules Stack, Brooklyn.

HARNESS RACING

Horse of Year—Fresh Yankee.
2-Year-Old Trotter—Quick Pride.
2-Year-Old Pacer—Albatross.
3-Year-Old Trotter—Timothy T.
3-Year-Old Pacer—Most Happy Fella.
Aged Trotter—Dayan.

Aged Pacer—Laverne Hanover.
Leading Money-Winner—Fresh Yankee.
Leading Driver (Heats) —Herve Filion.
Leading Driver (Earnings) —Herve Filion.
Hambletonian—Timothy T.
Yonkers Futurity—Victory Star.
Kentucky Futurity—Timothy T.
Dexter Cup—Marlu Pride.
Colonial—Timothy T.
Messenger Stakes—Most Happy Fella.
Cane Pace—Most Happy Fella.
Little Brown Jug—Most Happy Fella.
Adios—Most Happy Fella.

HOCKEY

Stanley Cup—Boston Bruins.
National League—Chicago Black Hawks (East), St. Louis Blues (West).
American League—Buffalo Bisons.
Eastern League—Clinton.
International League—Dayton Gems.
Allan Cup—Spokane Jets.
National Collegiate—Cornell.
Memorial Cup—Montreal Canadiens.
Ivy League—Cornell.

HORSESHOE PITCHING

World Champions

Men—Dan Kuchcinski, Erie, Pa.
Women—Ruth Hangen, Buffalo.

HORSE SHOWS

American Horse Shows Association Champions

Roadsters—R. W. Kuhne's Miss Dean Key.
Children's Three-Gaited—Mr. and Mrs. Robert Meyer's The Entertainer.
American Saddle-bred Pleasure—Mrs. Alan Robson's Social Butterfly.
Open Five-Gaited—Julianne Schmutz's Chapel Belle.
Open Fine Harness—Mrs. A. W. Zelinka's Tashi Ling.
Walking Horse—V. G. Gochneur's Mr. FFT.
Welsh Pleasure—Mrs. J. L. duPont's Liseter Twinkle.
Stock—Mrs. Katherine Haley's Shirley Chex.

Trail—Red Cantleberry's Katy O'Grady.
Western Pleasure—Jane Gray's Poco Lonnie.
Hackney Pony—Mrs. Victoria Armstrong's Callaway's Limerick Lad.
Harness Pony—Mrs. Armstrong's Fashions Miss Alice.
Regular Conformation Hunter—Marvin Van Rapoport's Spindletop Showdown.
Green Conformation Hunter—Mrs. A. C. Randolph's Lord Sutler.
Regular Working Hunter—Cornelia Guest's Li-Ke.
Green Working Hunter—Jane Womble's Sign The Card.
Amateur-Owner Hunter—Sign The Card.
Small Pony Hunter—Mrs. Lorraine Baroody's Shenandoah Flintstone.
Amateur Owner Jumper—Melanie Smith's The Irishman.
Junior Hunter—Michele McEvoy's Amabette.
Park Morgan—Mr. and Mrs. W. L. Orcutt's Orland John Darling.

ICE SKATING

FIGURE

World Champions

Men—Tim Wood, United States.
Women—Gabriele Seyfert, East Germany.
Pairs—Irina Rodnina and Aleksei Ulanov, U.S.S.R.

United States Champions

Men—Tim Wood, Colorado Springs.
Women—Janet Lynn, Rockford, Ill.
Pairs—Ken Shelley and Jo-Jo Starbuck, Downey, Calif.
Silver Dance—Gerard Lane, Boston, and Mary Bonacci, Rye, N.Y.
Gold Dance—Jim Sladky, Rochester, and Judy Schwomeyer, Indianapolis.

SPEED

World Champions

Men—Ard Schenk, Netherlands.
Women—Attje Kuelen-Deelstra, Netherlands.

United States Champions

Men's Outdoor—Pete Cefalu, West Allis, Wis.

Men's Indoor—Barth Levy, Brooklyn.

Women's Outdoor—Sheila Young, Detroit.

Women's Indoor—Cathy Crowe, St. Louis.

JUDO

National AAU Champions

139-Pound—Larry Fukuhara, So. Pac. AAU.

154-Pound—Paul Maruyama, U.S. Air Force.

176-Pound—Hayward Nishioka, S. Pac. AAU.

Under 205-Pound—Rodney Haas, C. Cal. AAU.

Over 205-Pound—Allen Coage, Met. AAU.

Open—Kensuka Kobayashi, Met. AAU.

Grand Champion—Allen Coage.

LACROSSE

Club—Long Island Athletic Association.

Intercollegiate—Johns Hopkins, Navy, Virginia (tie).

North-South—South.

MODERN PENTATHLON

World—Peter Kelemen, Hungary.

World Team—Hungary.

World Military—Bo Jansson, Sweden.

World Military Team—Sweden.

U.S. Ind.—Lieut. Charles Richards, U.S. Army.

MOTORBOATING

World Offshore Races

South Africa—Francesco Cosentino, Italy.

Sam Griffith (Miami)—Bill Wishnick, New York.

Bahamas 500—Doug Silvera, Bahamas.

Wills (England)—Vincenzo Balestrieri, Italy.

Naples—Vincenzo Balestrieri.

Yugoslavia—Tommy Sopwith, England.

Viarregio (Italy)—Vincenzo Balestrieri.

Hennessy Grand Prix—Bob Magoon, Miami.

Dauphin d'Or (France)—Tommy Sopwith.

Long Beach Hennessy (California)—Bill Wishnick.

Gettingloppet (Sweden)—Joergen Book.

Cowes-Torquay (England)—Tommy Sopwith.

Deauville (France)—Tim Powell, England.

Miami-Nassau—Vincenzo Balestrieri.

Hennessy Key West—Bob Magoon.

Unlimited Hydroplanes

Sun Coast (Tampa)—Miss Budweiser.

President's Cup (Washington)—Myr Sheet Metal.

Kentucky Cup (Owensboro)—Myr Sheet Metal.

Dodge Memorial (Detroit)—Myr Sheet Metal.

Indiana Cup (Madison)—Miss Budweiser.

Atomic Cup (Pasco, Wash.)—Pay'N Pak L'il Buzzard.

Seafair (Seattle)—Miss Budweiser.

Gold Cup (San Diego)—Miss Budweiser.

MOTORCYCLING

United States Champions

Grand National Champion—Gene Romero, San Luis Obispo, Calif.

50-Mile National—Gene Romero.

20-Lap Half-Mile National—Mark Brelsford, San Bruno, Calif.

PARACHUTING

World Champions

Accuracy—Donald E. Rice, United States.

Style—Aleksei Jacmenev, U.S.S.R.

Over All—Aleksei Jacmenev.

Women's Accuracy—Zdena Zarybnicka, Czechoslovakia.

Women's Style—Valja Zakoreckaja, U.S.S.R.

Over All—Marie-France Baulez, France.

Team—Czechoslovakia.

Women's Team—Czechoslovakia.

United States Champions

Accuracy—Bill Hayes, St. Louis.

Style—Doug M. E. Metcalfe, Chardon, Ohio.
Over All—Clayton Schoelpple, Washington.
Women's Accuracy—Martha Huddleston, Washington.
Women's Style—Mrs. Susie Joerns, Houston.
Over All—Martha Huddleston.

POLO

Open—Tulsa Greenhill Farm.
20-Goal—Oak Brook, Oak Brook, Ill.
16-Goal—Cloudy Clime Farm, San Antonio.
12-Goal—Spokane, Wash.
Intercollegiate—Yale.

RACQUETS

National Champions

Singles—G. W. T. Atkins, England.
Doubles—D. McLernon, Montreal and M. Sales, Detroit.
Tuxedo Gold Racquet—D. McLernon.

ROLLER SKATING

World Champions

Men (Figures) —Michael Obrecht, West Germany.
Women's (Figures) —Christine Kreutzfeldt, West Germany.
Dance Pairs—Richard Horne and Jane Pankey, United States.
Mixed Pairs—Ron and Gail Robovitsky, United States.

Rink Operators Association Champions

Men—Michael Jacques, Norwood, Mass.
Women—Kathy Miller, Haverhill, Mass.
Pairs—Ron and Gail Robovitsky, Detroit.
Dance—Sanja Pulitz and R. Manns, Indianapolis.
Figures—Gary Lintz, Everett, Wash.
Women's Figures—Margaret Lucas, Riverside, N.J.
Speed—Pat Bergin, Dallas.
Women's Speed—Jan Irwin, Dallas.

Amateur Roller Skating Association Champions

Men—Randy Dayney, Levittown, L.I., N.Y.
Women—Colleen Giacomo, South Amboy, N.J.
Mixed Pairs—T. Abell and Gigi Fox, Harvey, Ill.
Women's Pairs—Barbara Francesconi and Barbara Kaffka, N.Y.
Dance—Richard Horne and Jane Pankey, Livonia, Mich.
Figures—William Boyd, Marion, Ind.
Women's Figures—Barbara Francesconi.

ROWING

United States Champions

Single Sculls—James W. Dietz, New York A.C.
Pairs With Coxswain—Union B.C., Boston.
Pairs Without Coxwain—Union B.C.
Fours With Coxwain—New Zealand.
Fours Without Coxswain—Vesper B.C., Philadelphia.
Eights—Vesper B.C.
Double Sculls—Long Beach (Calif.) R.A.
Team—Vesper B.C.

Intercollegiate Champions

Intercollegiate R.A.—Washington.
Dad Vail Trophy—St. Joseph's.
Eastern Sprint—Harvard.
Harvard-Yale—Harvard.
Oxford-Cambridge—Cambridge.
Western Sprint—UCLA.

RUGBY

World—South Africa.
Eastern U.S.—Manhattan R.F.C.
Collegiate—Army.

SHOOTING

World Rifle Champions

Small-Bore Prone—Laszlo Hammer, Hungary.
Small-Bore 3-Position—Vital Parkimovitch, U.S.S.R.

Small-Bore 3-Position Team—U.S.S.R.
Women's Prone Standard—Desanka Perovic, Yugoslavia.
Women's Prone Standard Team—Yugoslavia.
Men's Standard—John Writer, United States.
Men's Standard Team—U.S.S.R.
Women's Standard—Margaret Murdock, United States.
Women's Standard Team—United States.

United States Rifle Champions

National High Power—Ronald G. Troyer.
Service High Power—W.O. Robert L. Goller, U.S. Marine Corps.
Civilian High Power—Ronald G. Troyer.
Women's High Power—Pauline S. Tubb.
National Trophy Ind.—S.F.C. Myles G. Brown, U.S. Army.
National Trophy Team—U.S. Marine Corps.

World Pistol Champions

Men's Standard—Renart Suleymanov, U.S.S.R.
Men's Standard Team—United States.
Women's Standard—Judy Trim, Australia.
Women's Standard Team—Australia.

United States Pistol Champions

National—W.O. Francis Higginson, U.S. Marine Corps.
Police—Tom Gaines, U.S. Border Patrol.

Trapshooting Champions

Grand American—Charles Harvey, Oskaloosa, Iowa.
Women's Grand American—Carol Harmon, Roanoke, Tex.
Men's All-Round—Gene Sears, El Reno, Okla.
Women's All-Round—Mrs. Loral I. Delaney, Anoka, Minn.
Men's Over All—Larry Gravestock, Wichita Falls, Tex.
Women's Over All—Mrs. Loral I. Delaney.

United States Skeet Champions

All-Round—Tony Rosetti, Biloxi, Miss.
Women's All-Round—Karla Roberts, Bridgeton, Mo.
12-Gauge—John Durbin, Kirkwood, Mo.
20-Gauge—Harry Stilwell, Oreland, Pa.
28-Gauge—Wayne Ray, Galveston, Tex.
.410-Gauge—William Lawson, Malden, Mass.

SKIING

World Nordic Champions

Men's 15-Kilometer Cross-Country—Lars Ausland, Sweden.
Men's 30-Kilometer Cross-Country—Vyacheslav Vedenin, U.S.S.R.
Men's 50-Kilometer Cross-Country—Kalevi Oikarainen, Finland.
Men's 40-Kilometer Cross-Country Relay—U.S.S.R.
Combined—Ladislav Rygl, Czechoslovakia.
70-Meter Jumping—Gary Napalkov, U.S.S.R.
90-Meter Jumping—Gary Napalkov.
Women's 5-Kilometer Cross-Country—Galina Kulakova, U.S.S.R.
Women's 10-Kilometer Cross-Country—Alevtina Olyunina, U.S.S.R.
Women's 3x5-Kilometer Relay—U.S.S.R.

World Alpine Champions

Men's Slalom—Jean-Noel Augert, France.
Men's Giant Slalom—Karl Schranz, Austria.
Men's Downhill—Bernard Russi, Switzerland.
Women's Slalom—Ingrid Lafforgue, France.
Women's Giant Slalom—Betsy Clifford, Canada.
Women's Downhill—Anneroesli Zryd, Switzerland.

National Alpine Champions

Men's Slalom—Bob Cochran.
Men's Giant Slalom—Tyler Palmer.
Men Downhill—Rod Raylor.
Women's Slalom—Patty Boydstun.

Women's Giant Slalom—Susan Corrock.
Women's Downhill—Ann Black.

National Nordic Champions

Jumping—Bill Bakke, Madison, Wis.
Men's 15-Kilometer Cross-Country—
Mike Gallagher, Killington, Vt.
Men's 30-Kilometer Cross-Country—
Mike Gallagher.
Women's 5-Kilometer Cross-Country—
Martha Rockwell, Putney, Vt.
Women's 10-Kilometer Cross-Country—
Martha Rockwell.
Combined—Jim Miller, Mexico, Maine.

National Collegiate Champions

Slalom—Mike Porcarelli, Colorado U.
Giant Slalom—Otto Tschudi, U. of
Denver.
15-Kilometer Cross-Country—Ole Hansen, U. of Denver.
50-Meter Ski Jump—Jay Rand,
Colorado U.
Nordic Combined—Jim Miller, Ft.
Lewis A & M.
Team—University of Denver.

SOCCER

United States Champions

Open—Elizabeth (N.J.) S.C.
Amateur—Chicago Kickers.
Junior—St. Barth's, St. Louis.
North American League—Rochester
Lancers.
National Collegiate—St. Louis.
NAIA—Davis and Elkins.

Other Champions

World Cup—Brazil.
English Division One—Everton.
English F.A. Cup—Chelsea.
Scottish Division One—Glasgow Celtic.
Scottish F.A. Cup—Aberdeen.

SOFTBALL

Amateur Association Champions

FAST PITCH

Men—Raybestos, Stratford, Conn.
Women—Lionettes, Orange, Calif.

SLOW PITCH

Men—Little Caesars, Detroit.

Women—Rutenschroeder, Cincinnati.
Industrial—Pharr Yarn, McAdenville,
N.C.

SQUASH RACQUETS

United States Champions

Singles—Anil Nayar, Bombay, India.
Doubles—Ralph Howe, New York, and
Sam Howe 3d, Philadephia.
Veterans Singles—Henri Salaun, Boston.
Seniors (50 and over)—Calvin Mac-
Cracken, Englewood, N.J.
Senior Doubles—Hastings Griffin and
Newton Meade, Philadelphia.
Team—Ontario.
Women's Singles—Mrs. Nina Moyer,
Pennington, N.J.
Women's Doubles—Mrs. Terry The-
sieres and Mrs. Nathan Stauffer,
Cynwyd, Pa.
Intercollegiate—Larry Terrell, Harvard.
Intercollegiate Team—Harvard.

SQUASH TENNIS

U.S. Open—Pedro A. Bacallao, Princeton Club.
U.S. Open Doubles—William A. Riesenfeld, Yale Club, and Aaron
Daniels, City A.C.
U.S. Amateur—Pedro A. Bacallao.
U.S. Veterans—David Smith, New York.

SURFING

United States Champions

All-Round—Corky Carroll, Dana Point.
Men—Brad McCaull, Huntington
Beach.
Women—Jericho Poppler, Long Beach.
Senior—Les Williams, Dana Point.
Masters—Barry Ault, San Diego.
Junior—Dane Silzle, S.J. Capist.
Mixed Tandem—Hal Sachs and Patty
Crawford.

SWIMMING

Men's National Long-Course Champions

100-Meter Free-Style—Frank Heckl.
200-Meter Free-Style—Mark Spitz.
400-Meter Free Style—John Kinsella.

1,500-Meter Free-Style—John Kinsella.
100-Meter Backstroke—Mike Stamm.
200-Meter Backstroke—Mike Stamm.
100-Meter Breaststroke—Brian Job.
200-Meter Breaststroke—Brian Job.
100-Meter Butterfly—Mark Spitz.
200-Meter Butterfly—Gary Hall.
200-Meter Medley—Gary Hall.
400-Meter Medley—Gary Hall.
400-Meter Free-Style Relay—Los Angeles A.C.
800-Meter Free-Style Relay—Phillips 66.
400-Meter Medley Relay—Santa Clara S.C.
One-Meter Dive—Jim Henry.
Three-Meter Dive—Jim Henry.
Platform Dive—Rick Early.
High-Point Award—Gary Hall.
Team—Phillips 66, Long Beach, Calif.

Men's National Short-Course Champions

100-Yard Free-Style—David Edgar.
200-Yard Free-Style—John Kinsella.
500-Yard Free-Style—John Kinsella.
1,650-Yard Free-Style—John Kinsella.
100-Yard Butterfly—Mark Spitz.
200-Yard Butterfly—Gary Hall.
100-Yard Breaststroke—Brian Job.
200-Yard Breaststroke—Brian Job.
100-Yard Backstroke—Mike Stamm.
200-Yard Backstroke—Gary Hall.
200-Yard Medley—Gary Hall.
400-Yard Medley—Gary Hall.
400-Yard Free-Style Relay—Southern California.
800-Yard Free-Style Relay—Southern California.
400-Yard Medley Relay—Santa Clara S.C.
Team—Santa Clara S.C.

Women's National Long-Course Champions

100-Meter Free-Style—Cindy Schilling.
200-Meter Free-Style—Ann Simmons.
400-Meter Free-Style—Debbie Meyer.
1,500-Meter Free-Style—Debbie Meyer.
100-Meter Backstroke—Susie Atwood.
200-Meter Backstroke—Susie Atwood.
100-Meter Breaststroke—Linda Kurtz.
200-Meter Breaststroke—Claudia Clevenger.

100-Meter Butterfly—Alice Jones.
200-Meter Butterfly—Alice Jones.
200-Meter Medley—Lynn Vidali.
400-Meter Medley—Susie Atwood.
400-Meter Free-Style Relay—Santa Clara S.C.
800-Meter Free-Style Relay—Arden Hills S.C.
400-Meter Medley Relay—Lakewood A.C.
One-Meter Dive—Cynthia Potter.
Three-Meter Dive—Micki King.
Platform Dive—Cynthia Potter.
High-Point Award—Susie Atwood.
Team—Santa Clara S.C.

Women's National Short-Course Champions

100-Yard Free-Style—Wendy Fordyce.
200-Yard Free-Style—Wendy Fordyce.
500-Yard Free-Style—Debbie Meyer.
1,650-Yard Free-Style—Debbie Meyer.
100-Yard Butterfly—Lynn Colella.
200-Yard Butterfly—Lynn Colella.
100-Yard Breaststroke—Kim Brecht.
200-Yard Breaststroke—Linda Kurtz.
100-Yard Backstroke—Susie Atwood.
200-Yard Backstroke—Susie Atwood.
200-Yard Medley—Lynn Vidali.
400-Yard Medley—Debbie Meyer.
400-Yard Free-Style Relay—Jack Nelson S.C.
400-Yard Medley Relay—Lakewood A.C.
800-Yard Free-Style Relay—Arden Hills A.C.
Team—Santa Clara S.C.

National Collegiate Champions

50-Yard Free-Style—David Edgar, Tennessee.
100-Yard Free-Style—David Edgar.
200-Yard Free-Style—Juan Bello, Michigan.
500-Yard Free-Style—Mike Burton, UCLA.
1,650-Yard Free-Style—Mike Burton.
100-Yard Backstroke—Larry Barbiere, Indiana.
200-Yard Backstroke—Mitch Ivey, Long Beach, Calif.
100-Yard Breaststroke—Brian Job, Stanford.
200-Yard Breaststroke—Brian Job.

100-Yard Butterfly—Mark Spitz, Indiana.
200-Yard Butterfly—Mike Burton.
200-Yard Ind. Medley—Frank Heckl, USC.
400-Yard Ind. Medley—Gary Hall, Indiana.
400-Yard Free-Style Relay—USC.
800-Yard Free-Style Relay—USC.
400-Yard Medley Relay—Stanford.
One-Meter Dive—Jim Henry, Indiana.
Three-Meter Dive—Jim Henry.
Team—Indiana.

TABLE TENNIS

United States Open Champions

Singles—Dal Joon Lee, Cleveland.
Women's Singles—Violetta Nesukaitis, Toronto.
Doubles—Glen Cowan, Los Angeles, and Dal Joon Lee.
Women's Doubles—Wendy Hicks, Santa Barbara, and Patty Martinez, La Mesa, Calif.
Mixed Doubles—Dell and Connie Sweeris, Grand Rapids, Mich.
Senior Men—Max Marinko, Toronto.
Senior Women—Jenny Marinko, Toronto.
Junior Men—Mitchell Sealtiel, Trenton.

TENNIS

International Team Champions

Davis Cup—United States.
Wightman Cup (Women) —United States.
Federation Cup (Women) —Australia.

Wimbledon Champions

Men—John Newcombe, Australia.
Women—Mrs. Margaret Court, Australia.
Men's Doubles—John Newcombe and Tony Roche, Australia.
Women's Doubles—Rosemary Casals, San Francisco, and Mrs. Billie Jean King, Long Beach, Calif.

U.S. Open Champions

Men—Ken Rosewall, Australia.
Women—Mrs. Margaret Court.
Men's Doubles—Nikki Pilic, Yugoslavia, and Pierre Barthes, France.

Women's Doubles—Mrs. Judy Dalton and Mrs. Court, Australia.

United States Clay-Court Champions

Men—Cliff Richey, San Angelo, Tex.
Women—Linda Tuero, Matairie, La.
Men's Doubles—Arthur Ashe, Gum Spring, Va., and Clark Graebner, New York.
Women's Doubles—Rosemary Casals and Gail Chanfreau, France.

United States Indoor Champions

Men—Ilie Nastase, Rumania.
Women—Mrs. Mary Ann Curtis, St. Louis.
Men's Doubles—Author Ashe and Stan Smith, Pasadena, Calif.
Women's Doubles—Nancy Richey, San Angelo, Tex., and Peaches Bartkowicz, Hamtramck, Mich.

Other Foreign Open Champions

Australian Men—Arthur Ashe.
Australian Women—Mrs. Court.
Italian Men— Ilie Nastase.
Italian Women—Mrs. King.
French Men—Jan Kodes, Czechoslovakia.
French Women—Mrs. Court.

THOROUGHBRED RACING

Horse of year—Personality and Fort Marcy.
Older Horse—Nodouble.
3-Year-Old Colt—Personality.
3-Year-Old Filly—Fanfreluche and Office Queen.
2-Year-Old Colt—Hoist the Flag.
2-Year-Old Filly—Forward Gal.
Steeplechase—Top Bid.
Turf Course—Fort Marcy.
Best Sprinter—Ta Wee.

TRACK AND FIELD

Men's National Senior Outdoor Champions

100-Yard Dash—Ivory Crockett.
220-Yard Dash—Ben Vaughan.
440-Yard Run—John Smith.
880-Yard Run—Ken Swenson.
One-Mile Run—Howell Michael.
Three-Mile Run—Frank Shorter.

Six-Mile Run—Frank Shorter and Jack Bacheler (tie).
3,000-Meter Steeplechase—Bill Reilly.
120-Yard High Hurdles—Tom Hill.
440-Yard Hurdles—Ralph Mann.
High Jump—Reynaldo Brown.
Pole Vault—Bob Seagren.
Long Jump—Bouncy Moore.
Triple Jump—Milan Tiff.
Shot-Put—Randy Matson.
Discus Throw—Jay Silvester.
Hammer Throw—George Frenn.
Javelin Throw—Bill Skinner.
Team—Southern California Striders.
Two-Mile Walk—Tom Dooley.
All-Round—Brian Murphy.
Decathlon—John Warkentin.
Pentathlon—Mike Hill.
10,000-Meter Walk—Dave Romansky.
15,000-Meter Walk—Dave Romansky.
25,000-Meter Walk—Dave Romansky.
50,000-Meter Walk—John Knifton.
One-Hour Walk—Larry Walker.
Two-Mile Walk—Tom Dooley.

Men's National Senior Indoor Champions

60-Yard Dash—Lieut. Charlie Greene, Army.
60-Yard High Hurdles—Willie Davenport.
600-Yard Run—Martin McGrady.
1,000-Yard Run—Juris Luzins.
One-Mile Run—Marty Liquori.
Three-Mile Run—Arthur Dulong.
One-Mile Relay—Sports International.
Two-Mile Relay—Chicago Track Club.
Sprint Medley Relay—Rutgers.
One-Mile Walk—Dave Romansky.
High Jump—Otis Burrell.
Pole Vault—Bob Seagren.
Long Jump—Norm Tate.
Triple Jump—Norm Tate.
Shot-Put—Brian Oldfield.
35-Pound Weight Throw—George Frenn.
Team—Southern California Striders.

National Collegiate Outdoor Champions

100-Yard Dash—Eddie Hart, California.
220-Yard Dash—Willie Turner, Oregon State.
440-Yard Run—Larry James, Villanova.

880-Yard Run—Ken Swenson, Kansas State.
One-Mile Run—Marty Liquori, Villanova.
Three-Mile Run—Steve Prefontaine, Oregon.
Six-Mile Run—Bob Bertelsen, Ohio U.
120-Yard Hurdles—Paul Gibson, Texas at El Paso.
440-Yard Hurdles—Ralph Mann, Brigham Young.
3,000-Meter Steeplechase—Sid Sink, Bowling Green.
440-Yard Relay—California.
One-Mile Relay—UCLA.
High Jump—Pat Matzdorf, Wisconsin.
Pole Vault—Jan Johnson, Kansas.
Long Jump—Arnie Robinson, San Diego State.
Triple Jump—Mohinder Gill, California Poly.
Shot-Put—Karl Salb, Kansas.
Discus Throw—John Van Reenan, Washington State.
Hammer Throw—Steve DeAutremont, Oregon State.
Javelin Throw—Bill Skinner, Tennessee.
Decathlon—Rick Wanamaker, Drake.
Team—California.

Intercollegiate AAAA Outdoor Champions

100-Yard Dash—Bill Krouse, West Chester.
220-Yard Dash—James Reed, Amherst.
440-Yard Run—Larry James, Villanova.
880-Yard Run—Andy O'Reilly, Villanova.
One-Mile Run—Marty Liquori, Villanova.
Three-Mile Run—Dick Buerkle, Villanova.
3,000-Meter Steeplechase—Des McCormack, Villanova.
120-Yard High Hurdles—Kwaku Ohne-Frempong, Yale.
440-Yard Hurdles—Rich Weaver, PMC Colleges.
440-Yard Relay—Maryland.
One-Mile Relay—Villanova.
High Jump—Joe David, Maryland.
Pole Vault—Tom Blair, Pennsylvania.
Long Jump—Noel Hare, Harvard.

Triple Jump—Mike Neff, Maryland.
Shot-Put—John Hanley, Maryland.
Discus Throw—Paul Corrigan, Maryland.
Javelin Throw—Bob Kouvolo, Pittsburgh.
Hammer Throw—Dick Narcessian, Rhode Island.
Team—Villanova.

Women's National Outdoor Champions

100-Yard Dash—Chi Cheng.
220-Yard Dash—Chi Cheng.
440-Yard Run—Mavis Laing.
880-Yard Run—Cheryl Toussaint.
1,500-Meter Run—Francie Larrieu.
100-Meter Hurdles—Mamie Rallins.
200-Meter Hurdles—Pat Hawkins.
440-Yard Relay—Tennessee State.
880-Yard Medley Relay—Mayor Daley Y.F., Chicago.
One-Mile Relay—Atoms T.C.
High Jump—Sally Plihal.
Long Jump—Willye White.
Javelin Throw—Sherry Calvert.
Discus Throw—Carol Frost.
Shot-Put—Lynn Graham.
Team—Mayor Daley Y.F.

VOLLEYBALL

National AAU Champions

Men—Chart House, San Diego.
Women—Renegades Green, Los Angeles.

U.S. Volleyball Association Champions

Men—Chart House.
Women—Shamrocks, 1, Long Beach, Calif.

WATER POLO

United States Champions

Outdoor—DeAnza, Cupertino, Calif.
Indoor—New York A.C.
Y.M.C.A.—Macomb, Ill.

WATER SKIING

United States Champions

Over All—Mike Suyderhoud, San Anselmo, Calif.

Women's Over All—Liz Allan, Winter Park, Fla.
Slalom—Suyderhoud.
Women's Slalom—Liz Allan.
Jumping—Suyderhoud.
Women's Jumping—Liz Allan.

WEIGHT LIFTING

National Champions

Flyweight—S. del Rosario, Philippines.
Bantamweight—M. Nassiri, Iran.
Featherweight—J. Benedek, Hungary.
Lightweight—Z. Kaczmarek, Poland.
Middleweight—V. Kurentsov, U.S.S.R.
Light Heavyweight—G. Ivanchenko, U.S.S.R.
Middle Heavyweight—V. Kolotov, U.S.S.R.
Heavyweight—Y. Talts, U.S.S.R.
Super Heavyweight—V. Alekseyev, U.S.S.R.

National AAU Champions

Flyweight—Eugene Casasola, York (Pa.) B.B.C.
Bantamweight—Salvador Domingues, Arizona B.B.C.
Featherweight—Fernando Baez, Puerto Rico.
Lightweight—James Benjamin, Columbus (Ohio) Y.M.C.A.
Middleweight—Fred Lowe, York B.B.C.
Light Heavyweight—Mike Karchut, Sayre Pk.
Middle Heavyweight—Phil Grippaldi, Keasby Eagles.
Heavyweight—Bob Bednarski, York B.B.C.
Super Heavyweight—K. Patera. Multnomah A.C.

WRESTLING

World Free-Style Champions

105.5-Pound—Ebrahim Javadi, Iran.
114.5-Pound—Ali Riza Alan, Turkey.
125.5-Pound—Hideaki Yanagida, Japan.
136.5-Pound—Shamsseddin Syedabassi, Iran.
149.5-Pound—Abdollah Movahed, Iran.
163-Pound—Wayne Wells, United States.
180.5-Pound—Yoirix Shachmuradon, U.S.S.R.

198-Pound—Gennadi Starchov, U.S.S.R.
220-Pound—Vladimir Gulutkin, U.S.S.R.
Heavyweight—Aleksandr Medved, U.S.S.R.

National AAU Free-Style Champions

105.5-Pound—Bob Orta, Nebraska.
114.5-Pound—John Moreley, New York A.C.
125.5-Pound—Rich Sanders, Multnomah A.C.
136.5-Pound—Mike Young, Utah.
149-Pound—Dan Gable, Iowa State Grapplers.
163-Pound—Wayne Wells, Oklahoma.
180-Pound—Jay Robinson, New York A.C.
198-Pound—Wayne Baughman, U.S. Air Force.
220-Pound—Larry Kristoff, Mayor Daley Y.F.
Heavyweight—Greg Wojciechowski, Toledo U.
Team—New York A.C.

National Collegiate Champions

118-Pound—Greg Johnson, Michigan State.
126-Pound—Dwayne Keller, Oklahoma State.
134-Pound—Darrell Keller, Oklahoma State.
142-Pound—Larry Owings, Washington.
150-Pound—Mike Grant, Oklahoma.
158-Pound—Dave Martin, Iowa State.
167-Pound—Jason Smith, Iowa State.
177-Pound—Chuck Jean, Iowa State.
190-Pound—Geoff Baum, Oklahoma State.
Heavyweight—Jess Lewis, Oregon State.
Team—Iowa State.

YACHTING

International

America's Cup (12-Meter)—Intrepid Syndicate's Intrepid, United States.
International Catamaran Challenge Trophy—Bruce Proctor and Graham Candy with Quest III, Australia.
Scandinavian Gold Cup (5.5-Meter)—Robert E. Turner, Atlanta.

Onion Patch Trophy (team)—United States (Carina, Equation, Bay Bea).
America-Australia Challenge Cup (6-Meter)—Tom Blackaller's St. Francis IV, San Francisco.

Long Distance

Newport-Bermuda—Richard S. Nye's Carina, Greenwich, Conn.
Stamford Y.C. Vineyard Trophy—Carina.
Storm Trysail Club Block Island—Sumner A. Long's Ondine, Larchmont, N.Y.
Bayview-Mackinac Island—Jesse Phillips' Charisma, Chicago.
Chicago-Mackinac Island—Lynn Williams' Dora.
Southern Ocean Racing Conference—Robert E. Turner's American Eagle, Atlanta.
Mohegan Island—James L. Madden's Gesture.
San Pedro-Papeete, Tahiti—G. Norman Bacon's Widgeon, Santa Barbara, Calif.
San Diego-Acapulco—J. Greene's Yellow Jacket.
Storm Trysail Club's Governor of Rhode Island Cups—Paul Hoffmann's Thunderhead and William Ziegler 3d's Gem.

North American YRU Champions

Mallory (men)—Dr. John Jennings, St. Petersburg (Fla.) Y.C.
Prince of Wales (match racing)—Dr. John Jennings.
Adams (women)—Mrs. Jan O'Malley, Mantoloking (N.J.) Y.C.
O'Day (single-handed)—Robert Doyle, Harvard University.
Sears (junior)—Danny Williams, Houston (Tex.) Y.C.

One-Design Champions

National Unless Otherwise Indicated

Atlantic—Lou Michaels. Cedar Point, Conn.
Blue Jay—Bill Pagels, Sayville, L.I., N.Y.
Comet (N. Am.)—Don McPherson, Ithaca.

Comet (Int.) —Jack Boehringer, Cooper River, N.J.

Cottontail—Reginald Page, Stamford, Conn.

Dragon (N. Am.) —Buddy Friedrichs, Jr., New Orleans.

Ensign—Rollie Whyte, Narra Bay, R.I.

Etchells 22—Timothea and Dave Larr, Oyster Bay, L.I., N.Y.

Finn (N. Am.) —Carl Van Duyne, Naval Academy.

5-0-5 (N. Am.) —Dennis Surtees, Los Altos, Calif.

5.5-Meter—Ted Turner, Atlanta.

5-5-Meter (World) —David Forbes, Australia.

Flying Dutchman (N. Am.) —David Croshere, San Francisco.

Flying Dutchman (World) —Rodney Patterson, England.

420 (World) —John Gilder, Australia.

470 (World) —Yves and Harve Carre, France.

Jet 14—Peter Jones, Washington.

Lightning (N. Am.) —Tom Allen, Buffalo.

Luders 16 (Int.) —Leroy Sutherland, Newport Beach, Calif.

Moth (N. Am.-Women) —Kathy Mullen, Surf City, N.J.

Moth (N. Am.-Sr.) —Bob Peterson, Sea Isle City, N.J.

One-Design (World) —Stuart B. Rowe, Jr., Larchmont, N.Y.

110—Mark O'Connor, Marblehead, Mass.

Raven—Bill Pagels, Sayville, L.I., N.Y.

Rhodes 19—Martha Martin, San Francisco.

Shields—Lance McCabe, Balboa, Calif.

Snipe—Earl Elms, San Diego, Calif.

Snipe (N. Am) —August Diaz, Miami.

Soling (N. Am.) —Dave Curtis, Marblehead, Mass.

Soling (World) —Stig Wennerstrom, Sweden.

Star (N. Am.) —Durward Knowles, Nassau, Bahamas.

Star (World) —Bill Buchan, United States.

Sunfish (N. Am.) —Dick Griffith, Virgin Islands.

Sunfish (World) —Gary Hoyt, San Juan, P.R.

Tempest—John and James Linville, Larchmont, N.Y.

Thistle—Kent Foster, Cincinnati.

210—Norman Cresy, Marblehead, Mass.

Windmill (Int.) —John Dane 3d, New Orleans.

THE PRIZE WINNERS

ART SPANDER (They Were Singing "God Save the Queen"), winner of the news-coverage award, has been with the *San Francisco Chronicle* since May, 1965. He is a graduate of UCLA with a degree in political science. He started newspaper work with the United Press (Los Angeles) and moved to the *Santa Monica* (Calif.) *Evening Outlook* sports department before he came to the *Chronicle*. His writing has earned him prizes from the Golf Writers Association and two inclusions in *Best Sports Stories*. Favorite beats are football and basketball.

ROBERT LIPSYTE (Dempsey in the Window), the news-feature winner, is one of the two winningest authors in *Best Sports Stories*. By capturing the 1971 feature newspaper award with his column on Jack Dempsey, he has garnered five prizes. He is a graduate of the Columbia School of Journalism and has been with *The New York Times* for over 13 years. He is the author of many books. His latest, *Assignment Sports* (Harper and Row) is for young people dealing in sport assignments. In 1966, he won the Mike Berger Award for distinguished reporting.

BILL BOUSFIELD (The Housebreaker), the magazine award winner, was born on the family farm near Jarvis, Ontario, in Canada. After active service in the Canadian Army as a motorcycle instructor, he purchased and operated an auto repair garage in New Toronto. In 1951 he moved with his wife and two children into the forest areas of Lac Seul and built a hunting lodge out of virgin bush. His business stationery makes interesting reading: "Lac Seul, Onaway Lodge: The Home of Record Northerns and Excellent Walleyes." He has earned citations for catches in deep-sea fishing. This is his first appearance in *Best Sports Stories*.

OTHER CONTRIBUTORS (In Alphabetical Order)

BOB ADDIE (As the Coach Laying Dying) won the *Best Sports Stories* feature award in 1963 with his moving account of blind children at a baseball game. After his graduation from the University of Alabama, he began his career with the old *New York Journal-American* and then went to *The Washington Post,* where he is a sports columnist. He can handle all major sports and features with facility and insight. He was president of the Baseball Writers Association of America in 1967. He has merited many inclusions in this sports anthology.

NEIL AMDUR (Campus Crossfire) was born in Wilkes-Barre, Pennsylvania, attended the University of Missouri and received a degree in journalism. He spent six years on the sports staff of the *Miami Herald* and received the Florida Sportswriters Association award for general excellence in 1966. In 1968, he joined the staff of *The New York Times* and has been covering college football, tennis and track and field. This marks his second appearance in *Best Sports Stories.*

BOB BARNET (A Torpedo Named Dust Commander), a perennial favorite of readers of *Best Sports Stories,* has just won a first-place award in the 1970 Indiana Associated Press Managing Editors newswriting contest. He is the sports editor of *The Muncie* (Ind.) *Star.* Besides his many civic and honorary involvements, he has been president of the Indiana Sports Writers and Radio Broadcasters Association, director of the Indiana Trotting and Racing Horse Association and holder of the 1965 George A. Barton Award for greatest contributions to the national Golden Gloves program.

FURMAN BISHER (8-9-10 and Out) has been honored by *Time* magazine by being named as one of the outstanding sports columnists in this country. He is sports editor of *The Atlanta Journal* and has merited many appearances in this series of sports stories. He has written for all major periodicals and lately has had two books published: *Miracle in Atlantia* (World Publishing) and *Strange but True Baseball Stories* (Random House).

HAL BODLEY (Blind Spot to the Right) became the sports editor of the *Wilmington* (Del.) *News* and *Journal* papers in 1969. He is a native of Smyrna, Delaware, and was graduated from the University of Delaware. He has been selected Delaware sports writer of the year on five different occasions, and his column has won several regional awards. This marks his second appearance in *Best Sports Stories.*

PETER BONVENTRE (The Ladies Who Love the Knicks) is a newcomer to *Best Sports Stories.* Born in New York City and graduated from the University of Pennsylvania in 1967 as a journalism major, he came to *The New York Times* as a news clerk. In 1968 he was assigned to the sports desk. One year later he went to *Newsweek* as assistant sports editor. He already has been published in *McCalls, Signature* magazine, *West Magazine* (the Sunday *Los Angeles Times*) and *Sport.*

NELSON BRYANT (A Sportsman's Daydream) is a twice-wounded World War II paratrooper veteran and the hunting and fishing sports columnist

for *The New York Times*. He is a graduate of Dartmouth College, class of
'46, and received his newspaper start as managing editor of the *Claremont*
(N.H.) *Eagle*. At one time he was a fish and game commissioner in New
Hampshire. His treks have led him from fishing in James Bay, Ontario,
and Costa Rica, to red grouse shooting on the moors of Scotland. McGraw-
Hill is publishing a book of his *Times* columns, called *American Heritage*,
in the spring.

Si Burick (The Best Victory) is a highly-thought-of veteran writer of
America's central area who has been selected as Ohio's Sports Writer of the
Year for six consecutive years (1963–68). At his present paper, *The Dayton Daily News*, he has covered every facet of the sporting scene. He began
writing for that paper at the age of 19 and has been with it for over 41
years. He is also a member of the board of directors of Dayton Newspapers, Inc.

Dwight Chapin ("Batman" and "Robin" Fall Before "Superman") was
graduated from the University of Idaho and received his MA in journalism
from Columbia University. His newspaper work consists of stints with the
Lewiston (Idaho) *Morning Tribune, Vancouver* (Wash.) *Columbian,
Seattle Post-Intelligencer,* and for the last four years the *Los Angeles
Times*. He has received national honors for his articles on college basketball and baseball in Washington and California.

Jack Chevalier (The Stanley Cup at Last) resigned as *The Philadelphia
Inquirer's* hockey writer last June to become a sports columnist for *The
Baltimore Evening Sun,* a paper for which he had originally worked. His
father, J. Earl, is a retired hockey, boxing and baseball writer from
Springfield, Massachusetts. Jack Chevalier is a University of Massachusetts
graduate who in 1956 began his newspaper career with the *Springfield
Daily News*. This marks his third appearance in *Best Sports Stories*.

Bill Conlin (The Old Grad Goes Back to the Big Game) has been writing for *The Sacramento Union* since his graduation from Stanford University in 1934, except for three years service as a Navy officer. He has
been sports editor for some 20 years and has been editor and city editor
of this newspaper that describes itself as "The Oldest Daily West of the
Rockies." His present piece marks his first appearance in *Best Sports
Stories*.

Glenn Dickey (Super Chiefs Shock Super Bowl) was graduated from the
University of California, Berkeley, in 1958 and went to work shortly afterward as editor of the *Watsonville* (Calif.) *Register-Pajaronian*. In 1964,
he joined the *San Francisco Chronicle* as a sports writer and is there at the
present time. This marks his third appearance in *Best Sports Stories*.

Frank Dolson (Who's Got a Dime?) is making his fourth appearance in
Best Sports Stories. He was graduated from the University of Pennsylvania
in 1954, spent six months with *Sports Illustrated* and then went to *The
Philadelphia Inquirer* in 1955. He began to write occasional columns for

that paper in 1959, and since 1966 he has been a regular sports columnist there, covering a wide range of topics.

JOSEPH DURSO (The Orioles Begin Another Dynasty), who writes for *The New York Times,* is a Phi Beta Kappa from New York University with a master's degree from Columbia. After three years in the Air Force and three years in radio news and sports, he came to *The Times* in 1950. He has been assistant to the national news editor there and assistant city editor. He is also an associate professor in the Columbia Graduate School of Journalism and is the author of *Casey* and *The Days of Mr. McGraw.* This marks his second apearance in *Best Sports Stories.*

PHIL ELDERKIN ("I Win with My Overall Game") started with *The Christian Science Monitor* in 1943 and soon worked his way into the sports department. He is also the NBA columnist for *The Sporting News.* His specialty lately is doing a lot of first-person stories for the *Monitor.* He has driven in a stock-car race, coxed the MIT heavyweight crew, taken a parachute jump, played Australia's No. 1 Davis Cupper in singles and soloed a hot-air balloon. This is his first appearance in *Best Sports Stories.*

DWAIN ESPER (The Leprechauns Change Color) has been with the *Pasadena Independent Star News* since 1965. Before that he worked for the *El Centro* (Calif.) *News Press, Hayward* (Calif.) *Daily Review, San Francisco News,* and *Los Angeles Examiner,* and edited the now defunct magazine *Sports Review.* Among his writing honors are citations by The Associated Press and California Newspaper Publishers Association and inclusions in *Best Sports Stories.*

RAY FITZGERALD (A Solid Vote for Baseball) is a graduate of Notre Dame. For the past 19 years he has been writing sports, the last five of them at the *Boston Globe.* He lives in the seaside town of Scituate, Massachusetts, eschews water sports and doesn't even own a boat. In 1963 he was named Massachusetts Sportswriter of the Year. This marks his second appearance in *Best Sports Stories.*

STANLEY FRANK (Put Your Money on That Man in the Striped Shirt) is a native-born New Yorker who is both a veteran newspaperman and a free-lance writer. He worked for the *New York Post* as a sports columnist and later as a World War II correspondent in the European Theater. Upon his return to this country, he left the *Post* and has continued to write for many of the top magazines. His fine writing has merited many inclusions in *Best Sports Stories.*

JOE GERGEN (Jim Hickman: Authentic American Hero) was graduated from Boston College in 1963 and joined United Press International in New York. After five years with the UPI he became in September, 1968, baseball and football writer at *Newsday,* on Long Island, and he is still there. He is a frequent contributor to baseball and football magazines. This marks his second appearance in *Best Sports Stories.*

BOB GREENE (Who's on First? Who Cares?) is a June, 1969, graduate of the Northwestern University Medill School of Journalism who is making his first appearance in *Best Sports Stories*. He went to work for the *Chicago Sun-Times* in July of that year as a general assignment reporter and was transferred to the feature department in January, 1971. His first free-lance story for *Midwest*, the *Chicago Sun-Times* Sunday magazine, won the award as the best Sunday magazines story of 1970. This is only his second sports piece. Married early in 1971, he returned from his honeymoon to find that his piece had been accepted for this anthology.

PAUL HEMPHILL (How Jacksonville Earned Its Credit Card) was born and raised in Birmingham, Alabama, and was graduated from Auburn University. His career as a sports writer started with the *Birmingham News* and he later continued as sports editor with the *Augusta Chronicle* and the *Tampa Times*. His last newspaper stint was the writing of a general column, "Second Front Page," for *The Atlanta Journal*. At present he is devoting himself completely to free-lance writing, and his book, *The Nashville Sound,* published by Simon & Schuster, received warm acclaim from the critics.

STAN HOCHMAN (Florida Fats) is a former schoolteacher who became hooked on sports and left education for the athletic scene. He was born and raised in Brooklyn, graduated from New York University, had his teacher fling for two years, and started writing stints in Georgia, Texas and California. He returned East and in 1959 went to work for the *Philadelphia Daily News,* where he does much of his writing in his own column.

STAN ISAACS (Green and Leafy Football) is represented this year in *Best Sports Stories* by a magazine piece after many inclusions of his newspaper articles. In 1962 his column, "Out of Left Field," won the National Headliners Award. His writing is done for Long Island's *Newsday*. He broke into newspaper writing with a Nebraska daily, the *Chelm Avenger*. He is the author of a book, *Careers and Opportunities in Sports,* published by E. P. Dutton & Co.

PHIL JACKMAN (The Brooks Robinson Story) was graduated from Providence College in 1958, worked for the *Worcester* (Mass.) *Telegram* until 1965 and then joined his present paper, *The Baltimore Evening Sun*. In 1968 he was voted the Maryland Sports Writer of the Year. His major beat in Baltimore is the world champion Orioles, although he is at home in all the major sports. This is his first appearance in *Best Sports Stories*.

ROGER KAHN (The Life and Hard Times of Jim Bouton) has won three magazine story awards in *Best Sports Stories*. The first article was won in 1960 and the second in 1969. His winning *Esquire* piece in the 1970 volume on Willie Mays was a deeply discerning study of a great outfielder. He broke into newspaper work with the late *New York Herald Tribune* as a sports reporter and then went to *Newsweek* as sports editor. He spent a short time with *The Saturday Evening Post* as a senior editor and now is free lancing and writing books that cover subjects from college revolutions to ethnic problems.

DAVE KLEIN (Harlem Playground) has been a sports writer and sports columnist for the *Newark Star-Ledger* for 10 years, with his major output concerned primarily with pro football and college basketball. As a free-lance writer he has contributed to several of the better known magazines, among them *Jock, Sporting Guide, Sport* and *Sports Illustrated.* He is also the author of four sports books, including *The Making of an NBA Rookie,* and a biography of Vince Lombardi, *The Coach.* He attended the University of Oklahoma and Fairleigh Dickinson University in New Jersey.

RICHARD KOSTER (The Sad Passing of an Era) is a 1960 graduate of the University of Missouri who has been with *The St. Louis Globe-Democrat* for eight years. Prior to that he worked for two years at the *Detroit Free Press.* He covers all major sports, with emphasis on pro football. He also writes a column and devotes about half his time to the *Globe's* Sunday feature department.

HAL LEBOVITZ (Wanna Take a Taxi?) has merited inclusion in *Best Sports Stories* many times. Western Reserve is his alma mater. He started as a high-school chemistry teacher but his avid interest in sports led him to the *Cleveland News* and later to the *Cleveland Plain Dealer* where he is now the sports editor. His column, "Hal Thinks," is supplemented by his "Ask Hal" column, and both have earned him numerous writing honors. He is a past president of the Baseball Writers Association of America.

BILL LEE (Those Three Terrible Left Hooks) has done all of his newspaper work in Connecticut, although he is originally from Brooklyn. He started his career in Bridgeport and later joined the *Meriden Journal,* where he became sports editor. In 1925, he joined *The Hartford Courant* and he has never been uprooted. He has been the sports editor of that paper since 1939. In 1941 he married Melva Swarts, crack city-side reporter. This is his first appearance in *Best Sports Stories.*

ALLEN LEWIS (Saved by Lee May's Bat) was graduated in 1940 from Haverford College, where he played varsity football and baseball. He was also sports editor of his school paper. His newspaper background consists of stints with a Connecticut weekly and the *Philadelphia Ledger,* now defunct. He went to work for *The Philadelphia Inquirer* over 20 years ago and has been there ever since. He has been chairman of baseball's Scoring Rules Committee for many years.

BILL LIBBY (Maurice Morning Wills at Twilight) is making his fifth appearance in *Best Sports Stories.* Born in Atlantic City, New Jersey, and reared in Indianapolis, he now lives in Westminster, California. He was a prolific free-lance writer but has cut down on his magazine work to devote himself to sports book writing. Some of the books which have received warm critical acclaim are: *Mr. Clutch, Parnelli, Life in the Pit, Andretti* and *Great American Drivers*. One book, *The Man Behind the Clown's Mask*, had its genesis in a magazine article that was selected to appear in *Best Sports Stories 1963*.

Roy McHugh (The Making of the No. 1 Draft Choice) is the sports editor of the *Pittsburgh Press*. He began his newspaper career with the *Cedar Rapids* (Iowa) *Gazette* after graduation from Coe College. He joined his present paper in 1947, and, after 14 years, went to Evansville, Indiana, as sports editor of the *Sunday Courier and Press*. He returned to the *Pittsburgh Press* in 1963 and became sports editor in 1969. He is also a free-lance magazine writer.

Jack Mann (The Boob-Tube Trap) broke into sports writing with Long Island's *Newsday* and in 1956 he became its sports editor. Later he joined the sports department of the defunct *New York Herald Tribune* and after two years moved to *Sports Illustrated*. In 1969, he went to *The Washington Daily News* after having free-lanced for many of the better national magazines. His writing has merited many inclusions in *Best Sports Stories*.

William Murray (Fore Play), who makes his first appearance in *Best Sports Stories*, is a free-lance writer who lives in Malibu, California, and writes on a variety of subjects other than sports. His recently published books include a novel, *The Americanos*, and *Previews of Coming Attractions*, a book about the way things are in Southern California, which appeared in June, 1970.

Lou O'Neill ("Thank You, Mr. President") won the news-feature prize award in 1968 with his probing analysis of the Mets. Mr. O'Neill is a veteran sports reporter who has spent 43 years in newspaper work, 24 of them as sports editor of the now defunct *Long Island Star-Journal*. When that paper was struck and subsequently died, he moved to the *Long Island Press* as a columnist. He has been an announcer of harness races at Yonkers Raceway and has been featured from there on radio and TV. This is his seventh appearance in *Best Sports Stories*.

Phil Pepe (The Baltimore Bulls Attack the Reds) is a graduate of St. John's University who became a member of the sports department of the late *New York World-Telegram* in 1957. The Yankees and college sports were his beat. In 1966, he worked for the now defunct *New York World Journal Tribune* as a three-days-a-week columnist, and free-lanced for a time. In 1968, he went to the *New York Daily News*. He is the author of five sports books, including one on Bob Gibson, Cardinal pitcher, *From Ghetto to Glory*. This is his fourth appearance in *Best Sports Stories*.

Shirley Povich (That Intoxicating Moment) attended Georgetown University, chose journalism as his profession and at the age of 20 became sports editor of *The Washington Post*, perhaps the youngest sports editor of any metropolitan daily. He won the *Best Sports Stories* news-coverage prize in 1957 with his story on Don Larsen's perfect World Series game against the Dodgers. His other prizes for fine writing have included the National Headliners Award and the Grantland Rice Award. His book, *All These Mornings*, was published in 1969 by Prentice-Hall. He has appeared in *Best Sports Stories* on many occasions.

JEFF PRUGH (The Ski Patrol) joined the *Los Angeles Times* staff nine years ago, upon his graduation from the University of Missouri, where he was president of his class in the School of Journalism. He concentrates on college football and basketball as well as the tennis tour He is first vice-president of the United States Basketball Writers Association. This is his second appearance in *Best Sports Stories.*

BILL ROBINSON (The America's Cup: An Incredible Series) was educated at Princeton ('39) and got his newspaper background as a sports writer and boat columnist with the *Newark Evening News* and the *Newark Star-Ledger,* where he remained until 1957, working two years on each paper. Since then he has been with *Yachting,* where he is executive editor. He has written a number of fine books on many phases of yachting—from instructional guides for both adults and children to books on the romance and adventure of this exciting sport.

GENE ROSWELL (Oh, Pancho) is a graduate of New York University and a native New Yorker. He worked as a stringer for the wire services and various New York dailies before going to the old *Bronx Home News.* Later he became the night sports editor of the *New York Post,* but soon joined the daylight forces to report major sporting activities. His son, Clint, a University of North Carolina student, was sports editor of that school's paper. This is Gene Roswell's second article for *Best Sports Stories.*

JOE SCALZO (Hell Week at Indy), a magazine and newspaper writer, is the author of two recently published books: *Racer* and *The Unbelievable Unsers.* A former motorcycle racer, he free-lanced for 10 years before joining Bond, Parkhurst and Bond, a publishing house in Newport, California, where he works as a feature writer. This marks his second appearance in *Best Sports Stories.*

JAY SEARCY (The Black-Draped Campus) attended East Tennessee State University and while a senior got his first newspaper job with the *Kingsport* (Tenn.) *Times-News.* Two years later he began to work for *The Chattanooga Times,* and in 1960 he became that paper's sports editor. Besides writing columns he covers Southeastern Conference athletics and writes a once-a-week column for the editorial page (quite a combination). He is a former winner of the Sportswriter of the Year Award in Tennessee. This marks his first appearance in *Best Sports Stories.*

NICK SEITZ (Ben Hogan Today) is making his sixth appearance in *Best Sports Stories* since graduation from the University of Oklahoma, where he majored in philosophy. He became sports editor of the *Norman* (Okla.)

Transcript at the age of 22, and later was named sports editor of the *Oklahoma Journal*. He is now associate editor of *Golf Digest* magazine and a free-lance writer for other magazines, including *Golf* and *Parents' Magazine*. He has won numerous prizes in golf and basketball writers' contests.

BLACKIE SHERROD (Through History with the American League) the executive sports editor of *The Dallas Times Herald,* has garnered just about every important sports writing prize in the country. To name a few: a National Headliners Award, seven out of 12 years as the outstanding sports writer by his newspaper, radio and TV colleagues, six Dallas Press Awards and 13 inclusions in *Best Sports Stories.* As a master of ceremonies and banquet speaker, he has appeared in 15 states, and during the football season he has his own radio and TV programs.

AL STUMP (Joe Kapp: Football's Fury) is a free-lance writer with a national reputation in magazine writing. In 1962, his magazine piece on Ty Cobb, *The Fight to Live,* won the *Best Sports Stories* magazine award. He is a native of the West Coast and received his education at the University of Washington. He later joined the *Portland Oregonion.* Besides his magazine work, he has collaborated with many great sports personalities in the writing of their biographies.

WELLS TWOMBLY (The Hero Sandwich of Sports) was the 1970 *Best Sports Stories* news-coverage winner with his article about the 1969 Super Bowl. *Newsweek* named him as one of the new sports columnists who are changing the whole style of sports writing. He is a most peripatetic journeyman, going from the *Willimantic* (Conn.) *Daily Chronicle* westward to the *Pasadena Star News,* then to the *North Hollywood Valley Times Today,* south to the *Houston Chronicle,* north to the *Detroit Free Press,* where he wrote his prize story, and finally back west to do a sports column for *The San Francisco Examiner.* He also is a regular weekly columnist for *The Sporting News.*

DICK YOUNG (The Joe Namath System) joined the *New York Daily News* in 1941 and appeared in 1941 in the first edition of *Best Sports Stories.* He was at that time one of the youngest sports reporters in New York City. Since then, he has become one of the two most consistent winners in this series with five *Best Sports Stories* awards: two prizes in news coverage, in 1959 and 1960; two for news features, in 1957 and 1966; and one magazine prize, in 1955. In addition to covering baseball, he writes a daily column for the *News* entitled "Young Ideas."

THE PHOTO WINNERS

JERRY RIFE (Expos' Last Stand) received a degree in education from San Diego College in 1964, and was the editor of that college's newspaper *The Daily Aztec*. Since 1965 he has been a staff photographer for *The San Diego Union* and *Tribune* and has won about 25 annual photographic awards from such organizations as the National Press Photographers, Press Photographers Association and the California Press Photographers Association. At present he is the editor of the California Press Photographers Association Monthly Newsletter. His photograph in this book is his first picture in *Best Sports Stories* and, by a coincidence, it won first prize.

PAUL J. CONNELL (A Time for Everything) makes himself a three-time winner in *Best Sports Stories* with this warm prize-winning shot. In 1961, he captured the action picture award and in 1968 he merited the feature prize. This year he has garnered the prize with another feature picture. In the past he has won over 80 prizes, regional and national, in all categories, and was cited three years in a row as the Photographer of the Year in his region. He has been with the *Boston Globe* since 1937.

OTHER PHOTOGRAPHERS (In Alphabetical Order)

MIKE ANDERSEN (Boston Baked Teams) has done photographic stints in Kansas and Iowa and now is in his second year with the *Boston Record-American*. He has won many awards, including New England Press Photographer of the Year and top place in the Pro Football Hall of Fame contest. This is his second appearance in *Best Sports Stories*.

JOHN E. BIEVER (Chi Chi Does the Cha-Cha) is at the University of Wisconsin and like his photographer dad, Vernon, does much free lancing. Already he has covered all five Super Bowls and his work has appeared in major magazines and sports books, particularly Jerry Kramer's best seller, *Instant Replay.*

JOHN CROFT (But Where's the Bat?), has been a staff photographer for the *Minneapolis Tribune* for the last 13 years, 10 of which have been in sports photography. He worked for WCCO-TV in Minneapolis before joining the *Tribune.* He resides in that city with his family.

DICK DARCEY (Demolition Derby), who won *Best Sports Stories* action award in 1967, is director of photography at *The Washington Post,* where he has worked since 1948. He began to cover major-league sports in 1956. His past honors have included *Look's* top sports picture of the year award and prizes in the National Press Photographers' competitions.

MALCOLM W. EMMONS (Who's Got the Ball?) is a New Englander now living in Ohio. He has a BS in agricultural marketing from Ohio State, where he is an instructor in photographic services at the Agricultural School. A free lancer, he has made many appearances in magazines as well as books and has had two inclusions in *Best Sports Stories.*

JOHN GREENSMITH (Keep on the Grass) is a staff photographer for the *Union* and the *Tribune* in San Diego. He was a news reporter for six years and in 1955 went over to photography. His work has merited a number of outstanding awards and the inclusion of eight pictures in this series of prize photos.

JACK GUNTER (And Now a Three-legged Player) has been a member of *The Nashville Banner's* photographic staff since 1948 except for three years he spent in the army. He was a photographer with the 45th Infantry in the Korean War. He is a native Nashvillian.

KENT KOBERSTEEN (Suddenly the Judge Was Racing—for Safety) has been a staff photographer for the *Minneapolis Tribune* since 1965. Prior to that he attended the University of Minnesota. This is his second appearance in *Best Sports Stories.*

CHARLES R. PUGH, JR. (Victory Ride), won the *Best Sports Stories* action photo award two years ago in his debut in the anthology. He started his photographic career with the *Johnson City* (Tenn.) *Press-Chronicle* and since 1956 has been with *The Atlanta Journal.*

FRANCIS ROUTT (Sock It to the Soccer Ball), a *Washington Star* staff photographer, is a member of the White House Newspaper Photographers Association and has received many awards in that organization, including a grand prize and five first-place awards. In the past two years he also has received first-place awards in the Football Hall of Fame contests. This marks his first appearance in *Best Sports Stories.*

WILLIAM SEAMAN (A Foot to the Jaw) has been with the *Minneapolis Star* since 1945. He garnered one of the most distinguished prizes in photography, the Pulitzer Prize, in 1959. He also has to his credit prizes from the Inland Daily Press Association, a 1956 Headliner Award and two prizes from the National Press Photographers Association. A number of his photographs have merited inclusion in *Best Sports Stories.*

CHRIS STRATTAN (Aw Phooey) was born in Indianapolis, Indiana. While in high school and college he was a staffer for a group of suburban weeklies, later becoming a stringer for the *Chicago Daily News* and the *Chicago Tribune.* At present he is on the staff of the *San Jose Mercury* and *News* in California.

RAYMOND F. STUBBLEBINE (A Flyer into the Net) is a 1968 graduate of Thiel College in Greenville, Pennsylvania, who was named to *Who's Who in American Colleges and Universities.* In college he worked as a public-relations photographer and edited his yearbook. He began his newspaper work for the *Philadelphia Evening* and *Sunday Bulletin* as a staff photographer.

JIM VINCENT (Cascading Down the Cascades) has been a staff photographer for *The* (Portland) *Oregonion* for five years. Previously he was employed in the same capacity by the (Portland) *Oregon Journal.* This marks his fourth appearance in *Best Sports Stories.*

Illustrations

AW PHOOEY

by Chris Strattan, *San Jose News*. The nine-year-old youngster on the ground isn't protesting a call by the umpire in this Little League game, but scored and ended up with a mouthful of dirt after a belly slide under the tag of the catcher. Reprinted by permission of the *San Jose News*.

DEMOLITION DERBY

by Dick Darcey, *The Washington Post*. Baltimore Orioles' pitcher Dave
McNally floats across the plate to a welcoming committee of ecstatic teammates and fans at Baltimore's Memorial Stadium after hitting a grand slam
homer against the Cincinnati Reds, thus becoming the first pitcher in the
history of World Series play to connect with the bases full. Copyright, ©,
1970, *The Washington Post*.

BUT WHERE'S THE BAT?

by John Croft, *Minneapolis Tribune*. Tony Oliva, outfielder for the Minnesota Twins has some trouble hanging onto the bat since he broke a finger
in 1969. Here he lets loose again, but this time no one was hurt, although
later in the year Oliva did hit Harmon Killebrew in the on-deck circle.
Copyright, ©, 1970, *Minneapolis Star and Tribune Company*.

BOSTON BAKED TEAMS

by Mike Andersen, *Boston Record-American*. Players from the Washington Redskins and Boston Patriots take time out when their exhibition game turned into a more heated game than expected. A rubbish fire underneath the wooden stands at Boston College Field spread quickly to the fans, who were forced to flee to the playing field for safety. No one was injured but the game was delayed 40 minutes before the blaze was extinguished. Copyright, © 1970, *Boston Record American-Sunday Advertiser.*

VICTORY RIDE

by Charles R. Pugh, Jr., *The Atlanta Journal.* Neither rain nor gloom of
night could stop these football warriors from West Virginia from carrying
their coach, Jim Carlin, to the dressing room after victory over South Carolina in the Peach Bowl. Copyright, ©, 1970, *The Atlantic Journal.*

A FOOT TO THE JAW

by William Seaman, *Minneapolis Star*. Pat Coleman of Benilde High School in Minneapolis gets the ball and a kick at the same time in the Catholic State basketball tournament. A teammate (No. 32) looks on aghast. Copyright, ©, 1970, *Minneapolis Star and Tribune Company*.

AND NOW A THREE-LEGGED PLAYER

by Jack Gunter, *The Nashville Banner.* There have been seven-foot basketball players, but none of three feet, as this illusive photo seems to show. Action was caught in the Alabama-Vanderbilt basketball game as the Crimson Tide's Dave Williams wrests a rebound from Vanderbilt's hidden captain, Perry Wallace. Copyright, ©, 1970, *The Nashville Banner.*

WHO'S GOT THE BALL?

by Malcolm W. Emmons, *Ohio State University*. Craig Barclay (No. 44) of
Ohio State looks a little bewildered as he tries to figure out whether he has
the ball or does the man guarding him have it. Reprinted by permission of
Malcolm W. Emmons.

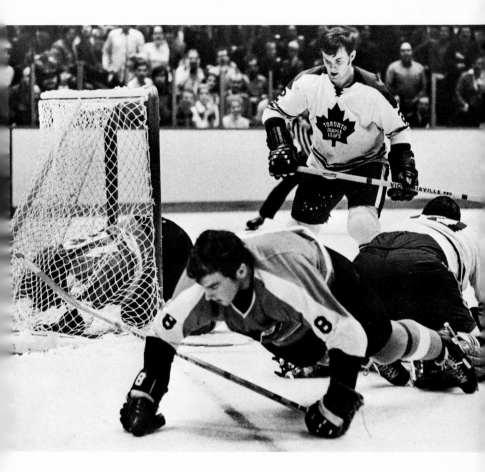

A FLYER INTO THE NET

by Raymond F. Stubblebine, *Philadelphia Bulletin*. Bobby Clarke of Philadelphia falling into the net (with puck) in game between Philadelphia Flyers and Toronto Maple Leafs, as Toronto goalie Bruce Gamble leaves his bailiwick to cover the puck. The only man left standing is Toronto's Ricky Ley. Copyright, ©, 1970, *Bulletin Co.*

CHI CHI DOES THE CHA-CHA

by John E. Biever, *Cedarburg* (Wis.) *News-Graphic*. Chi Chi Rodriguez does
a little dance step after a good fairway wood shot in the Greater Milwaukee
Open golf tournament. Reprinted by permission of *John E. Biever*.

SOCK IT TO THE SOCCER BALL

by Francis Routt, *The Washington Star*. Keith Aqui of Howard University flies through the air as he passes to a teammate during game against Maryland in the NCAA play-offs. Copyright, ©, 1970, *The Washington Star*.

SUDDENLY THE JUDGE WAS RACING—FOR SAFETY

by Kent Kobersteen, *Minneapolis Tribune*. Corner judge Dennis Chelberg abandons his tower when a racer skidded into his platform at the Minnesota State Fair's North Star 500. Chelberg was not injured. The driver, Fred Horn, just went on racing, but his car gave out before the finish. Copyright, ©, 1970, *Minneapolis Star and Tribune Company*.

KEEP ON THE GRASS

by John Greensmith, *The San Diego Evening Tribune*. This photo illustrates grass racing, which has become popular at the Del Mar Turf Club in California. Here the field is rounding the chute turn and onto the main track. Copyright, ©, 1970, *The San Diego Evening Tribune*.

CASCADING DOWN THE CASCADES

by Jim Vincent, *The* (Portland) *Oregonian*. Dave Kelsey of Orinda, California, fights his way down the rapids of the Wenatchee River during the national kayak championships near Leavenworth, Washington, in the Cascade Mountains. Copyright, ©, 1970, *The Oregonian*.